UNIVERSITY OF NORTH CAROLINA AT CHAPEL HILL
DEPARTMENT OF ROMANCE LANGUAGES

NORTH CAROLINA STUDIES
IN THE ROMANCE LANGUAGES AND LITERATURES

Founder: URBAN TIGNER HOLMES

Distributed by:

UNIVERSITY OF NORTH CAROLINA PRESS
CHAPEL HILL
North Carolina 27514
U.S.A.

NORTH CAROLINA STUDIES IN THE
ROMANCE LANGUAGES AND LITERATURES
Number 182

A STUDY OF NOMINAL INFLECTION IN
LATIN INSCRIPTIONS
A MORPHO-SYNTACTIC ANALYSIS

A STUDY OF NOMINAL INFLECTION IN LATIN INSCRIPTIONS

A MORPHO-SYNTACTIC ANALYSIS

BY

PAUL A. GAENG

CHAPEL HILL

NORTH CAROLINA STUDIES IN THE ROMANCE
LANGUAGES AND LITERATURES
U.N.C. DEPARTMENT OF ROMANCE LANGUAGES
1977

Library of Congress Cataloging in Publication Data

Gaeng, Paul A.
A study of nominal inflections in Latin inscriptions.

(North Carolina studies in the Romance languages and literatures; no. 182)
Bibliography: p.
Includes indexes.
1. Latin language—Noun. 2. Inscriptions, Latin.

I. Title. II. Series.

PA2181.G3   475   76-58868
ISBN 0-8078-9182-7

Published with the help of the Charles Phelps Taft Memorial Fund, University of Cincinnati

I.S.B.N. 0-8078-9182-7

DEPÓSITO LEGAL: V. 1.327 - 1977   I.S.B.N. 84-399-6529-X
ARTES GRÁFICAS SOLER, S. A. - JÁVEA, 28 - VALENCIA (8) - 1977

DILECTISSIMO MAGISTRO, AMICO ET SODALI
   MARIO PEI

CONTENTS

	Page
SYMBOLS AND ABBREVIATIONS … … … … … … … … …	13
BIBLIOGRAPHY … … … … … … … … … … …	15
INTRODUCTION … … … … … … … … … … …	21
CHAPTER 1: FIRST DECLENSION … … … … … … …	27
1.1 Singular … … … … … … … … … … …	27
1.11 Nominative … … … … … … … … …	27
1.12 Genitive … … … … … … … … … …	27
(a) *-e* for *-ae* … … … … … …	27
(b) *-aes* and *-es* for *-ae (-e)* … …	27
(c) *-is* for *-ae* … … … … … …	30
(d) Prepositional Construction with *de* … …	32
1.13 Dative … … … … … … … … … …	36
(a) *-es* for *-ae (-e)* … … … … …	36
(b) Prepositional Construction with *ad* … …	36
1.14 Accusative … … … … … … … … …	38
1.15 Ablative … … … … … … … … … …	43
1.2 Plural … … … … … … … … … … … …	46
1.21 Nominative … … … … … … … … …	46
1.22 Genitive … … … … … … … … … …	51
1.23 Dative … … … … … … … … … …	52
1.24 Accusative … … … … … … … … …	52
1.25 Ablative … … … … … … … … … …	53
1.3 Summary … … … … … … … … … … …	54
1.31 Singular … … … … … … … … … …	54
1.311 Nominative … … … … … … …	54
1.312 Genitive … … … … … … … …	54
1.313 Dative … … … … … … … …	55
1.314 Accusative … … … … … … …	55
1.315 Ablative … … … … … … … …	55
1.32 Plural … … … … … … … … … …	56
1.321 Nominative … … … … … … …	56
1.322 Genitive … … … … … … … …	56

				Page
	1.323	Dative	... ...	56
	1.324	Accusative	... ...	57
	1.325	Ablative	... ...	57

CHAPTER 2: SECOND DECLENSION 58

2.1 Singular 58

    2.11 Nominative 58
        (a) *-os* for *-us* 58
        (b) *-u* for *-us* 60
        (c) *-o* for *-us* 62

    2.12 Genitive 66
        (a) *-o* for *-i* 66
        (b) Periphrasis with *de* 73

    2.13 Dative 75
        (a) *-i* for *-o* 75
        (b) *-u* for *-o* 76

    2.14 Accusative 76
        (a) *-u* for *-um* 77
        (b) *-o* for *-um* 83

    2.15 Ablative 88
        (a) *-u* for *-o* 88
        (b) *-um* for *-o* 94

2.2 Plural 101

    2.21 Nominative 101
    2.22 Genitive 103
        (a) *-oro* for *-orum* 103
        (b) *-oru* for *-orum* 105
        (c) Prepositional Constructions 106

    2.23 Dative 107
    2.24 Accusative 107
        (a) *-us* for *-os* 107
        (b) *-is* for *-os* (*-us*) 113

    2.25 Ablative 114

2.3 Summary 119

    2.31 Singular 119
        2.311 Nominative 119
        2.312 Genitive 121
        2.313 Dative 121
        2.314 Accusative 122
        2.315 Ablative 122

    2.32 Plural 124
        2.321 Nominative 124

CONTENTS

Page

	2.322	Genitive	124
	2.323	Dative	125
	2.324	Accusative	125
	2.325	Ablative	126

CHAPTER 3: THIRD DECLENSION ... 127

- 3.1 Singular ... 127
  - 3.11 Nominative ... 127
  - 3.12 Genitive ... 131
    - (a) *-es* for *-is* ... 131
    - (b) *-e* for *-is* ... 132
    - (c) *-i* for *-is* ... 133
    - (d) Prepositional Replacement ... 136
  - 3.13 Dative ... 137
    - (a) *-e* for *-i* ... 137
    - (b) Periphrastic Construction with *ad* ... 139
  - 3.14 Accusative ... 139
  - 3.15 Ablative ... 144
    - 1. Ablatives in *-e* ... 144
      - (a) *-i* for *-e* ... 145
      - (b) *-em* for *-e* ... 147
    - 2. Ablatives in *-i* ... 150
- 3.2 Plural ... 152
  - 3.21 Nominative ... 152
  - 3.22 Genitive ... 159
  - 3.23 Dative ... 160
  - 3.24 Accusative ... 162
    - 1. Consonant stems in *-es* ... 162
    - 2. *i*-stems in *-is* ... 164
  - 3.25 Ablative ... 167
- 3.3 Summary ... 172
  - 3.31 Singular ... 172
    - 3.311 Nominative ... 172
    - 3.312 Genitive ... 172
    - 3.313 Dative ... 173
    - 3.314 Accusative ... 173
    - 3.315 Ablative ... 173
  - 3.32 Plural ... 174
    - 3.321 Nominative ... 174
    - 3.322 Genitive ... 175
    - 3.323 Dative ... 175
    - 3.324 Accusative ... 175
    - 3.325 Ablative ... 176

CHAPTER 4: FOURTH AND FIFTH DECLENSIONS ... 177

- 4.1 Fourth Declension ... 177
- 4.2 Fifth Declension ... 181

	Page

Chapter 5: GENERAL SUMMARY AND CONCLUSIONS ... 184

 5.1 Nominative Singular ... 184
  5.11 First Declension ... 184
  5.12 Second Declension ... 184
  5.13 Third Declension ... 185

 5.2 Genitive Singular ... 186
  5.21 First Declension ... 186
  5.22 Second Declension ... 186
  5.23 Third Declension ... 187

 5.3 Dative Singular ... 187
  5.31 First Declension ... 187
  5.32 Second Declension ... 188
  5.33 Third Declension ... 188

 5.4 Accusative Singular ... 188
  5.41 First Declension ... 188
  5.42 Second Declension ... 188
  5.43 Third Declension ... 189

 5.5 Ablative Singular ... 190
  5.51 First Declension ... 190
  5.52 Second Declension ... 190
  5.53 Third Declension ... 191

 5.6 Nominative Plural ... 192
  5.61 First Declension ... 192
  5.62 Second Declension ... 193
  5.63 Third Declension ... 193

 5.7 Genitive Plural ... 193
  5.71 First Declension ... 193
  5.72 Second Declension ... 193
  5.73 Third Declension ... 194

 5.8 Dative Plural ... 194
  5.81 First Declension ... 194
  5.82 Second Declension ... 195
  5.83 Third Declension ... 195

 5.9 Accusative Plural ... 195
  5.91 First Declension ... 195
  5.92 Second Declension ... 195
  5.93 Third Declension ... 196

 5.10 Ablative Plural ... 196
  5.101 First Declension ... 196
  5.102 Second Declension ... 197
  5.103 Third Declension ... 197

Concluding Remarks ... 198

Appendix ... 207

Index Nominum Rerumque ... 225

SYMBOLS AND ABBREVIATIONS

The following two symbols used in inscriptional examples call for comment:

(a) Letters enclosed in square brackets ([ ]), although supplied by the editor(s), are presumed to have existed on the original stone;

(b) Letters enclosed in parentheses are additions made by the editor(s) to facilitate comprehension, even though nothing is missing on the original inscription.

Note that a number immediately following an inscriptional example refers to the corresponding number in the Diehl collection. Numbers preceded by the letter "V" refer to the corresponding item in the Vives collection.

Other abbreviations used in this study are as follows:

Cat. = Catalan	Rum. = Rumanian
Cl. Lat. = Classical Latin	Sard. = Sardinian
Fr. = French	Sicil. = Sicilian
Eng. = English	Sp. = Spanish
It. = Italian	OFr. = Old French
Log. = Logudorese	OIt. = Old Italian
Port. = Portuguese	OProv. = Old Provençal
Prov. = Provençal	V.L. = Vulgar Latin

BIBLIOGRAPHY

Note: This selected bibliography with abbreviations includes only those sources and works that were frequently consulted in connection with this study.
Works referred to only occasionally are cited in full in the text.

I.—*Sources*

C. I. L. = *Corpus Inscriptionum Latinarum*. Berlin, 1862-1943.
DIEHL, *AI* = Diehl, Ernst (ed.), *Lateinische Altchristliche Inschriften*. 2nd. ed. Bonn, 1913.
DIEHL, *ICLV* = Diehl, Ernst (ed.), *Inscriptiones Latinae Christianae Veteres*. 3 volumes. Berlin, 1924-1931. 2nd. ed., revised. Berlin, 1961. *Supplementum* (vol. IV) edited by J. Moreau and H. I. Marrou. Berlin, 1967.
DIEHL, *VL* = Diehl, Ernst (ed.), *Vulgärlateinische Inschriften*. Bonn, 1910.
DÍAZ Y DÍAZ = Díaz y Díaz, Manuel C. (ed.), *Antología del latín vulgar*, Madrid, ^{1}1950, ^{2}1962.
LEBLANT = LeBlant, Edmond, *Nouveau Recueil des Inscriptions chrétiennes de la Gaule antérieures au VIIIe siècle*. Paris, 1892.
MULLER-TAYLOR = Muller, Henri F., and Pauline Taylor, *A Chrestomathy of Vulgar Latin*, New York, 1932.
PISANI, *Testi* = Pisani, Vittore, *Testi latini arcaici e volgari con commento glottologico*. 2nd ed., revised. Torino, 1960.
VIVES = Vives, D. José (ed.), *Inscripciones cristianas de la España Romana y Visigoda*, Barcelona, 1942.

II.—*Books and Articles*

ATZORI = Atzori, M. T., *La preposizione "de" del latino volgare*. Firenze, 1939.
BATTISTI = Battisti, Carlo, *Avviamento allo studio del latino volgare*. Bari, 1949.
BONNET = Bonnet, Max, *Le latin de Grégoire de Tours*. Paris, 1890.
BOURCIEZ, *De praepositione 'ad'* = Bourciez, Edouard, *De praepositione 'ad' casuali in latinitate aevi merovingici*. Paris, 1886.
BOURCIEZ, *Éléments* = Bourciez, Edouard, *Éléments de linguistique romane*. 4th ed., revised. Paris, 1956.

BOURCIEZ, *Phonétique* = Bourciez, Edouard, *Précis historique de phonétique française.* 9th ed., revised. Paris, 1958.
CARNOY = Carnoy, A., *Le latin d'Espagne d'après les inscriptions.* 2nd ed. Louvain, 1906.
COOPER = Cooper, Paul J., "The Language of the Forum Judicum." Unpublished Ph.D. dissertation, Dept. of French and Romance Philology, Columbia University, 1952.
DIEHL, *De m finali* = Diehl, Ernst, *De m finali epigraphica.* Leipzig, 1899.
ELCOCK = Elcock, W. D., *The Romance Languages.* London, 1960.
EWERT = Ewert, Alfred, *The French Language.* London, 1933.
GAENG, *Local Variations* = Gaeng, Paul A., *An Inquiry into Local Variations in Vulgar Latin as Reflected in the Vocalism of Christian Inscriptions.* Chapel Hill, 1968.
GRANDGENT, *Italian* = Grandgent, C. H., *From Latin to Italian.* Cambridge (Mass.), 1927.
GRANDGENT, *V. L.* = Grandgent, C. H., *An Introduction to Vulgar Latin.* Reprint. New York, 1962.
HEHL = Hehl, Albert, *Die Formen der lateinischen ersten Deklination auf den Inschriften.* Tübingen, 1912.
HIGGINS = Higgins, Robert K., "Research Into the Phenomena Involving Latin Final M." Unpublished Master's essay, Dept. of French and Romance Philology, Columbia University, 1951.
JENNINGS = Jennings, Augustus Campbell, *A Linguistic Study of the Cartulario de S. Vicente de Oviedo.* New York, 1940.
KONJETZNY = Konjetzny, Guilelmus, "De idiotismis syntacticis in titulis latinis urbanis conspicuis," *Archiv für lateinische Lexikographie und Grammatik,* XV (1908), 297-351.
LAUSBERG = Lausberg, Heinrich, *Romanische Sprachwissenschaft.* Vol. III: *Formenlehre.* Berlin, 1956.
LEHMANN = Lehmann, Winfred P., *Historical Linguistics.* New York, 1962.
LINDSAY = Lindsay, W. M., *The Latin Language.* Oxford, 1894.
B. LÖFSTEDT = Löfstedt, Bengt, *Studien über die Sprache der langobardischen Gesetze.* Stockholm, 1961.
LÖFSTEDT, *Peregrinatio* = Löfstedt, Einar, *Philologischer Kommentar zur Peregrinatio Aetheriae.* Uppsala, 1911.
LÖFSTEDT, *Syntactica* = Löfstedt, Einar, *Syntactica, Studien und Beiträge zur historischen Syntax des Lateins.* Vol. I: *Über einige Grundfragen der lateinischen Nominalsyntax.* 2nd ed. Lund, 1942.
MARTIN = Martin, Henry, *Notes on the Syntax of the Latin Inscriptions Found in Spain.* Baltimore, 1909.
MARUCCHI = Marucchi, Orazio, *Epigrafia cristiana.* Milano, 1910.
MIHĂESCU = Mihăescu, H., *Limba latină în provinciile dunărene ale imperiului roman.* Bucharest, 1960.
MOHL = Mohl, F. G., *Introduction à la chronologie du latin vulgaire.* Paris, 1899.
MULLER, *Chronology* = Muller, Henri F., *A Chronology of Vulgar Latin* (*Zeitschrift für romanische Philologie,* Beiheft 78). Halle/Saale, 1929.
MULLER, *Préposition "à"* = Muller, Henri F., *Origine et histoire de la préposition "à" dans les locutions du type "faire faire quelque chose à quelqu'un."* Poitiers, 1912.

NORBERG, *Beiträge* = Norberg Dag, *Beiträge zur spätlateinischen Syntax.* Uppsala, 1944.
NORBERG, *Synt. Forsch.* = Norberg, Dag, *Syntaktische Forschungen auf dem Gebiete des Spätlateins und des frühen Mittellateins.* Uppsala, 1943. (Uppsala Universitets Årskrift #9.)
PALMER = Palmer, L. R., *The Latin Language.* London, 1954.
PAULY-WISSOWA = *Paulys Real-Encyclopädie der classischen Altertumswissenschaft.* Neue Bearbeitung von G. Wissowa u.a., Stuttgart, 1894 ff.
PEI, *Accusative* = Pei, Mario A., "Accusative or Oblique," *Romanic Review*, XXVIII (1937), 241-267.
PEI, *It. Lang.* = Pei, Mario A., *The Italian Language.* New York, 1941.
PEI, *Texts* = Pei, Mario A., *The Language of the Eighth-Century Texts in Northern France.* New York, 1932.
PIRSON = Pirson, Jules, *La langue des inscriptions latines de la Gaule.* Brussels, 1901.
POLITZER, *Lomb. Docs.* = Politzer, Robert L., *A Study of the Language of Eighth-Century Lombardic Documents.* New York, 1949.
POLITZER, *Rom. Trends* = Politzer, Robert L. and Frieda N., *Romance Trends in 7th and 8th Century Latin Documents.* Chapel Hill, 1953.
PRINZ = Prinz, Otto, *De O et U vocalibus inter se mutatis in lingua latina.* Halle, 1932.
PROSKAUER = Proskauer, Carola, *Das auslautende -s auf den lateinischen Inschriften.* Strassburg, 1909.
REICHENKRON = Reichenkron G., *Beiträge zur romanischen Lautlehre*, Jena and Leipzig, 1939.
ROHLFS, *Vulgärlatein* = Rohlfs, Gerhardt, *Vom Vulgärlatein zum Altfranzösischen.* Tübingen, 1960.
RÖNSCH = Rönsch, H., *Itala und Vulgata.* 2nd ed. Marburg, 1875.
SAS = Sas, Louis Furman, *The Noun Declension System in Merovingian Latin.* Paris, 1937.
SCHUCHARDT = Schuchardt, Hugo, *Der Vokalismus des Vulgärlateins.* 3 vols. Leipzig, 1866-1888.
SITTL, *Mittellatein* = Sittl, Karl, "Zur Beurteilung des sog. Mittellatein," *Archiv für lateinische Lexicographie und Grammatik*, II (1885), 550-580.
TAGLIAVINI = Tagliavini, Carlo, *Le origini delle lingue neolatine.* 3rd ed. Bologna, 1959.
TAYLOR = Taylor, Pauline, *The Latinity of the Liber Historiae Francorum.* New York, 1924.
UDDHOLM = Uddholm, A., *Formulae Marculfi, Études sur la langue et le style.* Uppsala, 1954. (Uppsala Universitets Årskrift #2.)
VÄÄNÄNEN, *Inscr. pomp.* = Väänänen, Veikko, *Le latin vulgaire des inscriptions pompéiennes.* 3rd ed. Berlin, 1966. (Abhandlungen der Deutschen Akademie der Wissenschaften zu Berlin, 1958, 3.)
VÄÄNÄNEN, *Lat. vulg.* = Väänänen, Veikko, *Introduction au latin vulgaire.* 2nd ed., revised. Paris, 1967.
v. WARTBURG, *Ausgliederung* = von Wartburg, Walther, *Die Ausgliederung der romanischen Sprachraume.* Bern, 1950.
v. WARTBURG, *Évolution* = von Wartburg, Walther, *Évolution et structure de la langue française.* 5th ed., revised. Bern, 1958.

III.—*Historical and Descriptive Grammars*

ALLEN-GREENOUGH = Allen & Greenough's *New Latin Grammar*. Revised ed. New York, 1903.
BENNET = Bennet, Charles E., *Syntax of Early Latin*. 2 vols. Boston, 1914.
BRUNOT-BRUNEAU = Brunot, Ferdinand and Charles Bruneau, *Précis de grammaire historique de la langue française*. Fifth Edition. Paris, 1949.
DRAEGER = Draeger, A., *Historische Syntax der lateinischen Sprache*. Leipzig, 1878.
ERNOUT, *Morphologie* = Ernout, A., *Morphologie historique du latin*. 3rd ed. Paris, 1953.
ERNOUT-THOMAS = Ernout, A., and Fr. Thomas, *Syntaxe latine*. 2nd ed. Paris, 1953.
GARCÍA DE DIEGO = García de Diego, Vicente, *Gramática histórica española*. Madrid, 1951.
KIECKERS = Kieckers, Ernst, *Historische lateinische Grammatik*. 2 vols. München, 1931.
MAURER = Maurer, Theodoro Henrique, Jr., *Gramática do Latim Vulgar*. Rio de Janeiro, 1959.
MENÉNDEZ PIDAL, *Gramática* = Menéndez Pidal, Ramón, *Manual de gramática histórica española*. 10th ed. Madrid, 1958.
MEYER-LÜBKE, *Grammatik* = Meyer-Lübke, Wilhelm, *Grammatik der romanischen Sprachen*. 4 vols. Leipzig, 1890-1902.
MEYER-LÜBKE, *Ital. Grammatik* = Meyer-Lübke, Wilhelm, *Italienische Grammatik*. Leipzig, 1890.
NEUE, *Formenlehre* = Neue, Friedrich, *Formenlehre der lateinischen Sprache*. 2nd. ed. 2 vols. Berlin, 1877.
PISANI, *Grammatica* = Pisani, Vittore, *Grammatica latina storica e comparata*. 3rd ed., revised. Torino, 1962.
ROHLFS, *Grammatik* = Rohlfs, Gerhardt, *Historische Grammatik der italienischen Sprache*. 3 vols. Bern, 1949-1953.
SCHWAN-BEHRENS = Schwan E. and D. Behrens, *Grammaire de l'ancien français*. Trans. by O. Bloch. Leipzig, 1922.
SOMMER = Sommer, Ferdinand, *Handbuch der lateinischen Laut- und Formenlehre*. 3rd. ed. Heidelberg, 1948.
STOLZ-LEUMANN = Leumann, Manu, J. B. Hofmann and Anton Szantyr, *Lateinische Grammatik auf der Grundlage des Werkes von Friedrich Stolz und Joseph Hermann Schmalz*. Erster Band: Manu Leumann, *Lateinische Laut- und Formenlehre*. München, 1963.
STOLZ-HOFMANN = Leumann, Manu, J. B. Hofmann and Anton Szantyr, *Lateinische Grammatik*. Zweiter Band: J. B. Hofmann, *Lateinische Syntax und Stilistik*. Neubearbeitet von Anton Szantyr. München, 1965.
STOLZ-SCHMALZ = Stolz, Friedrich and Joseph H. Schmalz, *Lateinische Grammatik*. 4th ed. München, 1970 (Handbuch der Altertumswissenschaften II:2).
TEKAVČIĆ = Tekavčić, Pavao, *Grammatica storica dell'italiano*. 3 vols. Bologna, 1972.

IV.—*Dictionaries and Glossaries*

Blaise, Albert, *Dictionnaire latin-français des auteurs chrétiens*. Revised by H. Chirat. Strasburg, 1954.
Du Cange, D. D., *Glossarium Mediae et Infimae Latinitatis*. 8 vols. Reprint of 1883-1887 edition. Graz, 1954.
GODEFROY = Godefroy, F., *Dictionnaire de l'ancienne langue française*. 10 vols. Paris, 1880-1902.
LEWIS-SHORT = *A Latin Dictionary*. Founded on Andrews' edition of Freund's Latin Dictionary. Revised, enlarged and in great part rewritten by Charlton O. Lewis and Charles Short. Oxford, 1958.
REW = Meyer-Lübke, Wilhelm (ed.), *Romanisches etymologisches Wörterbuch*. 3rd ed. Heidelberg, 1935.
SCHÖNFELD = Schönfeld, M., *Wörterbuch der altgermanischen Personen- und Völkernamen*. Heidelberg, 1911.
THESAURUS = *Thesaurus Linguae Latinae*. Leipzig, 1900 ff.

INTRODUCTION

The favorable reception that our phonological study on local differences in Vulgar Latin [1] was accorded by reviewers [2] has encouraged us to pursue our linguistic inquiry based on Christian Inscriptions of the funerary type. In this study we are attempting to give an organic treatment of an important area of morphology: the *nominal flection*. Specifically, it has been our aim to determine the extent to which this inscriptional material reflects the transformation of the Classical Latin multi-case system into the eventual one-case system of the Western Romance languages. To what extent, in other words, do these inscriptions that cover the period from the early fourth to the early seventh (and in the case of the *Iberian Peninsula* even the late seventh) centuries reveal (a) the survival of the classical system, and (b) trends in the direction of a collapse of this system.

The salient points of the evolution of the classical system have repeatedly been outlined by leading Romanists of both past and present. [3] Some of their explanations have, of course, been challenged in a number of individual studies concerned with the morphology of

---

[1] *An Inquiry Into Local Variations in Vulgar Latin As Reflected in the Vocalism of Christian Inscriptions*. Chapel Hill, 1968.

[2] Pavao Tekavčić in *Revue roumaine de linguistique*, XV, 4 (1970), 404-411; Veikko Väänänen in *Romanistisches Jahrbuch*, XXI (1970), 196-197; Frank R. Hamlin in *Revue des langues romanes*, LXXIX (1970), 502-504; Luigi Romeo in *Romance Philology*, XXIV, 3 (1971), 516-518; Jakob Wüest in *Vox Romanica*, XXX (1971), 326-329; W. Rothwell in *Modern Language Review*, LXVII, 3 (1972), 604-605; Robert L. Politzer in *Language*, XLVIII, 3 (1972), 702-705; and Arnulf Stefenelli in *Zeitschrift für romanische Philologie*, LXXXIX, 4-6 (1973), 520-523.

[3] For a concise summary of the main points as outlined by such distinguished names of the past as Meyer-Lübke, Grandgent, Nyrop, etc., cf. Sas, 2-4. As to the present, Väänänen's *Introduction au latin vulgaire* remains a classic *mise au point*.

Late Latin texts [4] and there still exists a great deal of disagreement on many issues. [5] Much of this disagreement, we believe, is due to the fact that too often isolated cases are selected to prove the existence or non-existence of certain morphological forms, instead of evaluating them in the context of a quantitative analysis, comparing correct occurrences and deviations from the classical norm and then drawing conclusions from the ratio that exists between the two. [6]

---

[4] Such as those of Bonnet, Taylor, Pei, Sas, Politzer, B. Löfstedt, to name just a few important ones. (See Bibliography for details.)

[5] Not the least of them being the controversial question whether "the accusative case alone was normally the source of the Romance substantive" (Elcock, 6) or whether the latter is "the result of a merger of classical Latin accusative, ablative and dative, brought about by the phonetic equivalence of the singular endings in two of the three major declensions and then gradually extended, by a syntactic process of analogy, to cover the dative singular of the first declension, the genitive singular of the three declensions and those plural forms which could not phonetically coalesce" (Pei, *Accusative*, 241). (More will be said on this point in subsequent pages.)

[6] In an important article entitled "Aspects de la différentiation territoriale du latin sous l'Empire" (*Bulletin de la Société linguistique de Paris*, LX, 1 (1965), 54-70) the author, the Hungarian scholar József Herman, has indeed proposed a methodology for a comparative-quantitative analysis of inscriptional material based on deviations alone. Convinced that the numerical proportion of a deviation in a given region reveals no more than the relative level of orthographic correctness, Herman bases his comparison on the ratio between spellings that are likely to reflect a phonetic feature of the spoken language and the total number of all deviations in that same region. Thus, for instance, in his analysis of fifth and sixth century Christian inscriptions he finds 50 *consonantal* deviations out of an overall total of 304 deviations (both vocalic and consonantal) in *Gaul* (mainly *Vienne* and *Lyon*), a 16.4 % ratio, as against 122 *consonantal* deviations in *southern Italy*, out of a total of 288 deviations, i.e., a 53.5 % ratio, and 183 *consonantal* deviations in *Rome*, out of a total of 415 deviations (a 44.1 % ratio), and he concludes that "la Gaule, comparée en particulier à la région de Rome et à l'Italie du Sud, possédait au Ve siècle un consonantisme relativement bien conservé" (63). Interestingly enough, Herman shows that in the 5th century the orthographic confusion between stressed Latin /ō/ and /ŭ/ and /ē/ and /ĭ/ is considerably less frequent in *Rome* (and in *Italy* in general) than in *Gaul*, a finding which is in absolute accord with our own statistical data (arrived at quite independently of Herman's work by comparing correct spellings and deviations from the classical norm) for *Lugdunensis* and *Narbonensis* (cf. our *Local Variations*, 60).

A restatement of Herman's methodology is also found in his more recent "Essai sur la latinité du littoral adriatique à l'époque de l'Empire" (in *Sprache und Geschichte: Festschrift für Harri Meier zum 65. Geburtstag*. München, 1971, 199-266). While strongly embracing the principle of a quantitative analysis of inscriptional data, Herman takes exception to establishing a ratio between deviations and correct spellings; nevertheless, he concedes that "la

Deviations alone do not, to our mind, afford the significance of a given phenomenon and may well lead to assigning them exaggerated importance.

The methodology we propose to follow in this study is essentially the same as the one employed in our previous analysis of the vocalism of Latin Christian Inscriptions. Again, with Ernst Diehl's three-volume *Inscriptiones Latinae Christianae Veteres* and José D. Vives' *Inscripciones cristianas de la España Romana y Visigoda* as primary sources, we have counted all occurrences of each morphological phenomenon we propose to study according to Classical Latin standards and deviations therefrom and we have then compared the extent of deviations among the various areas. Since an attempt has also been made to establish a chronology wherever possible, the numerical analysis, shown in tables in the Appendix, is based only on dated material. However, examples of deviations from the classical norm are also taken from non-dated inscriptions, both to further illustrate a particular phenomenon observed in dated material and to support our conclusions.[7]

The inscriptional material we have chosen is divided into four main areas; these, in turn, are subdivided into regions corresponding to the old Roman provinces (*grosso modo* in accordance with the topographical classification of the *Corpus*), so as to be able to show more accurately the existence of possible local differentiations:

A. *Iberian Peninsula*: (a) *Baetica*; (b) *Lusitania*; (c) *Tarraconensis*
B. *Gaul*: (a) *Narbonensis*; (b) *Lugdunensis*
C. *Italy*: (a) *Northern*; (b) *Central*; (c) *Southern Italy*
D. *Rome*

While it is not our intention to repeat here the detailed description of individual areas given in our previous study (28-34), it may be appropriate, nevertheless, to summarize briefly some of our earlier comments.

---

proportion entre graphies fautives et graphies correctes peut être suggestive pour caractériser l'état de la langue d'une seule région" (205).

[7] For a justification of the validity of our methodology, cf. our *Local Variations*, 26-28.

A. *Iberian Peninsula*

The primary source for our analysis of inscriptional material from this area is the Vives collection of Christian inscriptions from Roman and Visigothic Spain, primarily because it contains about sixty epitaphs from a military cemetery at ancient *Tarraco* (present-day *Tarragona*) discovered only in 1924. These are not found in Diehl.

The total number of 362 funerary inscriptions found in this area is broken down by regions as follows:

(a) *Baetica*: 90 dated; 22 non-dated.
(b) *Lusitania*: 93 dated; 11 non-dated.
(c) *Tarraconensis*: 114 dated; 32 non-dated.

The number of dated inscriptions in centuries preceding the sixth is relatively small. Also, a large percentage of the dated material from *Tarraconensis* is made up of epitaphs from the *Tarragona* necropolis which are not specifically dated, although it has been determined that they originate from between the fourth and early sixth centuries.[8] Hence, we decided to treat all dated inscriptions of the fourth, fifth, and sixth centuries as *one* group, while those of the seventh century are dealt with separately.

Our material from this area also includes a special group of about 40 Visigothic coin inscriptions which, for the most part, are very short.

B. *Gaul*

Volume XII of the *Corpus* comprises *Narbonensis*, while Volume XIII also includes *Aquitania*, *Belgica* and the two *Germaniae*, beside *Lugdunensis*. For the sake of convenience, however, we have designated this whole area covered by Volume XIII as *Lugdunensis*. Except for *Augusta Treverorum*, the number of Christian inscriptions from *Belgica* is negligible and the handful originating from the two *Germaniae* were not included in our count, unless they come from a place where Romance speech developed, e.g., *Vesontia* in *Germania Superior*.

The total number of epitaphs taken from this area is 480, distributed as follows:

---

[8] Cf. Vives, 59-60.

INTRODUCTION 25

(a) *Narbonensis*: 104 dated; 110 non-dated.
(b) *Lugdunensis*: 84 dated; 182 non-dated.

For the purposes of our numerical analysis, the material from this area is divided into two groups: 4th-5th and 6th-7th century inscriptions. The bulk of dated material is from the 5th and 6th centuries.

C. *Italy*

The whole *Italian* area, excluding *Rome*, is broken up into three main regions: the *northern*, or *Cisalpina*, corresponding to Volume V of the *Corpus*, comprising *Liguria*, *Transpadana*, and *Venetia*; the *central* region, including *Aemilia*, *Etruria*, and *Umbria*, which makes up Volume XI; and the *southern* region in which we include all Christian inscriptions scattered over Volumes IX (*Calabria*, *Apulia*, *Samni*, and *Picenum*), X (*Lucania*, *Campania*, *Sicilia*, and *Sardinia*), and XIV (ancient *Latium*).

The total of 1183 epitaphs that we studied for this area is distributed as follows:

(a) *Northern Italy*: 190 dated; 228 non-dated.
(b) *Central Italy*: 127 dated; 153 non-dated.
(c) *Southern Italy*: 155 dated; 330 non-dated.

As will be seen in the tables, the inscriptional material from the *northern* region is grouped into 4th-5th and 6th centuries, whereas inscriptions from the *central* and *southern* regions are divided into three groups each: 3rd-4th, 5th, and 6th-7th centuries.

Actually, no precisely dated inscriptions are available from *Cisalpina* before the fifth century; however, the first group also includes about 70 epitaphs found in the military cemetery at *Concordia* dating back to a period extending from the end of the fourth to the first half of the fifth century.[9]

There is only one specifically dated epitaph from the third century in the *southern Italian* region. In *central Italy*, on the other hand, there are 18 inscriptions from the *St. Catherine* cemetery at ancient *Clusium* (present-day *Chiusi*) said to date back to the third century

---

[9] Pauly-Wissowa, IV, 831. The *Concordia* cemetery was destroyed by Attila's hordes in 452 A.D.

also.[10] The number of seventh century inscriptions in both these regions does not exceed half a dozen.

D. *Rome*

The separate treatment of *Rome*, the metropolis, and in many ways the focal point of linguistic innovation, seems to be justified on the basis of the abundance of material, if for no other reason. Out of a total of 1818 epitaphs selected, 744 are dated. The bulk of these (393) goes back to the fourth century; their number decreases to 299 in the fifth and 99 in the sixth centuries. This is quite in contrast to other areas where the bulk of dated material is found in either the fifth or sixth centuries. The number of epitaphs that date back to the seventh century is so small as to be almost negligible.[11]

The pros and cons of the value of inscriptional material, in general, and Christian inscriptions, in particular, have been discussed elsewhere.[12] Suffice it to say that even those scholars who have pointed out the severe limitations of inscriptions as a source of our knowledge of the state of the Latin language in the centuries following the "Golden Age" have generally admitted that with sufficient amount of material it is often possible to catch a glimpse of what the spoken language may have looked like. Admittedly, the language of inscriptions is at times little more than a mixture of formulae in which stone masons strive to imitate the classical language; but these same stone masons unconsciously make "slips" due to the influence of the vulgar language of the people. It is these "slips" or "errors" that we have attempted to bring into a coherent morphological pattern. At the same time, we have also tried to ascertain what morpho-syntactic features that differentiate Western Romance languages can be traced to local variations in Vulgar Latin.

---

[10] Cf. Pauly-Wissowa, IV, 118.

[11] The same situation also obtains for *Gaul* and the rest of the *Italian* area. Without attempting to speculate on the possible causes for the sharp decline in inscriptional material around the end of the sixth century, these might be sought in the decline of Latin culture in *Gaul* and *Italy* as a result of Germanic invasions. In the *Iberian Peninsula*, on the other hand, the strong Roman-Visigothic monarchy was no doubt responsible for the survival of Latin tradition and culture until the Moslem onslaught in the early eighth century.

[12] Cf. our *Local Variations*, 34-40.

CHAPTER I

FIRST DECLENSION

1.1 SINGULAR

A summary of morphological endings is given in table #1 of the Appendix.

1.11 *Nominative*

Whenever this case occurs in our material, both dated and non-dated, it is always spelled with -*a*.

1.12 *Genitive*

The following orthographic replacements are found for the Classical Latin -*ae* ending:

(a) -*e* for -*ae*: The -*e* spelling is very frequent in all areas under study and presumably reflects the monophthongization of the classical diphthong /aj/,[1] while the -*ae* spelling is a mere *graphie archaïsante*. This change is of no morphological significance.

(b) -*aes*, and -*es* for -*ae* (-*e*): There is ample evidence of the orthographic substitution of -*aes* and -*es* for -*ae* (or -*e*) in feminine *agnomina* and *cognomina*, which has been called "an expression in Roman letters of the Greek Genitive-ending -ης (with open E)."[2]

---

[1] Cf. Gaeng, *Local Variations*, 247-252. For orthographic -*ae* > -*e* in Pompeian and pagan inscriptions, cf. Väänänen, *Inscr. pomp.*, 18-19, and Hehl, 14-15, respectively.

[2] Lindsay, 381. Palmer (241) states that the ending -*aes* is a combination of -*ae* and -*ās*. In the same vein also Kieckers, II, 19. Proskauer, however,

This transfer of Latin feminine proper names to a "declinatio semi-graeca"[3] is particularly widespread in the *central* and *southern Italian* areas, including *Rome*. Completely absent from *Northern Italy*, *Tarraconensis*, and *Lusitania*, we found an occurrence each in *Baetica*, *Narbonensis*, and *Lugdunensis*, respectively:[4]

> memoria Fundanianes (V14, 4th/early 5th cent., *Hispalis* or *Emerita*)[5]
> filia bonememoriaes Quelioles (283, *Massilia*)[6]
> depos. Selentioses (3039, a. 334, *Lugdunum*)

Examples from the *Italian* area (except the *north*) are quite numerous. Here is a rather extensive sampling showing the exact location of each epitaph, in order to give some indication as to the geographical concentration of these graecized forms:

(a) Ce. Italy: depositio Locries Magnes (3034N ad., 3rd/4th cent., *Clusium*)[7]
locus Ianuari et Victories (3526, *Toscana*)
Romanes mes. unius (3999A, *Pisaurum*)
(b) So. Italy: depossio infates Aselies (3029, a. 401, *Stabiae*)[8]
filius ... Marturi et Catelles (140, a. 552, *Capua*)

---

sides with Lindsay when she states: "-*aes*, ein nach griechischem Muster gebildeter Genitiv" (124-125).

[3] Expression used by Carnoy to designate "l'usage de la déclinaison en *e* pour les noms propres d'origine grecque" (236).

[4] Carnoy (237) notes the frequent transfer of Latin feminine names to this "declinatio semi-graeca" in pagan inscriptions from Spain. For the use of Latin names with the Greek genitive in -*es* on the analogy of Greek *cognomina* in inscriptions from *Gaul*, cf. Pirson, 128 ff.

[5] This genitive form presupposes a graecized nominative *Fundaniane*, which means that the attested Latin cognomen *Fundania* was drawn into the Greek - ανή class. It is not a case of a mere morphological substitution of -*es* for -*ae*. For the shift of Latin names ending in -*ia* to the Greek -*ane* pattern, cf. Hehl, 6 and 17.

[6] From a nominative form *Caeliola* or *Coeliola*. Notice the Greek genitive extension to the adjective *bonememoria*.

[7] The nominative form *Locria Magna* is attested in an epitaph that comes from the same place, #4145G.

[8] Sc. *depositio infantis*.... The form *depossio*, which is frequently found on inscriptions from the *Italian* area (including *Rome*), is to be interpreted as an assimilation of *depostio* built, it would seem, on a syncopated past participle form *depostus*, just as *depositio* is built on the classical *depositus*. Cf. Pavao Tekavčić in his review of our *Local Variations* in *Revue roumaine de linguistique*, XV, #4 (1970), 4c9.

FIRST DECLENSION 29

                    positi in cimiterium Generoses (2000, 7th cent., Ostia)
                    Probiani v. i. Epifanies c. v. (203, Portus Ostiensis Augusti) [9]
                    dep. Sapriciaes (3016, near Ostia) [10]
                    dormitione Veneriaes (3237A, Ostia)
                    loc. Aphrodisiaes (3882, Ostia)
(c)   Rome: *depossio Petronies* (775, a. 375)
                    loc. Glorioses (2978D, a. 389)
                    dep. Amanties (3003A, a. 395)
                    [dep.] Victories (4217A, a. 367)
                    hunc locum... Anastasies h.f. (694, a. 522) [11]
                    Seberes filia Urbica (3405) [12]
                    in prima Minerbes mil. ann. V (532) [13]

Here are a few examples from this latter area showing the use of the Greek genitive ending with common nouns and adjectives:

    mire bonitatis et totius innocenties (4328, a. 387)
    depositus.... natale domnes Sitiretis (2115, a. 401) [14]
    sub presentia nonnes Cutties ancille dei (1137a, a. 521)
    alumno.... Valentines filies mees (577)
    liberti puelles Sures (766A) [15]
    locus Sirices bidues (3811F)
    fides Val. Lorubies Felicesimes nofites (4338C) [16]

It has been pointed out that the Graeco-Latin hybrid in *-aes* and the Greek genitive in *-es* were primarily used with *cognomina* of slave girls and women from the lower strata of society "dans lesquels l'influence du grec peut le plus facilement se faire valoir, en raison de

---

[9] One would expect *Epifania* to be designated as *c.f.* (= *clarissima femina*) rather than c. v., i.e., *clarissimus vir*.

[10] Both the name *Sapricia* and the masculine form *Sapricius* are attested.

[11] An abbreviation for *honesta femina*.

[12] Nominative form is *Severa*.

[13] *Sc. legione*. The deceased had served five years in the first "Minerva" legion.

[14] For the use of *natale* to refer to the 'day of death' rather than 'birthday' cf. Betty I. Knott, "The Christian 'Special Language' in the Inscriptions," *Vigiliae Christianae*, X (1956), 65-79. *Domina Soteris* is said to have been a "sancta Romana."

[15] This appears to be the signature on the epitaph. Probably to be interpreted as 'the free children of the slave girl Sura.'

[16] For *neophytae*.

la provenance étrangère de ceux-ci." [17] Our material would seem to suggest, however, that these graecized Latin forms are no longer confined to epitaphs of the uneducated classes; funerary inscriptions for *spectabiles, clarissimae,* and *honestae feminae* would rather suggest that the Greek genitive (more likely to be spelled with *-es* than with *-aes*) had seeped up into the more educated strata of society as well, reflecting the strong non-Latin tradition irradiating from the Greek centers of the South.

(c) *-is* for *-ae*: recessit.... die Lunis (V199, 4th/5th cent. *Tarragona*), *Tarraconensis*

d(e)positum ... diae Lunis (3527, *Aquileia*), *No. Italy*

de(p) XVI kal Mai die Lunis (4206, *Mediolanum*), *No. Italy*

defunt. die Lunis (582, a. 392, *Canusium*), *So. Italy*

difuncta est ... dies Lunis (2146a, a. 395), *Rome*

ripausaut Quintilla ... die Lunis (1617N),[18] *Rome*

[dep ...] Iulias die Lunis (4392A), *Rome*

The replacement of the expected *-ae* (or *-e*) ending by the third declension singular genitive *-is* ending in the first declension feminine *Lunae* has been explained by analogy of (*die*) *Martis, Jovis,* and *Veneris.*[19] Thus, our material seems to confirm the fact that the Catalan form *dilluns* continues the Latin *die Lunis* rather than *Lunae*,[20] and that it is this sigmatic genitive which lives on in some

---

[17] Väänänen, *Inscr. pomp.*, 83. Cf. also Sommer, 326; Lindsay, 381, and Pirson, 128.

[18] For *repausavit*, probably in the meaning of 'died' or 'was put to rest.' Cf. Rum. *răposa* 'to die' (Sextil Puşcariu, *Etymologisches Wörterbuch der rumänischen Sprache*, Heidelberg, 1905, 127). For the development of *-avit* > *-aut* and the origin of the Romance perfect of the It. *-ò*, Sp. *-ó*, and Port. *-ou* types, and its attestation in Pompeian inscriptions, cf. Väänänen, *Inscr. pomp.*, 45. For the form *dedicaut*, cf. also Pirson, 57.

[19] Elcock, 52.

[20] Menéndez Pidal (*Gramática*, 187) derives Sp. *lunes* from a hypothetical *Lunae-s* (by analogy of *Martis*) while García de Diego (204) derives it from *Lunis*, although, he says, this form is not attested. Because of the wide distribution of the analogical *Lunis* form, as shown in our inscriptional material, it would seem reasonable to assume that this form was also widespread in the *Iberian* area.

Old Fr. *luns* (Godefroy, V, 53) is obviously derived from *Lunis*, so that it is quite legitimate to postulate the ultimate derivation of Fr. *lundi* from

modern North Italian dialects, as in Lig. *lünesdi* and Pied. *lunes*.[21] Though the reflex of a final -*s* no longer survives in Tuscan (and standard Italian) *lunedì*, our evidence seems to show that the analogical *Lunis* form must have been in use also in those *Italian* areas which are generally identified with the loss of -*s* in the Vulgar Latin period.[22] This is probably the reason why *Lunae die* is usually given as the historical form of *lunedì*[23] but one wonders whether its derivation from *Lunis die* would not be just as legitimate. The evidence would seem to point in this direction.

Nor is *Lunis* the only analogical sigmatic genitive we found in connection with the days of the week. Although not properly belonging in a discussion of first declension nouns, a brief mention of the forms *Mercuris* and *Saturnis* (for classical *Mercurii* and *Saturni*) may be in order, in view of the similarity of the problem involved, namely the analogical extension of the -*is* ending. Except for one example found in *Sardinia: recessit in pace diem mercur(i)s* (1358, a. 415),[24] all occurrences of these analogical forms appear on *Roman* epitaphs:

> *difunctus est... dies Saturnis* (2146b, a. 395)
> *natus est... die Saturnis* (3650, a. 368)
> *depositus... die Mercuris* (4394, a. 399)
> *recessit die Mercuris* (701, a. 452), etc.[25]

In view of the foregoing, it may be said that the survival of forms like *Lunis, Mercuris,* and *Saturnis* in the *Italian* area, especially *Rome,* attested as late as the fifth century (and is there any reason to assume that they were lost shortly thereafter?) is a striking feature of our inscriptional material with what we believe to be important implications for the allegedly early fall of final -*s* in the *Italian* area (except

---

V.L. *Lunis dies* rather than *Lunae dies*, as indicated in some standard manuals, e.g., Ewert, 45, 125, 317; Elcock: "The Latin basis of French and Italian is *Lunae diem*" (169).

[21] The form *lünesdi* is also found in eastern Lombardy and the Tessin, cf. Rohlfs, *Grammatik*, I, 498; II, 23.

[22] Elcock, 51 ff.

[23] Cf. Pei, *It. Lang.*, 76; Elcock, 61. The form *Lunae*, as a matter of fact, occurs only *once* in our material, #4460 a. 355 (*Rome*).

[24] Surviving in Log(udorese) *merkuris* (REW #5519), just as Lat. *lunis* is reflected in Log. *lunis* (REW #5164).

[25] The analogical genitives *Mercuris* and *Saturnis* occur in the following ratio with respect to the classical *Mercuri(i)* and *Saturni:* 5 to 3 and 6 to 1 in favor of the sigmatic forms.

northern Italy, of course) in the Vulgar Latin period.[26] For, had there indeed been a trend to discard final -*s*, one would rather expect to find *Lunae* (or *Lune*), *Mercuri(i)*, and *Saturni* intact and maybe cases of *Marti, *Iovi, *Veneri or even (*dies*) *Soli (by analogy of genitives in -*i*?). As it is, not a single case of the loss of final -*s* was found in any of these forms.[27] The use of the analogical (sigmatic) genitives, then, may just be one more piece of evidence to support the contention that inscriptions generally give good proof of the survival of final -*s* in the spoken language.[28]

(d) *Prepositional Construction with "de"*: Grandgent states that the genitive was little by little supplanted by other constructions "generally by the ablative with *de*" (43). He espouses Meyer-Lübke's view to the effect that "the genitive probably ceased to be really popular, save in set combinations, by the beginning of the third century" (43-44).[29] Menéndez Pidal, on the other hand, takes a more cautious stand when he says that "El genitivo.... se perdió también en fecha incierta, pero seguramente anterior a la época romance. La relación de dependencia se expresó con la preposición *de*" (*Gramática*, 206).[30]

Examples of a construction with *de* followed by the ablative as a substitute for various genitive functions may be found from Plautus

---

[26] Cf. v. Wartburg, *Ausgliederung*, 21 ff. For an opposing view, cf. Rohlfs, *Grammatik*, I, 497 ff.

[27] These names of the days of the week occur with the following frequencies: *Martis* (3), *Iovis* (5), *Veneris* (6), and *Solis* (6).

[28] Cf Proskauer's conclusions based on the study of inscriptional material extending from 200 B.C. to 700 A.D. "In ganz Italien, also grade auf dem Boden, wo in der späteren Sprachentwicklung -*s* geschwunden ist, finden sich nur ganz wenige Inschriften die vulgären Abfall des -*s* zeigen" (175). Cf. also Politzer, "Final -*s* in the Romania," *Romanic Review*, 38 (1947), 156-166, and Väänänen, "A propos de l's final dans les langues romanes," *Boletim de Filologia*, 11 (1950), 33-40.

[29] Here is what Meyer-Lübke has to say on the subject: "*de* statt des Genitivs in verschiedenen Funktionen ist seit Plautus bei allen weniger sorgfältigen Schriftstellern zu finden und zwar wohl um 200 schon allgemein vorherrschend" ("Die lateinische Sprache in den romanischen Ländern" in *Gröbers Grundriss*, I, 374). In the same vein, García de Diego claims that the Latin genitive was "olvidado en el latín popular desde principios del siglo III" (320), except for fixed expressions like *pedis ungula*.

[30] For the breakdown of nominal flections and the concomitant changes in sentence structure with increasing reliance on prepositions, cf. Ernout-Thomas, 7 ff. Also the recent treatise by Tekavčić, II, 35-48.

onward,[31] becoming increasingly frequent in the post-classical period.[32] Of these, "les premiers à céder à la phrase prépositionnelle étaient les emplois marquant la notion partitive et celle de relation," Väänänen notes (*Lat. vulg.*, 121), but he underscores the fact that "l'ancien génitif continue à subsister, et la construction prépositionnelle exprimant l'unique idée de possession est rare même dans les textes les plus barbares" (*loc. cit.*).[33]

Instances of the use of *de* followed by what appears to be the classical ablative form to replace the genitive are far from being numerous in our material. For the first declension, no examples were found in the *Iberian* area and in *Gaul*. As for the *Italian* area, except for one non-dated example from *Ostia* (*So. Italy*), namely *prepositus mediastinorum de moneta oficina* (702),[34] all occurrences of the periphrastic genitive were found in *Roman* inscriptions. Thus, side by side with the correct genitive in *Cinnamius Opas lector tituli Fasciole* (1296 a. 377),[35] we find *Pascentius lector de Fasciola* (1296 ad., a. 398/404). Other, similar examples are the following:

lector de Pallacine (1267ᵇ a. 348);[36] *lector de Pudentiana* (1270 a. 384)[37]

---

[31] E.g., *dimidium de praeda* in Plautus, cf. Palmer, 166.

[32] For an exhaustive list of examples in Late Latin authors (but none from inscriptional material), cf. Atzori, 100-114.

[33] Cf. also his important *mise au point* concerning this problem: "La préposition latine *de* et le génitif. Une mise au point," *Revue de Linguistique Romane*, XX (1956), 1-20. For a similar view, cf. also Th. Maurer who notes that only "na fase final do período vulgar" did the preposition *de* come to express possessive relationship proper (*Gramática*, 87). Similarly, Ernout-Thomas state that "la préposition *de* est attestée, par exemple, avec valeur partitive dès l'époque républicaine, alors qu'on chercherait vainement dans la latinité proprement dite un exemple du type *liber de Petro* marquant la possession" (34).

[34] Note the adjectival use of *moneta*. The deceased was most likely 'chief janitor' at the mint.

[35] For the use of *titulus* with the meaning of *ecclesia* in Roman inscriptions, cf. Diehl, *ILCV*, III, 414.

[36] Sc. *de titulo* (or *ecclesia*) *Pallacinae*. Cf. *lector tituli Fasciole* (1269). Concerning *Pallacinae vicus* 'eine Strasse im alten Rom,' cf. Pauly-Wissowa, XVIII, 156. According to Marucchi: "Il titolo di *Pallacine* corrisponde alla odierna chiesa di S. Marco" (209).

[37] The *ecclesia Pudentiana* is also known as *titulus Pudentis* after the name of its founder, a Roman Christian by the name of *Pudens*. *Pudentiana* is said to have been his daughter. Cf. Pauly-Wissowa, XXIII, 1941.

praepositus de via Flabinia (361);[38] *exorcista de katolika* (1259)[39]
lector de Savina (1274 ad.);[40] *Alexio lectori de fullocines* (2159)[41]

The *curator de sacra via* type construction that Menéndez Pidal cites from inscriptional material (without specific reference, however)[42] to show the loss of the synthetic genitive in Vulgar Latin seems to have been a rather late creation, at least in some areas. Carnoy makes no mention of it at all in his work on inscriptions from Spain. Martin gives a few examples of prepositional constructions to replace the classical genitive, but specifically states that the frequency of the use of *de* to supplant the genitive "is best illustrated in late Christian inscriptions where the best defined examples may be seen" (42).[43] Cooper (75) reports that in the eighth-century *Forum Judicum* the possessive genitive is never replaced by a prepositional construction, while the partitive genitive is replaced by *de* twice out of six occurrences. In his study of the tenth/eleventh century *Cartulario*, on the other hand, Jennings (145-146) finds that the use of *de* and the oblique as a genitive substitute is quite frequent, especially for expressing possession.

Pirson's examples of the *de* + ablative periphrasis to replace the classical genitive are taken from Christian inscriptions, the earliest

---

[38] Translated by Díaz y Díaz (²1962) as 'encargado de la circulación por la vía Flaminia' (126).

[39] Sc. *ecclesia*. Cf. *Lector ecclesie catolice* (1268 a. 362).

[40] The Church of Santa Sabina in Rome. Cf. *locus presbyteri Basili tituli Sabine* (1143).

[41] Presumably *titulo* or *ecclesia* to be understood. "Questo titulus Fullocines — Marucchi comments — è interamente sconosciuto e prese forse tal nome da una *fullocina* vicina" (208). For the *-es* genitive ending, *v. supra*, p. 27 ff.

[42] Cf. his *Gramática*, 205.

[43] Except for one inscription found on a church column at *Acci (Tarraconensis)*, probably dating back to the second half of the seventh century (also included in the Vives collection), all of Martin's examples are taken from post-Visigothic inscriptions. In his view, these examples "mark an advance over the same or similar constructions found in classical Latin in that here the *de* phrase and the genitive are not only parallel, but practically equivalent, as shown by their use in the same sentence" (*loc. cit.*). Thus, in the inscription referred to we read *recondite sunt ic reliquie [de] cruore d̄n̄i .... [de] pane d̄n̄i.... [de] cruce d̄n̄i..... de sepulcro.... sce crucis* (V303ᵇ). Further examples will be found in Martin, 42-43.

dating back to the middle of the fifth century (196).[44] (There are no examples from *Gaul* involving first declension nouns. *V. infra,* 2.12, p. 66, and 3.12, p. 131). Bonnet (609-611) still finds infrequent use of this genitive substitute in Gregory of Tours, but it seems definitely on the increase by the end of the seventh century. Sas reports that in the early eighth-century manuscript of the *Andecavenses* the analytic *de* + *-a* is the favored substitute for the classical genitive "where it constitutes 30 percent of all genitives noted in the first declension" (469). This development is also confirmed by Pei, *Texts,* 245.

For the periphrasis with *ad* to express possessive relationship, *v. infra,* 2.22, p. 103.

The earliest dated example of the use of a periphrastic construction with *de* to express a genitive relation comes from *Rome,* as was seen. In fact, it can be said that all occurrences of this analytic construction with *de* followed by the classical ablative to substitute for the expected genitive are concentrated in this general area (the only example found outside of Rome having been found at *Ostia,* near the capital city). While this may be a coincidence and essentially due to the fact that material from Rome is more abundant than it is from other areas and that genitives expressing this kind of relationship are more likely to occur here than elsewhere,[45] it is nevertheless true that comparable phrases in other areas make exclusive use of the classical genitive.[46]

---

[44] Pirson also cites, from what appear to be non-dated pagan inscriptions, *de gente mea solus* (CIL XII 218) and *de studentibus* (CIL XIII 2038) to illustrate the substitution of a *de* + ablative construction for the partitive genitive. *De* — as well as *ex* or *e* — followed by the ablative is, however, an acceptable substitute for the partitive genitive in classical Latin also (Allen-Greenough, 39), so that these examples do not really represent a deviation from the classical norm. But they do show the increased use of the preposition *de* at the expense of *ex* or *e* (cf. Grandgent, 39; Atzori, 73 ff.), as in *magister primus de numero Erolorum* (= *Herulorum*) (464), versus *ducenario ex numero armaturarum* (497), or *Iovinus de scola carrucarum* (375) versus *scutar(ius) e* [*scola*] *prima* (496), in addition to indicating place of origin, like *de civitate Mursese* (37) (but *e vico Atarca* (674)) or *quem ordinabit venire de Triento* (= *Tridento*) (202).

[45] Note, however, that this relationship is not consistently expressed by a periphrasis in Roman inscriptions either. In addition to *lector tituli Fasciole* cited above (p. 33), we read *lector eclesie catolice* (cf. our note #39), *lictor tt.* (= *tituli*) *sce marturis Caeciliae* (1273), *prepositus basilice* (1308 a. 526), etc.

[46] E.g., *notarius aeclesiae* (1315 a. 386/422), *Ce. Italy; lector sanctae aeclesiae Aeclanensis* (1276 a. 494), *So. Italy; primicirius scolae lectorum* (1287 a. 551), *Lugdunensis; princeps cantorum sacrosancte aeclesiae Mertilliane* (V93 a. 525), *Baetica,* etc.

The evidence, then, would seem to suggest that the genitive written -*ae* or -*e,* but certainly pronounced [e], was still very much alive during the period covered by our inscriptional material.[47] On the other hand, the significance of these periphrastic genitives, limited as they may be in terms of regional distribution, should be duly recognized since they reflect what Pei has called "the analytic tendencies of Vulgar Latin speakers" (*It. Lang.,* 111).

1.13 *Dative*

In all areas under investigation this case seems to be intact, although, like the genitive, it is just as likely to be spelled with -*e* as with -*ae,* the two endings frequently occurring concurrently in the same inscription.

(a) In one instance, however, the dative is spelled with -*es*: *Amelia Cresentianes ... benemerenti* (2650, *Rome*), probably under the influence of the frequent substitution of -*es* for -*ae* (-*e*) in the genitive of feminine *cognomina.*

(b) *Replacement of the Dative by a Prepositional Construction with "ad"*: Väänänen states that in its indirect object function "le datif alternait depuis Plaute avec le tour *ad* + acc." and illustrates this phenomenon with the oft-quoted phrase from Plautus: *hunc ad carneficem dabo* (*Lat. vulg.,* 120). Grandgent declares that similar constructions were freely used by classical authors, a practice which was fostered by fear of ambiguity "inasmuch as the dative in the singular of most nouns and in the plural of all, was identical in form either with the ablative or with the genitive" (44). Politzer believes that with the creation of a single form for all oblique cases in the course of the Vulgar Latin period, direct and indirect objects became identical, so that "the necessity to preserve the intelligibility of the dative function forced the language to take recourse to the analytic construction" (*Lomb. Docs.,* 109). Finally, Väänänen suggests that the analytic dative construction was a convenient expedient for use with indeclinable proper names (biblical names, in particular) and that a phrase

---

[47] Even as late as the eighth century Politzer finds only an overall 11 % replacement of the classical genitive by an analytic construction with *de* (*Lomb. Docs.,* 107).

like *locutus est ad Noe* may have favored its extension (*Lat. vulg.*, 121).

It has been said that in the Vulgar Latin of the West [48] the analytic dative construction with *ad* had gradually displaced the classical dative by the fifth century, [49] a view which does not, however, seem to have universal acceptance. [50] Researchers working on Late Latin and pre-Romance documents have all noted this analytic construction, occurring with varying frequency. [51] Their findings seem to agree on one thing, namely that the *ad* replacing the classical dative is pretty much restricted to nouns, while the synthetic dative generally survives in pronouns. [52]

This "periphrastic dative" construction with *ad* is very poorly represented in our material. There is not a single occurrence of it in the whole *Iberian* area [53] and only a handful of examples in *Gaul* [54]

---

[48] Let us recall that Rumanian has preserved traces of the synthetic dative-genitive to this day, cf. Väänänen, *Lat. vulg.*, 117.

[49] Cf. v. Wartburg's statement: "Depuis le 5ᵉ s. on remplace de plus en plus le datif à terminaison, *amico*, par un datif analytique, *ad illu(m) amicu(m)*" (*Évolution*, 37). As pointed out by Tekavčić, analytic constructions of the *ad amicum* type of identical semantic content with the corresponding synthetic forms (*amico*, in this case) were no doubt originally felt as "varianti affettive, stilistiche, delle sole forme casuali" (II, 38). However, as the preposition became the sole means of expressing syntactic function, any affective connotation of the prepositional periphrasis disappeared (*ibid.*, 40).

[50] For instance Muller (*Préposition* "*à*", 62 ff.) who, as far as *Gaul* goes, places the gradual substitution of the analytic dative construction for the synthetic dative in the Merovingian period (i.e., after the 6th century) and B. Löfstedt (224) who places this phenomenon in the 7th-8th centuries as far as the *Italian* area is concerned.

[51] Thus, Politzer reports percentages ranging from 40 %-60 % in his documents (*Lomb. Docs.*, 109), while Sas, who breaks up his figures not only by groups of documents but also by declensions, reports spreads of 45 %-76 % for the first, 38 %-47 % for the second (100 % in the second decl. neuter in one group of documents), and 31 %-52 % for the third declension (470-471). Cooper reports but one replacement of the classical dative by *ad* (75), whereas Jennings notes that in his documents (10th-11th centuries) the replacement of the classical dative by *ad* with the oblique is "especially frequent" (149).

[52] Pei, *Texts*, 237; Politzer, *Lomb. Docs.*, 109; B. Löfstedt, 225; Jennings, 149.

[53] This fact may explain why neither Carnoy nor Martin make any kind of a reference to this dative construction in their respective studies.

[54] Pirson (195) reports the replacement of the classical dative by a periphrastic construction with *ad* after the verbs *dare* and *concedere* on two pagan inscriptions: *ad cujus templi ornamenta.... dederunt; locum ad istum coenubium concessit*. The French scholar also records two examples from Christian

and the *Italian* area (including *Rome*), none of which involve first declension nouns. [55]

The scarcity of this "analytic" dative is no doubt due to the formulaic nature of inscriptional material. The most frequent use of the synthetic dative occurs in the formula *filiae, filio, uxori, matri, patri*, etc. *fecit* (often followed by an epithet such as *pientissimae/-o, dilectissimae/-o, incomparabili*, etc.); but even with the verb *dare* the synthetic dative seems to be preferred, as one can see in the frequent penalty formula *si quis .... violaverit dabit fisco*, where an occasional *ad fiscum* might reasonably be expected but is never found. Whatever the chronology of the extension of this dative substitute may have been, the gradual disappearance of the classical dative by the fifth century, as proposed by v. Wartburg, is not supported by inscriptional evidence.

1.14 *Accusative*

The *-am* ending is often replaced by *-a* both after verbs and prepositions. Here are some examples gleaned from each area:

A. *Iberian Peninsula*

  (a) *Baetica: accepit penitentia* (V142 a. 536)

  (b) *Lusitania: Sinticio. . . . traens linea Getarum* (V86 a. 632)

  (c) *Tarraconensis: filio. . . . memoria posuit* (V1 a. 354) [56]
                    requivit per bona confessione (V259 a. 562)
                    sorori in memoria posuit (V4)

---

inscriptions where the dative is expressed by a periphrasis with *ad* followed by the adjectives *aptus* and *paratus: ad nunc martiribus sedem tribuentibus aptam* (2172) and *Carusus qui fuit ad dei officio paratus* (1169 a. 557? 626?). These examples, however, were not included in our material in view of the fact that "adjectives of *fitness* or *use* take oftener the Accusative with *ad* to denote purpose or end" (Allen-Greenough, 238), as well as those denoting "mental preparation" (Lewis-Short, 1305), e.g., *aptus ad rem militarem, homo ad omne facinus paratissimus* (quoted by these authors), and thus are not particularly illustrative of the popular trend to substitute the classical dative case by a periphrastic construction.

Concerning *ad dei officio* for the expected *officium*, v. *infra*, 2.14, accusatives in *-o* for *-um*, p. 76.

[55] The few examples will be given under the appropriate declension.

[56] For the shift of meaning of *memoria* as used in Christian inscriptions of all areas to denote the 'tomb,' cf. Pirson, 259-260.

On two non-dated liturgical artifacts we read *fa(muli) Ameri vita Xps custodiat* (V514) and *Auildi vita Ds concedat* (V 515).

B. *Gaul*

(a) Narbonensis: *fondabet* (= *fundavit*) *hanc basilica* (1808 a. 530)

(b) Lugdunensis: *parentes.... memoria aeterna facerunt* (3701)
Porcaria quae mundana reliquit (3327 a. 454) [57]
longa moruit.... vita (1075 a. 630)
ter denus et lustra gesserat annus (1218 a. 548/621) [58]

There are also a few examples of the omission of final *-m* in non-dated inscriptions. The concurrent use of forms in *-am* and *-a* may be seen in *transierunt ad veram ... vita* (4827).

---

[57] Sc. *mundanam vitam*. In the same inscription we also read *tradedit animā dō*.... Since a dash over a letter or a group of letters is frequently used as an orthographic alternative for the purpose of saving space, e.g., $\overline{ann}$ (= *annos*), $\overline{cs}$ (= *consule, consulatus*), $\overline{di}$ (= *dei*), $\overline{e}$ (= *est*), $\overline{i}$ (= *in*), etc. (cf. *Abkürzungsverzeichnis* in Diehl, *AI*, 79 ff.), it is likely that the dash over the letter "a" is used here to mark a final *-m*, especially since the word occurs at the end of a line. On the other hand, the word *mundana*, which also occurs at the end of a line, does not carry such a symbol over the letter "a" and one wonders, therefore, whether the form *animā* is to be interpreted as a legitimate accusative form indicating that the stonecutter may have been conscious of final *-m* as a morphological marker. A similar case occurs in an inscription from *Lusitania* where we read, in part, *novā construxit ianue portam* (V358 a. 661?) with the difference that *novā* does not end the line but *portam* does. (In the same inscription we also read *virginū mater* with the first word occurring in the middle of the line.) Here the question arises as to why the dash to mark the missing *-m* in one instance and not in the other. Could it be that it was put in as an afterthought to bring it in line, at least orthographically, with *portam* (an agreement that the stonecutter failed to make in the case of *mundana* and *animā*) and that the *m*-less forms give some indication in the direction of the spoken language, reflecting actual pronunciation, whereas those with final *m* represent an archaic and learned spelling device? On the basis of the evidence presented in the following pages we would tend to answer this question in the affirmative. In any event, because of the speculative interpretation of *novā* and *animā*, these and other similar forms were omitted from our count.

[58] The form *lustra* would seem to be treated here as a feminine noun showing the assimilation of neuter plurals to the feminine singular. Väänänen reports a couple of such shifts already in Pompeian inscriptions (*Inscr. pomp.*, 82). For numerous instances of neuter plurals shifting to feminine singulars in Merovingian documents, cf. Pei, *Texts*, 163 ff.

C. *Italy*

(a) *Northern*: Occurrences of the accusative after verbs in 4th-5th cent. material are abundant (a total of about 100) because of a large group of inscriptions from the *Concordia* military cemetery mainly concerned with the purchase of *arcae*. Despite the strongly formulaic nature of these epitaphs and the constantly recurring *arcam sibi comparavit* and the penalty formula beginning with *si quis eam arcam aperire voluerit*, the final *-m* is omitted in 23 % of all cases. In this group the concurrent *-am* and *-a* spelling for the accusative is also frequently found. A few examples will suffice:

> *si aliquis eam arca aperire voluerit* (370)
> *arcam conpar* (= *comparavit*) ... *si quis ea* (480)
> *arca sibi posuit si quis eam* ... (506)
> *si quis eis iniuriam det det auro libra una* (836)
> *iuxta et poena capitis* (473) (but *arcam*)

In 6th century material only two occurrences of the accusative were found, both spelled with *-a*, e.g., *per ind.* (= *indictionem*) *tertia* (1162A a. 525).

The omission of final *-m* is also seen on a number of non-dated inscriptions, e.g.,

> *fecit sivi* (= *sibi*) *cum sua coniuge memoria* (1337)
> *non effugiant ira dei* (2019)
> *in mente havite* (= *habete*) *Maria* (3349)

An instance of an apparent ablative for an expected accusative after the preposition *in* may be observed in

> *si quis voluerit in hunc locum poni dabit in scola argenti* (508)

also from *Concordia* (but note *arcam fieri iussit* in the same epitaph). Latin grammars tell us that when the governing verb did not imply the idea of motion, the preposition *in* was to be followed by the ablative case, otherwise by the accusative (Allen-Greenough, 133-134). It seems, however, that the subtle distinction between *terminus in quo* and *in quem* was not always observed in the spoken language even during the classical period (Ernout-Thomas, 96-98, 103), so that it is not surprising that we should find a reflex of this confusion in epigraphic material. (Further examples illustrating this confusion will be given in our discussion of accusative and ablative in other declensions.)

This hesitation in the proper case government after *in* is also shown in the phrase *in hunc locum poni* where, according to the rules of grammar, we should expect the ablative case required by the presence of the verb *ponere* (Allen-Greenough, 273).

(b) *Central*: There are less than ten occurrences of this case in dated material. Deviations occur in 6th-7th century inscriptions where forms in -*a* predominate, as well as in non-dated material:

>   *basilica.... a fundamentis edificavit* (1795 a. 547)
>   *si quis ista sepultura.... iusserit aperire* (3895, 6th-7th cent.)
>   *vita refrigerat tibi deos* (2312)
>   *super aqua refectionis edocavit me* (2404ᵃ) [59]

(c) *Southern*: Except for one epitaph whose dating is disputed (we place it in the fifth century), the spelling -*a* is found in 6th-7th cent. material, to the exclusion of -*am*. About half a dozen deviations also occur in non-dated material, e.g.,

>   ... *ta] bula ipsei posuit* (3702A between a. 337-503) [60]
>   *ut ni qui* (= *ne quis*) *sepoltura mea violet* (3869 a. 558)
>   *memoria sibi fecerunt et suis* (3602)
>   *per inditione* (= *indictione*) *quarta* (4302)

(d) *Rome*: The -*a* spelling for -*am* is quite frequently attested after verbs and prepositions in both dated and non-dated material. Here are a few examples:

>   *numquam mecum discordia habere potuit* (4311 a. 367)
>   *queius familia malitia non meminit* (4330A, ca. 4th cent.) [61]

---

[59] The Vulgate has *super aquam* (Ps. 23, 2).

[60] The feminine dative form *ipsei* is probably built on the analogy of *quei* for *cui*, v. *infra*, note #61.

[61] The genitive form *queius* used with a feminine antecedent, already attested in pagan inscriptions (e.g., *de queius castitate unquam questus sum*, CIL IX, 1524) is not infrequently found in Christian inscriptions from *Rome* and *southern Italy*. The genesis of the feminine form is most likely due to an analogical proportion such as *qui* : *cuius* :: *quae* (*que*) : *queius*; or,

locum ad mesa beati martur is (2128 a. 409)
secundu arcu iuxta fenestra (2144 a. 404)
ad vita perbenit (1454B ad.)
ante domna Emerita (2137 a. 426)
sedet ad dextera patris (2462)
cum quo.... bona vita bixi (666)
per innocentia sua.... tulita est de saeculo (2767)[62]
anatema de Iuda et repra.... abeat (3866),[63] etc.

A great deal has been written on the omission of final *-m* in postclassical Latin and there seems to be general agreement on the loss of /m/ in the spoken language. It is on the chronology of its disappearance that there seems to be no consensus.[64] It is a well-known fact that in his *De m finali epigraphica*, devoted to the question of final *-m* exclusively, Diehl had attempted to set up a number of criteria to explain the possible reasons for omitting this consonant, such as abbreviations (see our note No. 57), lack of space (specifically in the end of a line, i.e., *margine urgente*), attraction to a following

---

perhaps, to an analogical reconstruction patterned after the Old Latin genitive *quoius*, just as the attested feminine dative form *quei* could be patterned after old dative *quoi*, classical *cui*. Mohl, who seems to have been the first to draw attention to the existence of the *cuius - queius* and *cui - quei* pairs (and censured Meyer-Lübke for not including them in his *Einführung*), urged half a century ago that they be included in any treatment of Vulgar Latin morphology "d'autant plus qu'il faudra de toute façon compter désormais avec ce couple *cuī : queī* pour expliquer le roman *lui : lei*" (Review of *Einführung in die romanische Sprachwissenschaft* by W. Meyer-Lübke in *Zeitschrift für romanische Philologie*, XXVI (1902), 593-620, specifically p. 619). The Romance forms *lui* (It. *lui*, Fr. *lui*, Rum. *lui*) and *lei* (OFr. *lei, li*, OProv. *lei*, It. *lei*, Rum. *ei*) are manifestly derived from V.L. *illui* and *illei* which, in turn, seem to be analogical forms built on *cui* and *quei*, respectively. Cf. also Grandgent, 163-165. For the theory that dative *illaei* is due to a contamination of *illi* and *illae*, cf. Väänänen, *Lat. vulg.*, 130; also Elcock, 80.

[62] For the analogical new formation *tollitus* for *sublatus* (cf. It. *tolto*, OFr. *tolt*), cf. Väänänen, *Lat. vulg.*, 154.

[63] Notice the shift of gender from neuter to feminine in *anatema* and the resulting change in declensional class.

Repra for *lepra*. For other instances of rhotacism in inscriptions, cf. Diehl, VI, 51 and 77.

[64] For bibliographical references, cf. Pei, *Texts*, 107-108. Among more recent works dealing with the question of final *-m*, cf. Väänänen, *Inscr. pomp.*, 71 ff.; Rohlfs, *Grammatik*, I, 487, 492; Politzer, *Lomb. Docs.*, 57 ff.; B. Löfstedt, 115 ff.; Higgins, Chapter 4, 16 ff.

word in a different case, etc.⁶⁵ Yet, the German professor himself had to admit after an exhaustive study of the question that in over one thousand cases the omission of final -*m* could not be accounted for. Before drawing our own conclusions, at least as far as the first declension goes, let us consider the situation in the ablative case.

1.15 *Ablative*

This case quite regularly appears spelled with -*a*, both in absolute constructions and after prepositions. The following exceptions should be noted, however.

A. *Iberian Peninsula*

(a) *Baetica*: Out of a total of four occurrences in 4th-5th cent. material, three are spelled with -*am* (two of them on the same inscription), as follows:

Aurelius Iulianus nationem Afram qui (V139)⁶⁶

where, in accordance with the Classical Latin norm, we would expect a so-called ablative of origin,⁶⁷ and

tabernacula in gloriam trinitatis. . . . aedificata (V303 a. 594)

for *in gloria*. There are no deviations in 7th cent. inscriptions and none in non-dated ones.

(b) *Lusitania*: No deviation.

(c) *Tarraconensis*: There are a total of seven occurrences of this case in dated material, spelled four times with -*am*, as follows:

---

⁶⁵ *De m finali*, 190 ff. Concerning the omission of final -*m* at the end of a line, Väänänen's remark is quite significant: "Cependant les omissions de -*m* en marge ne sont faites à dessein que dans des *tituli* de caractère officiel, selon la coutume qu'ont eue les lapicides romains de suspendre le mot à la dernière ou à l'avant-dernière lettre en fin de ligne *margine urgente* ou par le désir de maintenir la symétrie de l'inscription" (*Inscr. pomp.*, 71, note #2). The Finnish scholar clearly implies thereby that accusative forms without -*m* in inscriptions of a less official nature (and what could be less official than a funerary prose epitaph!) this omission indeed reflects spoken language habits.

⁶⁶ Vives comments: "Muy antigua, probablemente del siglo IV. . . ." (44).

⁶⁷ Allen-Greenough, 251.

recessit.... die Lunis oram tertium (V199, 4th-6th cent.) [68]
cum comparem suam Nonnitam (V205, 4th-6th cent.) [69]
inclusi tenerum corpus aeternam in sedem (V292, 6th or 7th cent.) [70]

B. *Gaul*

(a) *Narbonensis*: No deviation in either dated or non-dated material.

(b) *Lugdunensis*: A single instance of an *-am* spelling for the expected *-a* in

requiiscit membri... Audolena bona karetate suam (3858) [71]

C. *Italy*

(a) *Northern*: A few examples of forms in *-am* for *-a* after prepositions,

F. Sindia... in eam arcam iacet (494, 4th-5th cent.)
cum comparem suam Ianuariam (4206 ad.)
cum comparem suam Ixuperia fecit (4237)

For the use of *-em* for *-e* in the ablative of third declension nouns, v. infra, 3.14, p. 139. It is worth noting that in the last example a form in *-am* occurs side by side with one in *-a* (see also our example from *Lugdunensis*), that is, the same kind of orthographic confusion that was also observed in the accusative indicating, it would seem, that in the mind of the average speaker the awareness of the accusative-ablative relationship has been lost.

---

[68] This is how the form appears on the inscription; presumably it should be *tertiam*. We would, of course, expect *hora tertia*, i.e., a so-called ablative of time within which rather than an accusative of extent of time. With an ordinal numeral, however, the accusative may also be found (cf. Allen-Greenough, 266). Whether or not the stonecutter is still aware of so sophisticated a rule is an interesting question. It seems to us that the concurrent use of classical ablative and accusative to express the general idea of time is but another indication of the collapse of accusative/ablative consciousness in the speaker's mind.

[69] For the use of *cum* followed by what appears to be the classical accusative, cf. also Väänänen, *Inscr. pomp.*, 121.

[70] The date of this inscription has been disputed. On the basis of a recent study, Vives places it in either the 6th or 7th centuries.

[71] For *requiescunt membra... Audolenae*. Noteworthy is the change of gender in *membri*.

(b) *Central*: No deviation.

(c) *Southern*: Only one non-dated example of a hypercorrect *-am* form in *hic requiesciet (sic) Modesta quem castam bixit* ... (3249A) (notice also the hypercorrect *quem* for *que*).

D. *Rome*

The *-am* spelling for the expected *-a* in the ablative occurs with some frequency, particularly after prepositions. In about half of all instances, however, the classical and "hypercorrect" ablatives are used concurrently. Here are a few examples:

>*feci bisomum in cruptam ad luminalem* (3334 ca. 4th cent.) [72]
>*cum uxorem suam Silvanam* (2883 a. 360)
>*cum virginiam suam* (4251)
>*se relictum ab eam orfanum* (3398)
>*de parbula mediocritatem nostram feci* (666)
>*et in pace aeternam* (1139 ad., a. 565/578)
>*cum compare suam* (3741); *cum patre suam* (3993)
>*cum coniugi* (= *coniuge*) *suam* (3697), etc.

In what purports to be an ablative absolute construction we read

>*locum quem sibi preparaberat se vibam* (3866)

for the expected *se viva*. [73]

A comparison of accusative and ablative cases seems to show that, on the whole, the *-a* spelling for *-am* is more frequent than the reverse phenomenon. In fact, all things being equal, we think it would be quite legitimate to assume that given the same number of occurrences of both cases the *-a* spelling for *-am* would still outweigh the hypercorrect *-am* spelling for *-a*. The evidence of non-dated inscriptions would also tend to support this conclusion. The trend in the direction of a general orthographic *-a* suggests that accusative and ablative have collapsed in speech to a single /a/ phoneme represented in writing

---

[72] Should be *ad luminare*? The existence of a lambdacized *luminale* form seems to be born out by Venitian *luminal* 'roof-window'; all other Romance forms go back to *luminare* or *luminaria* (REW #5162).

[73] For the origin of this absolute construction, cf. Konjetzny, 322 ff. and our note #85 (Chapter 2), p. 89.

by -*a* or -*am*, depending on the writer's training in formal grammar,[74] also encompassing the nominative in a sort of "Universalkasus" serving several syntactic functions. This "blurring" of case consciousness seems to be particularly evident in the indiscriminate use of forms in -*a* and -*am* after prepositions (though, here too the trend is toward a universal -*a*) whose case governance — either accusative or ablative — is very specifically prescribed by the tenets of traditional Latin grammar.

1.2 Plural

For a summary of morphological endings see table #2 of the Appendix.

1.21 *Nominative*

There are relatively few occurrences of this case in both dated and non-dated inscriptions. In some areas it does not occur at all. Whenever this case occurs in inscriptions from the *Iberian Peninsula* or *Gaul*, it is generally spelled with -*e* rather than -*ae*.

The striking feature, however, is the occurrence of the nominative plural in -*as* in the *Italian* area, specifically *Northern Italy* and *Rome*,[75] outweighing those in -*ae* or -*e*.[76]

---

[74] Cf. Higgins' appropriate comment: "It is not at all likely that scribes knew formal differentiation of one case from another but rather that they wrote as they spoke, attaching an occasional -*m* to the vowel ending because of its constant occurrence in such reading as they had done" (51).

[75] Hehl (37-39) reports several examples from CIL IX (encompassing parts of our *southern Italian* area), like *delicias* (#959), *alumnas* (#3105), and *collegas* (3387ª). The only reliable -*as* nominative occurrence in our *southern Italian* material was found in an inscription from *Sardinia*: *quen tumulant.... patronas* (753). On a garbled inscription found near *Nola* (in *Campania*) we read [...*reli*]*quie beatarum mar*[*tyrum?*] [...*reli*]*quias sanctor*[....] *Maias* (2101). Admittedly, this is not an absolutely reliable example of a nominative in -*as*; however, since the usual formula on these epitaphs concerned with *reliquiae martyrum* or *sanctorum* is a nominative plural followed by the name of the martyr or saint, we are tempted to interpret *reliquias* as being a nominative. If this interpretation is correct then we have here a good example of a concurrent use of two plural nominatives with different morphological endings, pointing to a conflict between an essentially written -*e* and a spoken -*as* form.

Hehl reports no example of the nominative plural in -*as* from the *central Italian* area either.

[76] Because of the particular interest that this feature presents, we have also included non-dated inscriptions in our count.

(a) *Northern Italy*: Out of a total of three occurrences of this case (including non-dated inscriptions), two are spelled with -*as*:

collegas sui comparaverunt (497, 4th-5th cent.)
bene requiescant reliquias (2101 ad.)

(b) *Rome*: While there are only two dated attestations of the nominative in -*as* (as against two correct occurrences), there are seven more in non-dated material out of a total of eleven occurrences of this case. Since most examples from this area have not been previously collected, [77] it may be worth while listing all of them:

filias intercedentes (3753 a. 400/405)
requiescent.... germanas unius utere natas (1707 a. 461/482) [78]
collegas karissimo posuerunt (448)
matri.... filias in pace fecerunt (2710)
Petronia et Martina.... depositas in pace (2954)
duas sorores dormint in pace (3213A ad.)
parentes filiabus que voluistis nobis esse inimicas (3887A) [79]
Anastasia et Laurentia puellas dei quas nos precesserun (1472)
duas sorores: Istercora.... Marciane (4024)
filias matri pientissime in pace (4264G)

First declension nominative plural forms in -*as* have been traced as far back as the second century B.C. Indeed, the occurrence of the form *matrona* on old inscriptions of *Pisaurum* (*CIL* I 173, 177) has

---

[77] The two dated inscriptions have also been reported by Sittl, *Mittellatein*, 565. In the meantime, our study concerning this question was published under the title of "A Postscript to the Problem of the -*as* Nominative Plural Ending in Latin and the Origin of the Feminine *e*-Plurals in Standard Italian" (*Rivista di Studi Classici*, XIX No. 2 (1971), 228-234) but we feel that the examples collected for this article bear repetition here.

[78] Sittl (*loc. cit.*) comments on the form *utere* as follows: "weil wir es mit einer italienischen Inschrift zu thun haben, *utere* nicht = *uteri*, sondern = *utero*." This would seem to suggest the use of a general oblique case (merger of dative-accusative-ablative) in the singular of second declension nouns by the latter part of the fifth century.

[79] The fact that *que* occurs side by side with a nominative plural form in -*as* suggests that the relative pronoun is felt to be identical in the singular and plural, much like Italian *che*.

been interpreted as "dialectal *-as* Nom. Pl.... with the *s* dropped." [80] In a verse from one of the *Atellanae* of Pomponius (ca. 100 B.C.) the forms *laetitias insperatas* have also generally been regarded as plural nominatives. [81] Pompeian graffiti and pagan inscriptions also attest to the *-as* nominative form. [82] Nor is its occurrence limited geographically. Although in our own material of Christian inscriptions examples of *-as* nominatives are limited to the *Italian* area and *Sardinia*, the oft-quoted *hic quescunt duas matres duas filias.... et advenas II parvolas* (3476) and a *fecerunt collegas* (670) come from epitaphs found in *Pannonia*, while an inscription on a tile originating in *Tocqueville* (*No. Africa*) reads *hic abetur reliquias martiris Bincenti* (2103). [83] Interpreted by some as an extension of the accusative case, [84] while

---

[80] Lindsay, 398. Cf. also Pisani: "Si tratta probabilmente di umbrismo" (157).

[81] Stolz-Leumann, 276; Sommer, 329. Pisani considers *laetitias insperatas* as "un oschismo" and adds "o ad ogni modo ci mostra la conoscenza delle forme osche nel latino del popolo della Campania" (*loc. cit.*).

[82] Väänänen, *Inscr. pomp.*, 84, cites only one clear-cut example of a plural nominative in *-as* from Pompeian inscriptions, the form *Asellinas* (#7863), although it seems to us that the form *nugas* (*tu mortus es tu nugas es*, CIL IV 5279) should also be interpreted as a nominative in *-as*. This is how Lausberg, III, 18, note #2 interprets it also; but cf. Väänänen, *ibid.*, 116, for an accusative interpretation of *nugas*. On the *-as* nominative plural in early Vulgar Latin, cf. Väänänen, "Le nominatif pluriel en *-as* dans le latin vulgaire," *Neuphilologische Mitteilungen*, XXXV (1934), 81-95.

[83] We have not found a single nominative in *-as* in either the *Iberian* area or *Gaul*. Carnoy (228) mentions *filias matri posuerunt* (CIL II, 38, 2nd cent.?, *Lusitania*) from a pagan inscription. Hehl (37) also cites *amicas* (CIL II, 5094) from a pagan and *viduas* (IHC 413) from an 8th cent. Christian inscription. Pirson, on the other hand, makes no reference to *-as* for *-ae* (*-e*) in the nominative plural function. Must we conclude *ex silentio* that the sigmatic nominative was not used in the area of *Gaul* before, say, the late sixth or seventh centuries? The absence of *-as* nominatives from Gaulish inscriptions may be a coincidence, of course, but as Norberg also points out it may well be that "der Nom. auf *-as* erst ziemlich spät nach Gallien kam" (*Synt. Forsch.*, 29). Evidence of the replacement of the nominative plural ending in *-ae* (*-e*) by forms in *-as* in Merovingian documents, however, would suggest that by the 8th century the latter had become the normal marker for this case. Cf. Pei, *Texts*, 137; Sas, 75-80.

[84] Cf. Franz Altheim, "Die Anfänge des Vulgärlateins," *Glotta*, XX (1932), 154 ff. who finds, mostly on the basis of early borrowings of Greek words in the accusative form, that "die angeblichen Nominative auf *-as* sind ein Beleg dafür, dass im 2., wenn nicht bereits im 3. Jahrhundert der Nominativ als Kasusform in der des Akkusatives aufgegangen is" (157-158). Cf. also Grandgent who adds that the use of the accusative plural form as a nominative plural "was due in the main to the analogy of the singular, where there was

others regard it as a reflex of the Indo-European nominative in *-*as* preserved in some Italic dialects (cf. Oscan *scriftas* versus Latin *scriptae*),[85] this sigmatic nominative plural form is increasingly attested in Late Latin texts from *Gaul* and *Italy*.[86]

While the nominative plural in -*as* has not given rise to particular comment regarding those languages which derive their first declension feminine plural from a sigmatic form generally interpreted as the Latin accusative case, e.g., Fr. *étoiles*, Sp. *estrellas*, Sard. *istellas*, etc., opposing It. *stelle* and Rum. *stele* which are said to derive from the Classical Latin nominative,[87] the survival of a plural nominative in -*as* in the Vulgar Latin of *Italy* and the possibility that the feminine -*e* plurals in standard Italian may, indeed, derive from this etymon rather than V.L. -*e* (Cl. L. -*ae*) has been the subject of some debate. Studies by Berengario Gerola,[88] Robert L. Politzer,[89] and Paul Aebis-

---

only one form, and of feminine nouns of the third declension, which had only one form in the plural" (*V.L.*, 149). These views had previously also been advanced by Sittl, *Mittellatein*, 565, W. Meyer-Lübke, *Grammatik*, II, 40, and Schwan-Behrens, 150, among others. Cf. also Battisti, 201, and Elcock, 62.

[85] Cf. Mohl, 286 ff. Also Väänänen, *Inscr. pomp.*, 83, and his references to studies by E. Löfstedt, Norberg, and Gerola. The Finnish scholar, however, does not dismiss the likelihood of analogical pressure exerted by the singular (nom. *filia* — acc. *filia(m)*) and by the plural of third declension nouns. "Mais l'analogie à elle seule ne saurait suffire pour expliquer la fortune de cette [*sc.* -*as*] forme" (*Lat. vulg.*, 116). Against the Oscan theory, as well as the "accusative theory," cf. H. Mihăescu, 126-127. The *raison d'être* of the nominative in -*as* is explained as follows: "Din cauză că terminaţia -*ae* (pronunţată *e*) a substantivelor feminine de la declinarea întîia se confunda uşor cu terminaţia în -*i* a substantivelor masculine de declinarea a doua s-a simţit nevoia unei distincţiuni clare şi s-a generalizat la pluralul substantivelor de declinarea întîia forma în -*as*, atît la nominativ cît şi la acuzativ" (126).

[86] Cooper makes no mention of plural nominatives in -*as* in his study of the eighth century *Forum Judicum*. Jennings (93) reports the replacement of the nominative plural in -*ae* (or -*e*) by -*as* in only a few personal names.

[87] Cf. Elcock, 62 ff. This fact, as is well known, has been taken as one of the fundamental criteria for separating "East" from "West" Romance speech. Cf. v. Wartburg, *Ausgliederung*, 21.

For the suggestion that OFr. -*es* and OProv. -*as* plural nominatives derive from V.L. nominative in -*as* rather than the accusative, cf. Sas, 80; Norberg, *Synt. Forsch.*, 28; Lausberg, II, 18; and Väänänen, *Inscr. pomp.*, 83.

[88] "Il nominativo plurale in -AS nel latino e il plurale romanzo," *Symbolae philologicae gotoburgenses*, in *Acta Universitatis Gotoburgensis*. Göteborgs Högskolas Årsskrift, LVI (1950), 328-354.

[89] "On the Origin of Italian Plurals," *The Romanic Review*, XLIII (1952), 272-281.

cher,[90] in particular, have seriously called into question the traditional viewpoint that Italian -e feminine plurals could only derive from classical Latin -ae.[91]

---

[90] "La finale -e du féminin pluriel italien. Etude de stratigraphie linguistique," *Studi linguistici italiani*, I (1960), 5-49.

[91] Holding on to the generally accepted theory that Tuscan and, by extension, standard Italian *rose* is a historical continuation of the Latin nominative plural *ROSAE*, Gerola, nevertheless, finds that "nei dialetti italiani ricorrono, o ricorrevano, filoni notevoli di plurale in -as" (342), reflexes of which are the feminine -i plurals found in some modern dialects (cf. also Rohlfs, II, 42 ff.), in accordance with Meyer-Lübke's phonetic principle of -ās > -i by way of an intermediate -ēs (cf. his *Ital. Grammatik*, 60). This leads the Italian scholar to conclude that the plural of *a*-stem nouns in the whole Italian area does not go back to a single morpheme but "è invece il risultato della stratificazione secolare di due uscite diverse: il nom. in -ae e il nom. in -as" (*loc. cit.*). In essence, then, Gerola postulates an -ae > -e : -as > -i dualism in the derivation of first declension feminine plurals, the standard Italian -e ending being both a "continuazione ininterrotta di una fase ereditata" (349) and the result of a gradual overlaying of a once extensive -as > -i plural stratum by a more prestigious -e plural type derived from Latin -ae, which must have been prevailing in urban centers.

Politzer shows, supported by statistical data culled from eighth-century Longobardic documents, that the Italian feminine plural in -e could not derive from the classical nominative in -ae but, in fact, is the historical continuation of what he regards as the accusative form in -as, "by way of a logical intermediary between -as and -e" (276), namely an attested form in -es. His evidence leads him to conclude that "at the beginning of the eighth century the nominative in -ae was quite dead also in the central Italian area, and could thus not possibly have furnished the Italian plural form" (*loc. cit.*).

The most exhaustive study on the subject is that of Aebischer. For him the plural in -as must have been the prevalent form in the Vulgar Latin of Italy from north to south (already thus postulated by Reichenkron, 188-189); it is, therefore, from this popular form that the Italian -e plural developed through an -es stage (an -as > -es > -e development) reflected in the frequent -es (and occasional -e) spelling of the nominative plural in medieval charters from central and northern Italy. Inscriptional data and considerations of linguistic geography (the bulk of -as nominatives and the presence of final -s in verb morphology in some modern southern Italian dialects, cf. also Rohlfs, II, 288 and 297-298) also point to a nominative in -as as the source of Italian feminine plurals in -e. (His thesis is repeated in a subsequent article in which Aebischer examines the outcome of V.L. -as nominative plural in the Romance languages in general: "Le pluriel -ās de la première déclinaison latine et ses résultats dans les langues romanes," *Zeitschrift für romanische Philologie*, LXXXVII (1971), 74-98.

A critic of Aebischer's -as > -es > -e theory writes: "If a medieval writer wavered between acc. pl. *capre, capres*, and *capras*, this means not that -as has become phonetically first -es, then -e, to the exclusion of -e form from PRom. /-e/ = Lat. -AE, but that he knew one should add -s to form a plural and did so when he remembered to. Sometimes, however,

Of interest to us is the fact that these scholars find an increasing frequency of the use of -*as* plurals in Late Latin documents from the *Italian* area at the expense of the Classical Latin -*ae* (V.L. -*e*) nominative, suggesting that this phenomenon spread from a southern focal point (presumably the *Roman* area) to the north. This movement from south to north seems to contradict Meyer-Lübke's theory to the effect that the -*as* plurals in the south and those in the north are unrelated phenomena, those in the south being attributable to Oscan influence, while those in the north arose through Rhetian or Gallic influence.[92] The total absence of -*as* plurals in both pagan and Christian inscriptions from *Central Italy* would seem to support the unrelatedness of what appears to be the same phenomenon. On the other hand, if Meyer-Lübke's theory is correct, that is, if the -*as* plural form was so widespread in the Galloroman area that it affected the plurals in the Vulgar Latin of *Cisalpina*, would we then not expect to find the sigmatic plural in inscriptions from *Gaul*? As it is, this case is represented by either -*ae* or -*e*. It is entirely possible, therefore, that the -*as* nominative plural form may not have reached *Gaul* before the sixth century,[93] seeing that this plural form does not seem to be attested in *Northern Italy* before the early fifth century. The spreading of this morphological innovation from south to north seems, therefore, entirely plausible.

1.22 *Genitive*

The occurrence of this case is very infrequent. Only one replacement of the classical -*arum* form was found in an epitaph from *Rome*: *capsararius de Antoninianas* (603).[94] Note that the preposition is followed by the classical accusative case, whereas in the singular it was found to be followed by the classical ablative.

---

adding -*s* to his normal pl. -*e*, sometimes to his normal sg. -*a*" (Robert A. Hall, Jr., "Latin -*s* (-*ēs*, -*ās*, -*ōs*) in Italian," *Romance Philology*, XV (1962), 242). For a view that *dues terres* (one of the many examples adduced by Aebischer to prove the shift from Lat. -*as* to -*es*) may be due to hypercorrection rather than showing phonological development, cf. also Tekavčić, I, 113, note #26.

For an intermediate [-aj] stage to account for the Lat. -*as* > It. -*e* change, cf. Reichenkron, 121.

[92] *Grammatik*, II, 41 and 43.
[93] V. supra, our footnote #83.
[94] Sc. de thermas Antoninianas (i.e., *thermas Caracallae*). For *capsararius* 'custos vestimentorum,' cf. *Thesaurus*, III, 362.

No other deviations were found.[95]

1.23 Dative

No occurrence of this case in dated material. In a number of non-dated inscriptions the forms *filiabus* and *libertabus* have been noted, e.g.,

> *comparavit sibi et filis filiabusque suis* (809A, Rome)
> *parentes filiabus sororibus Maxime.... Maximiane* (4172, Rome)
> *lib. libertab. posterisq.* (808A, Narbonensis)[96]

The frequency of these feminine forms in *-abus* in both dative and ablative functions, has been pointed out by Carnoy (215) and Pirson (115-116) in their respective studies. This ending, which evidently served to distinguish the feminine gender from the masculine,[97] must have been widely used with feminine nouns even when there was no necessity of gender distinction, as can be seen in *reliquiab[us....]* (2101, Ce. Italy) and even in an *agnomen*: *Aeliabus Serene et Noricae filiabus pientissimis P. Ael Noricus pater posuit* (4505, Rome).[98]

1.24 Accusative

This case, as will be seen from our table, is always correctly spelled. The single instance where it appears with final *-a*, in *deposita III kal. Gianuaria* (3122 a. 503) may be due to the fact that the word appears at the end of the line.

---

[95] For the survival of the classical genitive plural in general throughout the Vulgar Latin period, cf. Uddholm, 58 ff.

[96] An abbreviation of the formula *libertis libertabusque posterisque*.

[97] Pisani (158) specifically refers to a statement by Priscian concerning these dative/ablative forms: "differentiae causa... *bus* desinentia faciunt dativum et ablativum plurales... *nātābus, filiābus, deābus, equābus, mulābus, libertābus, asinābus*."

[98] Hehl calls these forms in *-abus* "vulgäre Neubildungen" (45). Judging from the studies of Carnoy (215-216) and Pirson (115-116) these forms must have been widely used in the *Iberian* area and in *Gaul* also.

1.25 *Ablative*

Occurrences of the plural ablative in *-is* have been found only in the area of *Rome*. The few deviations involve the use of an accusative form in *-as* when preceded by a preposition, namely

> .... *Valeria cum filias s[uas]* (4559 ad. a. 518)
> *dormet in pace cu filias suas duas* (3215)
> *comparavi ego.... in catacumras* (3757) [99]

For the expected ablative absolute construction *se vivis* (corresponding to the singular *se viva*) we find the accusative form *vivas*: [100]

> *emerunt se vivas Baler(i)a et Sabina* (2153)
> *Mercura, Laurentia se bibas compararunt* (3734A) [101]

This accusative substitution also occurs in an epitaph from Naples,

> *Maximina et Tigris sibi bibas fecerunt* (4151B) [102]

This evidence seems to indicate a definite trend toward the syntactic replacement of the feminine plural ablative by the accusative. The explanation for this is not difficult to find. With the development of the singular "Universalkasus" in *-a*, on the one hand, and the common *-as* ending of nominative and accusative plural, on the other hand, it was inevitable that the *-as* forms should have encroached upon the ablative because of the greater frequency of their use, coupled with the fact that the majority of prepositions governed the accusative case in Latin anyway. [103]

---

[99] For the earliest inscriptional examples of the use of the accusative with *in* to express state rather than motion, cf. Väänänen, *Inscr. pomp.*, 121.

[100] In one instance we find *se vibi* (= *vivi*) (for the expected *se vivae?*), even though two feminine proper names are involved. On the other hand, *se vivi* could also be taken as *se vivis* with omission of final *-s*, but v. *infra*, our note #173 under 2.25, p. 119. *Se vivas* could, of course, also be a nominative plural in view of the frequent *-as* nominative plurals in the *Italian* area.

[101] For the dropping of the syllable *-vē-* (*-ā(vē)runt* > *-aron(o)*) in the perfect ending, cf. Pei, *It. Lang.*, 98.

[102] Because of the preceding *sibi*, the form *bibas* (= *vivas*) could also be considered a dative replacement, cf. Konjetzny, 322, for *vivo sibi fecit* and our note #88 under 2.15, p. 89.

[103] Cf. Allen-Greenough, 130-131.

1.3 Summary

For the first declension, our findings may be briefly summarized as follows.

1.31 Singular

1.311 *Nominative:*

The *-a* ending is used consistently throughout our material.

1.312 *Genitive:*

(a) There is a constant alternation between the *-ae* and *-e* spellings in all areas, reflecting the conflict between the monophthongization of the classical /aj/ diphthong in speech and orthographic tradition. This, however, is of no morphological significance.

(b) The *-aes* and *-es* spelling of feminine proper names (the latter spelling occurring more frequently), patterned after the Greek genitive ending in -ης, is particularly widespread in the *central* and *southern Italian* areas, including *Rome*, with sporadic occurrences also in *Baetica* and the southern parts of *Narbonensis* and *Lugdunensis*, that is, in those regions where Greek influence was still fairly strong. Occasionally, these endings are also extended to common nouns and adjectives, particularly in the area of *Rome*.

(c) Noteworthy is the use of *Lunis* for *Lunae* (also *Mercuris* for *Mercurii* and *Saturnis* for *Saturni*) in those *Italian* areas where final *-s* is said to have fallen in the Vulgar Latin period and does not survive in modern dialects, contrary to some northern dialects which still show reflexes of a *Lunis* form. This analogically reconstructed form suggests that it was in general use in the spoken language and that standard Italian *lunedì* may ultimately derive from this sigmatic genitive rather than the generally postulated *Lunae dies*.[104]

---

[104] Cf. Elcock: "Ital. *lunedì* < LUNAE DIEM" (61). The question is an academic one since It. *lune* could derive from either Latin form (cf. *martedì* < *Martis die*; *giovedì* < *Jovis die*). However, it is insofar of interest since the possibility of *lunedì* deriving from a sigmatic genitive form has never been given serious thought; at least the standard manuals and treatises do not make room for such a possibility.

(d) A periphrastic construction with *de* to mark a genitive relation generally followed by what appears to be the classical ablative, is sporadically attested in *Rome* and surrounding area. It involves constructions of the *praepositus de oficina* and *lector de ecclesia* types, rather than an actual possessive genitive like *de Maria* for *Mariae*. While examples of this replacement are not plentiful, they are, nevertheless, significant since they clearly point to the general Vulgar Latin trend to make the expression of case relationships increasingly depend upon the use of prepositions.

Analogical substitutions and periphrastic constructions notwithstanding, the evidence suggests that the stonecutters were quite familiar with the classical genitive in *-ae* (e), which is still the predominant ending in our material.

1.313 *Dative*

This case, whenever it occurs, is just as likely to be spelled with *-ae* as with *-e*. (The comments made under 3.312 (a) are also applicable in this instance.)

1.314 *Accusative*

It was found that the *-am* of the classical accusative is often replaced by *-a*, both after verbs and prepositions, evidencing the loss of final *-m* as a morphological marker, and the emergence of what we believe to be a general oblique case ending in *-a*.

On the basis of the relatively few occurrences of this case in our material it is difficult to establish a chronology of the disappearance of final *-m*.

1.315 *Ablative*

The expected *-a* ending is sporadically replaced by a hypercorrect *-am*. Examples may be found in most areas under study (though few dated ones). The concurrent use of forms in *-a* and *-am* suggests that, on the level of content, the writer (and, of course, the speaker) is no longer conscious of the classical case system, although a vague reminiscence thereof is still reflected on the level of form.

This same thing also holds true for *mercoledì* which can also derive from *Mercuris die*.

The trend toward a general oblique form in *-a* to serve both classical accusative and ablative functions becomes quite evident when we compare the spellings that the stonecutter uses to represent these cases; the trend in the direction of final *-a* is unmistakable.

Thus, in the *singular* we seem to be left with two endings essentially, namely *-a* for nominative, accusative, and ablative, and *-e* for genitive and dative (also represented as *-ae* in accordance with traditional orthography).

1.32 PLURAL

1.321 *Nominative*

(a) In the areas where the classical nominative does occur, it is generally spelled with *-e*, although an occasional *-ae* spelling can still be found. Again, there is no morphological significance attached to this orthographic change.

(b) Noteworthy is the frequent use of a nominative in *-as* in the *northern* and *southern Italian* areas, and, particularly, in *Rome*, evidencing the survival of an archaic (probably dialectal) sigmatic form in competition with the classical literary form. Not attested in *Central Italy* (where no occurrences of the classical nominative were recorded), the *-as* nominative is also absent from the *Iberian* area (although sporadically attested in pagan inscriptions) and from *Gaul*, where no trace of this sigmatic form is found in pagan inscriptions either.

1.322 *Genitive*

Whenever this case occurs, it is spelled with the classical ending *-arum*. Of interest is the occurrence of a periphasis with *de* followed by the accusative in *-as* on a single *Roman* epitaph.

1.323 *Dative*

The frequency of new formations in *-abus* must be noted, primarily in the words *filiabus* and *libertabus*. This ending, however, is also found with feminine nouns where no necessity of gender distinction is involved (since *filiis* and *libertis* may refer to both genders), e.g., *reliquiabus*, and is even attested with proper names.

1.324 *Accusative*

Found mostly with expressions of date, this case is regularly spelled with *-as*.

1.325 *Ablative*

Deviations concerning the ablative in *-is* or *-abus* (these case endings have been found only in *Roman* inscriptions) involve the substitution of these endings by the classical accusative in *-as*, e.g., *cum filias*. Also, instead of the expected *se vivis*, corresponding to the ablative singular *se viva*, the accusative substitute *vivas* was found.

There seems to be a definite trend for the accusative to replace the ablative, particularly when preceded by a preposition (at least in the area of *Rome*, the only available evidence coming from epitaphs found here). This, we believe, is essentially due to the fact that with the development of the oblique singular form in *-a* the conditions were set for a plural oblique in *-as*, since the only factor differentiating singular from plural was the *-s* marker. The emergence of a plural oblique in *-as* at the expense of *-is* or *-abus* was, furthermore, favored by the morphological identity of nominative and accusative, as a result of the originally dialectal *-as* nominative that, on the level of speech, appears to have replaced the classical *-ae* ending.

The attestation of a seemingly popular form like *filiabus* suggests, however, that the *-as* form had not yet completely obliterated the classical ablative, for which it has, nevertheless, become an acceptable substitute (*cum filias* = *cum filiabus*).

Contrary to the trend to reduce the first declension singular to two endings (*-a* and *-e*), the situation in the plural appears to be more complex. In those areas where nominative and accusative have become identical (*Italy*), it can be said that the plural is reduced to essentially *three* endings, namely *-as* (nom./acc.), *-arum* (gen.), and *-abus* (dat./abl.) (assuming that the feminine *-is* form is little more than a literary reminiscence), while in those where nominative and accusative are kept distinct, we are left with *four* endings: *-e* (nom.), *-arum* (gen.), *-as* (acc.), and *-abus* (dat./abl.).

CHAPTER 2

SECOND DECLENSION

2.1 SINGULAR

A summary of morphological endings is given in table #3 of the Appendix.

2.11 *Nominative*

The masculine *-us* ending is, generally speaking, very well preserved. The following orthographic deviations should be noted, however:

(a) *-os* for *-us*: The nominative singular in *-os* occurs more frequently in proper names than in common nouns and adjectives, in both dated and non-dated inscriptions, e.g.,

> *Eulogios* (2889A a. 524?); *Exoperios* (= *Exsuperius*) (3984); *Teodemodos* (= *Teodemundus*) (4426) — southern Narbonensis
> *Lopecenos* (= *Lupicinus*) (3563 a. 523) — southern Lugdunensis
> *Marcellinos* (2287A); *Eioybianos* (= *Iovianus*) *Retos* (3170A) — No. Italy
> *Antiochos candidatus* (490 a. 450); *Asellos* (2999D); *Leontinos* (3013F)[1] — Rome

The *-os* ending in proper names has been attributed to Greek influence,[2] although this spelling, particularly in the areas of *Gaul* and

---

[1] In the same inscription we also find the gen. sing. form *Faustines*.
[2] Cf. Prinz, 103; Uddholm, 55.

No. Italy, may also reflect the merger of Latin /ŭ/ and /ŏ/ in the unstressed final syllable.[3]

Examples of *-os* for *-us* in common nouns and adjectives are quite few.

>   *Reccaredus rex iustos* (V447 a. 586-601), appearing on a
>   Visigothic coin from *Lusitania*
>   *bonememorios Leo[ni]dans* (2892A a. 582) — *Narbonensis*
>   *c. antestetis est tuos* (1075 after a. 630)[4] — *Lugdunensis*
>   *Disiderius comitiacos* (343 a. 432?) — *No. Italy*
>   *parvos* (2356 a. 544) — *No. Italy*
>   *vita refrigerat deos* (2312) — *Ce. Italy*
>   *dipositos in pace* (2927 a. 397)[5] — *Rome*

Prinz (106) explains the form *tuos* as a case of dissimilation, while Pirson (46) accounts for *parvos* as an "archaïsme dans la langue populaire" due to a preceding consonantal *v*. Since *bonememorios* and *comitiacos* occur in the Gallic area, they could represent a merger of unstressed /ŭ/ and /ŏ/ in the final syllable also, as suggested above. As to *iustos, deos* and *dipositos* found in the areas where this orthographic change occurs only in morphological endings, one wonders whether the final *-s* could not be an "afterthought," so to speak, the stonecutter having had *iusto, deo,* and *diposito* in mind, that is, an oblique form in the subject function (*v. infra, -o* for *-us*),[6] to which he then added an *-s* as a reminiscence of the classical nominative case. (It goes without saying that the same thing can also be said for forms like *bonememorios* and *comitiacos*.) It may well be that these forms in *-os* represent the beginning of a conflict between nominative and oblique case, a conflict which, as is well known, resulted in a single form in *-o* in the singular of *o*-stem nouns in Italian and Spanish.[7]

---

[3] Cf. Pirson, 47. It may be of interest to note that the *-us* > *-os* orthographic change in other than morphological endings occur only in these two areas, cf. our *Local Variations*, 220-221.

[4] A reconstructed imparisyllabic nominative for the expected *cui* (= *qui*) *antestis*. Cf. Battisti, 206. The *antestis* — *antistes* alternation is quite common in Christian epitaphs.

[5] But *positus est Victorianus* in the preceding lines.

[6] We take the expression *oblique* in the sense in which Pei defines it, namely "the single form resulting from the phonetic merging of classical Latin oblique cases, where such merging took place" (*It. Lang.* 76).

[7] Bourciez, *Eléments,* 444 and 519. An entirely different explanation is given by Uddholm for the forms in *-os* for *-us* in the nominative singular of

(b) *-u* for *-us*: The apparent omission of *-s* may be observed in the following examples:

A. *Iberian Peninsula*

In an inscription of uncertain origin — either from *Hispalis* (*Baetica*) or *Emerita* (*Lusitania*), hence the question marks in our table — we read, in part, *fecet.... Leucadius m(a)ritu* (V14, 4th or early 5th cent.).

In the area of *Lusitania*, the omission of *-s* occurs also in *Andreas famulu dei* (V93 a. 525). In both instances the word *famulus* ends a line, so that the omission of the letter *s* for lack of space is not unlikely.[8] In this particular area we counted 25 correct occurrences of *famulus*.

One of the characteristic features of Visigothic coin inscriptions is the frequent use of *iustus* and *pius* applied to the names of kings. On two such coins originating from the *Tarraconensis* (judging from the place name given on the coin where, presumably, it was minted) the final *-s* is omitted, namely *Svinthila... iustu* (V459 a. 621-631)[9] and *Wamba... piu* (V468 a. 642-80). The above remarks concerning *famulu* may also apply in this case, since both adjectives occur at the end of the line. In eleven other instances these adjectives are written with *-s*. The possibility, however, that the *-u* ending may also represent "a compromise between the popular oblique in *-o* and the learned form in *-us*"[10] should not be dismissed, especially in view of the form *iu(s)to* (in a nominative function) (V456, early 7th cent.) found in this group of coin inscriptions.[11] (*v. infra, -o* for *-us*, p. 62 ff).

Latin words: "On peut expliquer l'usage de *-os* pour *-us* comme une analogie, établie d'après le schème: *quietus* : *quietu* (acc.-abl.) — *quietos* : *quieto* (acc.-abl.). La désinence *-os* serait une forme prononcée" (55). Of interest is Uddholm's implication that the forms *quietu* and *quieto* are merely alternate spellings for a single oblique form in the singular (*v. infra*, accusative and ablative forms spelled with *-u*, p. 76 ff.).

[8] Cf. in this connection Proskauer, 51 ff.

[9] The name of the Visigothic king appears elsewhere as *Svinthilanus*, e.g., V375. Cf. Paul A. Gaeng, "A Note on the Declension of Germanic Personal Names On Latin Inscriptions from Visigothic Spain," *Romance Notes*, XIII, 3 (1972), 563-566.

[10] Jennings' interpretation of nominatives in *-u* found in his documents (94).

[11] The editor believes that the engraver meant to write *iustos* (Vives, 155), a form that also occurs on another coin, *v. supra*, V447.

B. *Gaul*

A single non-dated example of the omission of -s was found in Lugdunensis: *Flavius ... positu est ad sanctos* (1574). The word occurs at the end of a line.

C. *Italy*

(a) *Northern*: Two deviations in non-dated material,

> *filio. ... Claudius Crescentinu pater* (3749)
> *depositu idus Semtebres* (2963)

Here the -s is not omitted *margine urgente*.

(b) *Central*: No deviation.

(c) *Southern*: In a non-dated *acclamatio* we read: *Lupu biba!* (857B ad.).

D. *Rome*

Two reliable examples of the omission of final -s were found in dated material,

> *ic positu es Victor* (2927A a. 402)
> *Petrus innox. ... defunctu* (4597 a. 407)

the latter deviation occurring at the end of a line.

There are a number of examples of -s less nominatives in non-dated inscriptions. It may be of interest to note that of a total of 26 occurrences counted, 16 instances involve proper names. Furthermore, in only two cases does the word or name occur at the end of a line, which means that the omission of -s can seldom be attributed to an apparent lack of space. Here are a few illustrative examples:

> *Lidosu, Sotericu, Filipu*, occurring side by side with *Petrus, Erculanius, Severinus*, and *Rogatus* on a stone dedicated to the apostle Paul (1951)
> *Cristu Zesus* (1967A)
> *locu emit pisomu Celerianu* (3809) [12]

---

[12] For *bisomu(m)*. Lewis-Short (240) only give the noun *bĭsōmum* 'sarcophagus for two persons.' The adjective *bisomus*, however, is not infrequent in our material, e.g., Nos. 3799B, 3800, 3801, 3808, 3808A.

defunc(t)u annoru duoru mesoru III dieru VI (3574E) [13]
locus Ienuares emtu se biba (3744)
titulu factu a parentes (4475), etc.

Admittedly, these instances of the omission of *-s* are few in the face of the overwhelming majority of cases where the nominative is regularly written *-us*. Does the *-u* spelling represent a conscious omission of a letter for lack of space, an unconscious negligence on the part of the writer, or, indeed, the reflex of a morphological substitution? Any of these factors may of course be responsible for this deviation, though in view of the attested morphological substitution of *-o* for *-us*, sporadic as it may be, we would incline toward the view expressed by Jennings, namely "a compromise between the popular oblique in *-o* and the learned form is *-us*" (*loc. cit.*). Cf. also our concluding remarks on forms in *-u* under 2.15, p. 99 ff.

(c) *-o* for *-us*: There is little doubt that this orthographic change reflects a morphological substitution. An occasional example can be reported from nearly all areas.

A. *Iberian Peninsula*

(a) *Baetica*: No occurrences.

(b) *Lusitania*: *Cunde Marcianus famulo Dei* (V565, 5th cent.)

As stated above (p. 60), there are 25 correct occurrences of *famulus* which, as was seen, is spelled once without *-s* (V93 a. 525). The form *famulo* may be the more significant since it occurs in a high frequency word and a stereotyped formula which a stonecutter would not be too likely to misspell, unless there existed a real conflict in his mind between the nominative and oblique cases.

(c) *Tarraconensis*: On a Visigothic coin inscription we read

Condemarus (= *Gundemarus*) *iu(s)to* (V456 a. 610-612)

It will be remembered that in this particular group of coins the occurrences of *piu* and *iustu* were also noted (*v. supra*, p. 60), where

---

[13] But *titulus* in the first line. For an interpretation of *-oru* (also *-oro*) in the genitive plural, cf. Gaeng, *Local Variations*, 229 ff.

the *-u* spelling might conceivably stand for an [o] pronunciation as a result of the merger of back vowels in the unstressed final syllable. [14]

B. *Gaul*

(a) *Narbonensis*: One deviation in an undated epitaph,

titulo duor. fratrum (3578)

(b) *Lugdunensis*: Examples of apparent nominatives in *-o* are as follows,

requiescit bonememorio Felocalus (3562 a. 518) [15]
diacon. Emellio (= *Aemilio*) *nomine* (1218 a. 548/621)
puer nomene Valentiniano (1542)

In these constructions introduced by *nomine* (what seems to us clearly an "ablative of specification," cf. Allen-Greenough, 262), the proper name is usually placed in the nominative case, as in *nomine dictus Aper* (1236), *natu(s)* ... *nomine Pascasius* (1541), and *passim*. Cf. also "quae nunc nominatur nomine Argo" (Enn. *Trag.* 208) cited by Bennet, II, 341. The nominative form *Valentiano* is confirmed by Le Blant, 281.

C. *Italy*

(a) *Northern*: Two *-o* spellings for *-us* in non-dated material,

recyiescet bonomemorio Eioybanos (3170A)
cum filiis suis duo, uno anoro VII et u(n)o anoro III (3197C)

(b) *Central*: On a non-dated mosaic depicting the Savior and his apostles we read *Simon Cananeio* (1962d) (for the expected *Chananeus*). Another epitaph reads, in part, *Mercurio* ... *dormit in pace* (3299). In both instances the *-o* spelling for *-us* in the subject function is unmistakable.

---

[14] For the neutralization of /ŭ/ and /ō/ in Late Latin, cf. Lindsay, 237.
[15] The adjective *bonememorius*, formed, no doubt, on the genitive of quality *bonae memoriae*, followed by the name of the deceased is almost exclusively limited to *Gaul*. There are two instances of this formula in *northern Italian* epitaphs.

(c) *Southern*: The few orthographic substitutions appear primarily in proper names. However, some deviations may be more apparent than real, since they lend themselves to different interpretations. Reliable nominatives would appear to be

> *Ilaro* (= *Hilarus*) *dulcis anima* (897)
> *Quobuldeo* (= *Quodvultdeus*) *requievit in pace* (3137Aa)
> *Urso in bibo* (4157) [16]

The following examples, which appear to be nominatives at first sight, may also be interpreted as dative cases:

> *Lupelo qui vis(it) annu XI et disces*.... (2851D ad.) [17]
> *filio suo fecit*.... *deposito III kal Ianuarias* (2958A) [18]
> *Petronio deposito in pace* (2973G) [19]

D. Rome

The only reliable example of an *-o* spelling for the expected *-us* in subject function would appear to occur in the following epitaph, which we quote in full,

> *Petro et Marcellino in signo domini vivi sivi fecerum* (1545ad.)

Indeed, unless we interpret these proper names as nominatives, we would not know whom *vivi sivi* (= *sibi*) could refer to, since the names of those who provide for a tomb while they are alive are invariably mentioned, e.g., [...*e*]*t Secundina vibi sibi fecerunt* (3236C); *Alexius et Capriola fecerunt se vivi* (11270), and *passim*.

In the following examples, however, taken from short, non-dated epitaphs, the *cognomen*, generally followed by *in pace* only, could

---

[16] The consecrated formula is the following: proper name in the nominative followed by *se vivo* (sc. *fecit*). Noteworthy is the use of the preposition *in* with this construction.

[17] In the epitaphs that contain a similar formula indicating the number of years the deceased lived and the date he died (*discessit*), the name is usually in the nominative case, unless followed by *benemerenti* (dative). It is possible that due to lack of space the adjective was omitted.

[18] A dative in apposition? We would expect *depositus*, cf. *Fortunato benemerenti*.... *depositus XII k. Non* (2950 ad.).

[19] In this particular formula the name is usually in the nominative, followed by *depositus in pace*. Here, also, *Petronio* could be in the dative case (*benemerenti* being understood) with the participle *deposito* in apposition.

also be taken as a classical dative case, even though the more usual formula has the name in the nominative (cf. Diehl, *ICLV*, II, 166-167):

> *Fortunato in pace* (3258); *Maximino in pace* (3258 ad.)
> *Privato in pace* (3799C);
> *Megetio ... cibes Eliopolitanus ... in pace* (4461 a. 345)

The morphological extension of *-o* for *-us* in the nominative singular is very sporadic and the evidence would hardly justify the conclusion that this case was being usurped by the oblique. Rather, it would seem that the classical nominative in *-us* is still rather firmly established in the language, as reflected in the orthography. At the same time, the occasional oblique extension to the nominative should not be dismissed *a priori* as the mistake of a semi-literate stonecutter. It may indicate, as a matter of fact, that on the level of *parole* at least, there was a trend toward a morphological substitution of *-o* for *-us*.[20] In any event, it may be of some interest to note that in the *Italian* area where examples of -o and -u spelling for *-us* seem to be more frequent than in other areas, these substitutions are more likely to occur in proper names than in common nouns and adjectives. (But cf. also the forms *Emillio* and *Valentiniano* found in *Lugdunensis*.)

In addition to the masculine nominative singular in *-us*, there are sporadic occurrences of nouns in *-er*.[21] Except for an unreliable example of *puir* for *puer* (V266, *Tarraconensis*),[22] this ending always appears correctly spelled.

The occurrence of the nominative singular of neuter nouns in *-um* is extremely rare. Of the few occurrences in the area of *Rome*, mostly the nouns *testimonium, bisomum, arcisolium* (but also *arcusolius* with a shift of gender, cf. 3647 ad.), and *cubiculum*, four deviations involve the omission of final *-m*, namely *bisomu* (4460a; 385; 3799; 3799A) and *arcisoliu* (3647), while *erit tibi deus testimonio* (3878) gives evidence of the substitution of *-o* for *-um* which has already been ob-

---

[20] Proskauer states: ".... 'filio' statt 'filius' zeigt die vulgäre Aussprache" (170), i.e., a feature of *parole*.
[21] Occurrences of forms in *-er* in dated material are as follows: *Baetica* 3, *Lusitania* 1, *Tarraconensis* 3, No. Italy 3, Ce. Italy 3, So. Italy 2, Rome 18.
[22] The editors are not agreed on the transcription; "Transcripción incierta" comments Vives (78).

served in connection with masculines in -*us*. For the -*o* spelling for -*um* in the accusative singular, *v. infra*, p. 83 ff.

2.12 *Genitive*

The characteristic -*i* ending of -*o* stems is, generally speaking, quite stable. According to authorities,[23] the older form of the genitive singular of *io*-stems is also -*i*, the classical -*ii* ending being a "grammarians's restoration on the analogy of *o*-stems" (Lindsay, 383-384). Yet, we are told that even after the introduction of -*ii* for *io*-stems "das einfache -*i* bleibt weiter bestehen... namentlich bei Eigennamen" (Sommer, 338). This conflict between the -*i* and -*ii* genitive endings is very apparent in our material, particularly in proper names, as evidenced by the occasional concurrent use of both endings in the same inscription, as in *III kal Maias depossio Iuli Mercurii* (3034, 3rd-4th cent.), or by the obvious hypercorrection *diaconii* (V267). This deviation, however, is of no morphological consequence.

(a) -*o* for -*i*: Of considerably greater interest to us is the spelling -*o* for -*i* in the genitive singular that can be observed in some of our areas under study, notably *Gaul*, particularly the *Lugdunensis*, and the *Italian* area, including, of course, *Rome*.

B. *Gaul*

Pirson states

> ce qui contribue le plus à différencier les inscriptions païennes des inscriptions chrétiennes, c'est la tendance à remplacer le génitif classique par un autre cas indirect sous la forme du datif, accusatif ou ablatif, lorsqu'il s'agit d'exprimer un rapport de possession (189).

This phenomenon is reflected in our material as follows:

(a) *Narbonensis*: In a 6th cent. inscription we read

scs *Florentinus abbas monasterio nostro* (1664 a. 553)

(b) *Lugdunensis*: The bulk of examples comes from this area. Here is a representative sampling:

---

[23] Lindsay, 383 ff.; Sommer, 338 ff.; Stolz-Leumann, 268.

SECOND DECLENSION

transiet ... an XXXXVI rig. Clotario (1169 a. 557? 626?)
anno XV regno dom Theudorici (2912 a. 526)[24]
post consulato Inportuno (4823 a. 510)
in Χρο nomine (2456, ca. 7th cent.) (but *in Χρι nomine* in 2455)
in mensi Iulio diae Sabato (3129, ca. 6th cent.)

for the expected *Iulii*, i.e., 'in the month of July,' as in *IIII° idus Iulii* 'the fourth day before the ides of July.'

The *-o* spelling for *-i* in the genitive is used exclusively in the following oft-quoted epitaph:

membra ad duus fratres Gallo et Fidencio qui foerunt fili Magno (150)

probably of the seventh century (cf. Väänänen, *Lat. vulg.*, 122), which, in addition to what has been referred to as "genitivos del caso oblicuo merovingio" (Díaz y Díaz, ¹1950, 122) for the expected *Galli, Fidentii*, and *Magni*, respectively), also shows the replacement of the possessive genitive by a prepositional construction: *ad duus* (= *duos*) *fratres* for *duorum fratrum*. (*V. infra*, 2.22, p. 106.)

Here are two more non-dated examples of the apparent oblique extension to the genitive:

Ursiniano subdiacono ... ossa requiescunt (3453)
in hunc tetolo requiescit Roteldis Rodoberto (3597)[25]

---

[24] The use of *regno* for *regni* (e.g., *anno XXXVII rigni [do]mi Chlotarii regis* (1218 a. 548 or 621)) occurs in five more instances (Nos. 2913, 2915, 2916, 3303, and 1220) ranging from the early 6th to the early 7th centuries.

[25] *Roteldis* is either the wife or daughter of *Rodobertus*, a Latinized Germanic name.
Le Blant records in his *Recueil* (279-280) the forms TAVRV (#263) and TEOVALDO (#264) and states specifically that "les deux noms TAVRV, TEOVALDO.... malgré leurs désinences, me paraissent être au génitif" (280-281). These apparent genitives in *-o* (and *-u*) have, however, also been interpreted as so-called "datives of possession," cf. Sittl, *Mittellatein*, 573. Ernout-Thomas consider the phenomenon (already attested in Plautus, e.g., *Philocomasio amator*) as "un tour de la langue parlée" (63), while Bennett states that "In Early Latin the Dative of possession is a very common idiom" (159). For the encroachment of the dative on the genitive denoting possession, cf. also Maurer, 91, with examples.
According to Norberg, a form like *Rodoberto*, just like *Gallo, Fidencio*, and *Magno* in #150, would be a *dativus sympatheticus* which had lost its special dative connotation through frequent use and could thus easily replace

At this point, we may also mention a phenomenon which seems to be peculiar to this area, namely the use of *regnum* in the genitive function, e.g., *anno V regnum domni nost Chlodovei reg* (1463 a. 643?).[26] This form is found in similar formulas in other texts also; thus, the opening line of the *Formulae Andecavenses* reads *Annum quarto regnum domini nostri Childeberto reges*.[27] Muller-Taylor's linguistic comment upon it is of interest:

> In spite of the apparent confusion of forms, this first line obeys very clearly the linguistic laws. *Annum quarto* marks the merging of the accusative and the general oblique case; *regnum* for the genitive is due to the same law; however, the genitive of possession remains alive longer, and we find *domni nostri reges (regis) Childeberto,* which shows the tendency to discard all forms except the general oblique for proper names (186, note #1).[28]

With respect to the frequent replacement of forms in *-o* for those in *-i* in this case function, Pei has found that "the use of the oblique case for the genitive is one of the most striking and frequent phenomena in the syntax of our texts" (*Texts*, 218), further specifying that this phenomenon appears primarily in proper names "almost to the exclusion of the traditional genitive ending" as well as common nouns and adjectives used in connection with such proper names, but that "it also appears in a large number of instances where no proper

---

the possessive genitive. The Swedish scholar's argument runs as follows: "durch die häufige Verwendung dieses Dativs ging die spezielle Dativbedeutung, die eine grössere Innigkeit und Teilnahme ausdrückte, verloren, und er konnte den possessiven Gen. ohne weiteres ersetzen. In der 2. Dekl. Sing. konnte also die Endung *-o* statt aller anderen obliquen Kasusformen verwendet werden" (*Synt. Forsch.*, 44). Whether or not we agree with Norberg's dative interpretation of such forms in *-o*, the significance of his point is that on the morphological level a universal singular form in *-o* could express the function traditionally reserved for the genitive in *-i*. Hence, to attach such labels as "dative of possession" and "sympathetic dative" to Late Latin forms in *-o* in genitive function seems to us irrelevant. See also our note #47, *infra*, particularly as regards these forms in Merovingian documents.

[26] This genitive in *-um* appears in two more instances: *indictione XIII regnum domni nostri Theudoberti regis* (1219 a. 610), and *Indictione nona regnum domni Theodoberti reges* (2919A a. 546? 606?).

[27] Muller-Taylor, 186. For the date of composition of these *Formulae*, cf. *ibid.*, 185, and Díaz y Díaz, ²1962, 193.

[28] For other instances of forms in *-um* in the genitive function in Merovingian documents, cf. Sas, 107 ff.

name is concerned" (*loc. cit.*). The evidence of our inscriptions from this area seems to foreshadow this state of affairs, especially as far as proper names go.[29]

C. *Italy*

(a) *Northern*: The following epitaphs from the *Concordia* cemetery (4th-5th cent.) show forms in -*o* in a genitive function:

> *davit fisco viribus argenti p. (= pondo) V* (436)[30]
> *det auro libro una* (836)[31]
> *arca Ursicini lapedario* (654)

This same phenomenon is also attested in epitaphs from other northern areas, as in

> *consulato Aeti et Valerio* (343 a. 432)
> *consulato Honorio XII et Theodosio VII Augustorum* (200ᵃ a. 418)[32]

The concurrent use of forms in -*i* and -*o* in the genitive function (*Ursicini* — *lapedario*; *Aeti* — *Valerio*) is noteworthy because this morphological confusion is a rather good indication that side by side with the traditional (learned?) genitive ending in -*i*, the oblique form in -*o* is used as an acceptable alternative for expressing possessive relationship.

A particularly interesting deviation occurs in

> *p.c. [Lampa]di et Oresto* (1157 a. 531)

---

[29] Cf. the statistical data furnished by Pei (*Texts*, 220, 377), subsequently confirmed by those of Sas (114-115, 505). In this connection, cf. also Taylor, 75-76.

[30] The more usual penalty formula reads simply *dabit fisco, dabit in fisco*, or *inferat fisco* such and such an amount of *solidi*, or pounds of silver or gold. Cf. Diehl, *ILCV*, I, 98 ff. The stonecutter may have been influenced by this formula, even though *fiscus* stands in a genitive relationship to *viribus*. However, the formula *dabit fisci viribus* is not infrequent, cf. Nos. 464A, 514, 524, and 537.

[31] We would expect a "genitive of material" *auri*, cf. *argenti pondo* in #436. (Allen-Greenough, 213.)

[32] Note, however, the correct genitive plural *Augustorum* governed by *consulatu* 'in the consulship of.'

The correct form should obviously be *Orestis*, a third declension genitive. The *-o* ending, however, shows that the stonecutter treats the name as belonging to the second declension (*Orestus) and we feel justified in including it here because it gives evidence of the same kind of *-i* and *-o* confusion already noted, as in *consulato Aeti et Valerio* given above.

(b) *Central*: A few forms in *-o* for *-i*, primarily in proper names,

> *consulatu Arkadio VI P. Anicio Probo* (2258 a. 406) [33]
> *pos con. Aetio ter et Si(mma)co* (2829 a. 447)
> *reposita est super pectum abunculo suo* (846, ca. 6th cent.)

(c) *Southern*: Only one example was recorded in this area,

> *post con͞ss Honorio XIII et Theodosio X* (2370 a. 422)

D. *Rome*

(a) Instances of an *-o* spelling for the expected *-i* in other than those involving proper names in formulae indicating consular years are few, in both dated and non-dated inscriptions.

> *magnalia Xρο* (1139 a. 535)
> *dormitioni Eutychio.... fecit* (3236) [34]
> *ante tribunal d͞no Ze[su...]* (3858A)

In the following epitaph the genitive relationship is marked by *-u*:

> *in mesu* (= *medio?*) *et situ presbiteriu* (2129)

for the expected *presbyterii*.

Here are a few examples of proper names in *-o* in time expressions,

> *consulatum ... Balentiniano III* (2943 ad. a. 370) [35]
> *sub consulatu Modesto et F. Arinthe* (2976B a. 372) [36]

---

[33] The original epitaph shows the form *consulam*. We accept Diehl's reading because of the letter "a" which would seem to rule out the possibility of *consulibus* and an ablative absolute construction.

[34] But cf. *dormitioni Aureli Sabiniani* (3236A) and *dormitio Elpidis* (nom. *Helpis*) (3236B) showing correct classical genitive forms.

[35] But *consulatum dn. Honori VI* (1351 a. 404) and *consulatum Fl. Vincenti* (2115 a. 401) (for *consulatu*) with the correct genitive complement.

[36] The second name should be *Arintheo*.

post conss. Theodosio Aug. XIII et Valentiniano III (3505 a. 431)
consul. domini nostri Valentiniano ... et Abinio (= *Abieno*) *cos.* (490 a. 450), etc.

In connection with these proper names in *-o* occurring in time expressions in which the year is expressed by the name of the consuls, the following comments are in order. According to the classical Latin formula "The year is expressed by the names of the consuls in the ablative absolute, usually without a conjunction" (Allen-Greenough, 267) e.g., *Optato et Paulino consulibus* (3039 a. 334) or *consule Titiano* (2805 a. 337) in the case of one consul. Around the middle of the fourth century A.D. there begins to appear the formula *post consulatum* followed by the name of the consul(s) in the genitive, e.g., *pos(t) consulatum Amanti et Albini* (2627 a. 346) (the earliest example recorded by Diehl), as well as a construction introduced by *consulatu*, also followed by the name(s) in the genitive case. The earliest example seems to be *consulatu Eusebi [et H]ypati* (1505 a. 359).[37] As a result of the coexistence of these stereotyped formulae, it may not be surprising that there should have arisen a confusion in the stonecutters' minds as evidenced by such hybrid constructions as *consulatu Maximo [II et Pa]terio vv. cc. consulibus* (4387n a. 443), or *Dinami et Sifidi vv. cc. consulibus* (1059 a. 448) (for *Dynamio et Sividio*).

The interpretation of the various abbreviations used for *consule*, *consulibus*, and *consulatu*, which may range anywhere from *c.* to *cos.* (*coss.*) or *cons.* (*conss.*),[38] presents a further difficulty. (In the case of *post consulatum*, *sub consulatum*, or *in consulatu* — the first one often abbreviated to *p.c.* — the nature of the abbreviation is irrelevant because of the preceding preposition.) How, for instance, should we interpret *conss. dn. Arcadi Aug. II et Rufinio* (4219B a. 392)?[39] Is it to be *consulatu*, in which case *Arcadi* is correct and *Rufinio* is not, or was the stonecutter thinking of *consulibus* introducing an ablative absolute construction, as reflected in *Rufinio*? In the two construc-

---

[37] The consuls *Fl. Eusebius* and *F. Hypatius*. For *-ii* > *-i*, v. supra, p. 66.

[38] For a full account of abbreviations, cf. Diehl, *ILCV*, III, 219 ff.

[39] The second name presupposes a nom. *Rufinius* (the name of the consul in question being *Rufinus*) probably by analogy of *Arcadius*. The concurrent use of a genitive in *-i* and *-o* may also indicate that in the stonecutter's mind the latter had become an acceptable alternative to the classical model.

tions *conss. Maximi iterum et Pateri* (3506 a. 443) and *conss. Maximo iterum et Paterio* (1086ad. a. 443), both the forms in -*i* and -*o* are correct if we precede them by *consulatu* and *consulibus*, respectively. Similarly, in *cons. Petro* (1648B a. 516) as against *cons. Deci iun.* (1024 a. 529) the first abbreviation apparently stands for *consule* and the second for *consulatu*. Cases of this kind are very frequent, and it would be tempting to interpret them in this sense; yet, as in the example quoted above, instances in which both the genitive and ablative follow *conss.* makes us wonder whether such an assumption is really justified. In order, therefore, to avoid any pitfalls on account of an incorrect interpretation of an abbreviation we have only recorded those instances of deviations (-*o* for -*i*) which are clearly identifiable as to the case required by the preceding word (in case of abbreviations, the prepositions *post, sub,* or *in*).

Having thus eliminated all doubtful cases, we are, nevertheless, left with a number of instances that could be interpreted as an extension of a singular oblique form in -*o* to the genitive. However, a note of caution seems also to be in order. Our tables show that, indeed, for the *Italian* area at least, the -*o* spelling for -*i* occurs mainly in the fourth and fifth centuries, with very few or no examples in the 6th century, that is, precisely in those in which there seems to be the greatest confusion among the various formulae discussed in the foregoing paragraphs. The decrease in deviations in *Rome*, for example, is particularly striking (23.3 % → 6.6 % → 1.3 %) and would seem to strengthen the hypothesis of a syntactic confusion of these stereotyped phrases,[40] militating against a theory of the extension of the oblique in -*o* to the genitive. This does not mean that we should altogether discard the latter possibility, but simply that the interpretation of the use of an oblique case for the genitive singular — an interpretation that we would subscribe to in connection with the *Lugdunensis*[41] — must be advanced with some reservations.

---

[40] Cf. also Konjetzny, 330.

[41] Deviations (i.e., orthographic -*o* for -*i*) in 6th-7th cent. material amount to about 24 % in this area. There are only two instances of a formula expressing consular year (*p. c. Agapeto* (3562 a. 518) in addition to the example already cited), so that even if we disregard them as possibly being due to a syntactic confusion with an ablative absolute construction we are still left with a 20 % replacement of the classical genitive.

SECOND DECLENSION 73

(b) Periphrasis with *de*: An example each of the periphrastic construction with *de* followed by the apparent classical ablative form was found in *Tarraconensis* and *Narbonensis*, respectively,

reliquie.... de sepulcro d̄ni (V375^b ca. 7th cent.) [42]
minester de tempulo Gerosale (1303, ca. 5th cent.) [43]

The following three examples are attested in *Roman* epitaphs:

Leopardus de Belabru puer (617, ca. 4th cent.) [44]
locus ... lectoris de Belabru (1271 a. 461/482)
lectoris de d̄ Eusebi locus (1274) [45]

It is, obviously, difficult to decide whether the periphrasis in the first two examples is constructed with the classical accusative (minus *-m*) or an ablative in *-u*. As will be seen (*infra*, 2.15 (a), p. 88 ff.) the *-u* spelling for the expected ablative in *-o* is quite frequent in *Roman* epitaphs, reflecting, we believe, a rather close [o] in speech. For further comments and our interpretation of these ablatives in *-u*, *ibid.*, p. 92 ff.

For the analogical sigmatic genitive forms *Mercuris* and *Saturnis*, v. *supra*, 1.12, p. 30 ff.

Even if we disregard such frequent stereotyped genitives as *sancti, domini, dei,* and *Christi*, we must conclude that the classical genitive form in *-i* is still fairly well preserved in our material (and quite intact in the *Iberian* area), despite encroachments by an oblique form in *-o* which is particularly striking in 6th cent. inscriptions from *Lugdunensis*. [46] Indeed, it may be said that by this century, the northern

---

[42] Cf. Chapter 1, note #43, p. 34.

[43] I.e., *Hierusalem*. Cf. *Gerusale civitas* (2324^e) on a Roman inscription. An attempt to show palatalization?

[44] Sc. *de Velabro*, referring maybe to the church of S. Giorgio in the *Velabro* district. Cf. Pauly-Wissowa, VIII:2, 2396. Concerning the word *puer* Diehl comments in a footnote to this inscription: "de servo ecclesia fort. dicitur." The use of *puer* with this meaning seems to be confirmed by Marucchi: "I lettori avevano per ufficio di leggere pubblicamente nelle chiese le sacre scritture. A questo ufficio erano deputati spesso anche dei giovanotti" (207).

[45] Sc. *de dominico*. For the use of *dominicum* (sc. *aedificium*) as a synonym for *ecclesia*, cf. Diehl, *AI*, 76.

[46] If we assume with B. Löfstedt that "die Akkusativendung *-um* als *-o* ausgesprochen wurde" (224), in accordance with the /ŭ/ > /o/ development

Gallic area is farthest along the way to creating a *casus obliquus universalis*. [47]

As stated already in connection with first declension nouns, the few examples of periphrastic construction to mark a genitive function

---

in Vulgar Latin, and we add the three genitives in *-um* to our collection of forms in *-o*, we obtain a 36.5 % replacement for this region. Cf. also Sittl, *Mittellatein*: "Die Genitivendung *-um* [second and third declensions plural] lautete im Vo'ksmunde *o*" (562).

[47] Research on Late Latin documents from *Gaul*, *Italy*, and *Spain* would seem to confirm this. Thus, Pei concludes from his and other studies of Merovingian documents that "by the Eighth Century the classical genitive was being replaced by the oblique case to such an extent as to make its disappearance more than probable by the end of the century" (*Texts*, 222). Politzer, on the other hand, maintains on the basis of his study of eighth-century Longobardic documents that "the genitive ending *-i* is very stable" (*Lomb. Docs.* 73), although his statistics also show an encroachment of the *-o* and *-um* endings to the extent of anywhere from 15 % (*Codice Paleografico*) to between 22 % and 25 % (*Codice Diplomatico*), the *-o* ending being by far the more frequent one "which is not surprising in view of the fact that *-o* eventually became the general ending of masculine nouns" (*Rom. Trends*, 18). On the other hand, we found no reference to morphological replacement of the classical genitive in B. Löfstedt's study on Longobardic laws, so that we must assume, *ex silentio*, that this case is still quite stable in 8th century *northern* and *central* Italy. [We must remember, of course, that these are legal texts and that the Latin genitive survives mainly in stereotyped phrases such as *in nomine Domini* or the *parte Sancti Benedicti* of the otherwise Romance sounding sentence in the 10th cent. Monte Cassino documents "with hardly more awareness of the Latin genitive on the part of the scribe than the average lawyer of to-day has when he says *corpus delicti*" (Jennings, 148).] On the Spanish side, in the 8th cent. *Forum Judicum* Cooper reports 74 correct occurrences of the genitive in *-i* and only *one* replacement by a form in *-um*. [Again, this is an essentially legal document.] We have to wait until the 10th cent. to find any appreciable percentage (13 %) of the replacement of the genitive by an oblique form in *-o*, but even so, Jennings finds that "the genitive expressed by the simple oblique, characteristic of Vulgar Latin texts of France and later of Old French and Provençal, is the exception" (145). As a matter of fact, this scholar notes that the more usual substitute for the classical genitive is the oblique in *-o* preceded by the preposition *de* which by the 11th cent. reaches a figure of 43 % (147).

Cf. also Battisti's statement: "Nel secolo VIII il genitivo singolare della prima e seconda declinazione non esiste più, mentre esso, in quello precedente, ha ancora una discreta documentazione" (199). The Italian scholar's view is, of course, quite at variance with those of, say, Meyer-Lübke and Grandgent (who believe that the classical genitive ceased to be popular by the beginning of the 3rd cent.) and also with the researches of Politzer, B. Lofstedt, and Cooper; however, it is quite in accord with Pei's findings concerning the linguistic situation in Northern France. [Be it said in passing that Battisti cites examples from Pei's study exclusively to buttress his own conclusions.]

seem to indicate that this "analytic" genitive is also an acceptable substitute for the classical form.

2.13 Dative

The occurrence of this case is quite infrequent in some areas, both in dated and non-dated inscriptions. Generally speaking, however, it is spelled with -o throughout our material. A few sporadic deviations may be noted, nevertheless.

(a) -*i* for -*o*: On two epitaphs from the *Concordia* military cemetery in *Northern Italy* (4th-5th cent.) we read the following,

> *dabit poenam fisci auri p. duum* (504) [48]
> *Ateri Florenti et Iuliae Valeriae fecimus* (1942)

while on a non-dated inscription from this same area we noted

> *deo Cristo [devota et T]heodoto diaconi iuncta* (1719)
> (but *iuncta est marito* (586))

A single example of this phenomenon was also found in *Sardinia*,

> *spirito requiescenti karissimi amicorum omnium* (3400) [49]

In his *Beiträge*, Dag Norberg notes that in Late Latin

> der Genitiv besonders oft an die Stelle eines Dativs treten konnte, da diese beiden Kasus in vieler Hinsicht einander besonders nahestehen (34).

Indeed, Norberg adduces a goodly number of examples to illustrate this "dativische Funktion des Genitivs" in Late Latin texts (34 ff.) and finds a confirmation of this phenomenon in the genitive plural *illorum* (also *eorum*, *quorum*, etc., in later latinity), which in the Romance languages in which it has survived (Fr. *leur*, It. *loro*,

---

[48] *Duum* is most likely a hypercorrection, such as occasionally occurs in the ablative singular, v. *infra*, 2.15, the spelling -*um* for -*o*, p. 94.

[49] The phrase *amicorum omnium* is somewhat puzzling. One would rather expect *amico omnium* in this case, cf. *Maximinus amicus omnium* (622 ad.) and *omnium amico* (dat.) (706). In the next line we read *prestatori bono pauperum* 'for the good provider of the poor.'

Rum. *lor,* Cat. *llur*) also fulfills a dative function which "offenbar auf die... syntaktische Entwicklung des Genitivs zurückzuführen ist" (*ibid,* 39).⁵⁰ It would be reasonable to assume, therefore, that these few examples, particularly those noted in the *northern Italian* area (*karissimi* in the Sardinian example could be explained as an orthographic influence of the preceding *requiescenti*), are due to the kind of syntactic confusion that Professor Norberg has in mind. Let us also recall that in this same area the oblique form in *-o* (which some have interpreted as a dative case, *v. supra,* our footnote #25) is sporadically attested in lieu of the genitive in *-i*.

(b) *-u* for *-o*: This orthographic change occurs in three instances on non-dated inscriptions from *Rome*:

> *sibi comparavit ... et Exuperu collega ipsi* (3812)
> *Asellu benemberenti (sic) qui vicxit....* (1970ᵇ)
> *ante tribunal d̄n̄o Ze[su Xρo] [Nazar]enu* (3858A) ⁵¹

Since the *-u* ending for *-o* is frequently found in the ablative (*v. infra*), the influence of the latter would seem probable.

2.14 *Accusative*

With the fall of final *-m* and the merger of /ŭ/ and /ŏ/ in the unstressed final syllable, the accusative is said to have been assimilated to the ablative, giving rise to what was to become, in the second declension singular, the general oblique case in *-o*.⁵² Thus, an originally phonological phenomenon eventually turned into a morphological one.⁵³ However, the orthographic change from *-u* to *-o*, as a result of the disappearance of *-m,* a change which is clearly reflected in studies of Late Latin documents,⁵⁴ is far from characteristic of the

---

⁵⁰ The morpho-syntactic merger of genitive and dative is particularly evident in Rumanian nouns and pronoun-adjectives, cf. Alain Guillermou, *Manuel de langue roumaine* (Paris, 1953), 25-26.

⁵¹ This example was also given to illustrate the replacement of the classical genitive by an oblique form in *-o* (*v. supra,* 2.12, p. 66 ff.). We have included it under this heading also since *tribunal dno* etc. could also be interpreted as an extension of the dative case, a kind of possessive dative.

⁵² Pei, *Texts,* 106 ff. and 141 ff. with additional bibliographical references.

⁵³ Muller-Taylor, 54.

⁵⁴ Pei, *Texts,* 141 ff.; Sas, 124 ff.; B. Löfstedt, 226 ff.; Politzer, *Lomb. Docs.,* 73; Cooper, 51 ff.; Jennings, 95 ff.

earlier Vulgar Latin period, as shown in Diehl's study on the final *-m* in epigraphic material where instances of an *-u* ending in what appears to be the classical accusative case abound (*De m finali*, 268 ff.). [55]

Our table #3 (see Appendix) shows instances of the omission of final *-m*, as evidenced by the apparent accusative forms in *-u*, as well as the replacement of the accusative by what would seem to be the classical ablative form in *-o*, both after verbs and prepositions. Excluded from our tabulation, however, are cases of *anno* for *annum*, (e.g., *vixit anno uno*), which reflect the use of the so-called ablative of time within which for the accusative of time duration, since the latter is already expressed by the ablative occasionally in classical Latin (cf. Allen-Greenough, 266) and, hence, cannot really be considered a deviation.

(a) *-u* for *-um*: Except for the whole *Iberian* area where the omission of final *-m* is attested neither in dated nor non-dated inscriptions, this orthographic change is reflected as follows:

B. *Gaul*

(a) *Narbonensis*: No evidence of the omission of final *-m* in either dated or non-dated material.

(b) *Lugdunensis*: We found only one reliable example in dated material, [56]

[*de*]*o temens puruque co*[*r*] [*ge*]*rebat* (1340 a. 486)

In non-dated epitaphs, three occurrences of this ending were noted, involving the phrase *titulu posuit* or *fecit* (1655, 4161, 4162). [57]

---

[55] Cf. also Carnoy, 206 ff., and Pirson, 99 ff.

[56] In *accepit transitum suū* (1463 a. 645), also found in this region, the dash over the last word would seem to indicate that the stonecutter was aware of the final *-m* ending of the classical accusative, omitted for lack of space (*suū* occurring at the end of a line). In the same epitaph we also find *Augustā* and *septē*. For the use of a dash to show a missing letter, v. *supra*, 1.14, note #57.

[57] No. 4161 reads, in part: *pro caritatem filiae suae titulu posuit*. Notice the use of the classical accusative after *pro* but the omission of *-m* in *titulu*.

C. Italy

(a) *Northern*: The *-u* spelling appears in both dated and non-dated inscriptions. Here are a few examples:

> *post ovitu* (= *obitu*) *meu* (844, 4th-5th cent.) [58]
> *filiae titulu posuerunt* (3361)
> *Petrus cum suis votu solvet* (1882)
> *parentis contra votu ficierunt* (1366) [59]
> *vixit annu et dies L* (2693B)

It must be pointed out that even in non-dated epitaphs the accusative is more likely to show final *-m* than *-u*. Thus, in the region of *Aquileia*, the formula *votum solvit* (also *solvet, solvent, solverunt*) is recorded eight more times showing the correct accusative ending (1822 ad. (occurring twice), 1883, 1884, 1885, 1886, 1887, 1888), i.e., a ratio of 8 to 1. The phrase *contra votum fecit* (or *fecerunt*), which seems to be characteristic of epitaphs from both the *Aquileia* and *Mediolanum* regions, occurs a total of 21 times, always spelled *votum* in the latter region, [60] while in *Aquileia* we find two deviations (*cuntra votu* 3401, in addition to the above example) as against nine correct accusatives. [61]

Does the relatively great number of correct accusative forms indicate that at the time of this inscriptional material (Diehl, *AI*, 2, places non-dated inscriptions in the fifth and sixth centuries) final *-m* was still pronounced? Not necessarily. Let us remember that these are formulaic expressions involving high frequency words in which the retention of final *-m* as a written device may not reflect the true state of the spoken language at all. [62] In fact, as our subsequent discussion

---

[58] In the same inscription we also read *vixit mececu* (presumably for *mecu*). The phrase *post obitu* (for the expected *obitum*) occurs on two more epitaphs from this place (*Concordia*) (Nos. 432 and 520b); but *post hobitum eorum* in #521.

[59] Is the spelling *ficierunt* an attempt to indicate palatalization of the velar consonant?

[60] Nos. 1367, 4200, 4202, 4203, 4203 ad., 4206, 4206 ad., 4208, 4210.

[61] Nos. 4197, 4198, 4199, 4201, 4201 ad., 4204, 4207, 4209, 4210.

[62] Cf. in this connection Emil Seelmann, *Die Aussprache des Lateins nach physiologisch-historischen Grundsätzen* (Heilbronn, 1885), wherein the author states "Die vulgärsprache hat.... jedwedes M dem Schwunde preisgegeben" (357-358).

will show, we believe that the written *-m* no longer reflects a spoken [m] accusative marker but rather represents an orthographic tradition which some stonecutters continue to observe, in accordance with their training in Latin grammar.

(b) *Central*: A single instance of the omission of *-m* in dated material,

vixi(t) ann. unu (3294 a. 400/405)

as well as just a handful in non-dated inscriptions, e.g.,

qui bixit annu et meses IIII (3299)
maledictione avea (= *habeat*) *q. istu sepulcrom misere* (3852)[63]
ne quis velat (= *velit?*) *aperire Iulianete vel Lucentiu* (820)[64]

The form *annu* for what one would assume to be the accusative without final *-m* could, however, also stand for the ablative (for the occasional *-u* spelling for *-o* in the ablative, v. *infra*), despite the fact that where it is followed by the accusative plural forms *menses* and *dies*, this form has generally been interpreted as an equivalent of *annum* (Prinz, 122). The interchangeability and practical identity of accusative and ablative in expressions of time duration, however, as evidenced by the frequently concurrent use of both cases in the same inscription in all areas under investigation,[65] would also lend

---

[63] The verb form is incomprehensible. Diehl comments: "*num voluit laeserit? vix sepulcr. ommiserit.*" In an epitaph from *Capua* we read *qui meum nomine miserit* (3851) which editors have interpreted as a garbled form for *laeserit*.

For the interpretation of *-om* in *istu sepulcrom* as being an attempt to represent the nasal quality of the preceding vowel brought about by the fall of *-m*, cf. Max Niederman, *Historische Lautlehre des Lateinischen*. 2nd ed. (Heidelberg, 1911), 64. Another explanation, already advanced in connection with nominatives in *-os* for *-us* (v. supra, 2.11, p. 59), might be that following his pronunciation habits the stonecutter first wrote *sepulcro* (forms in *-o* to signal direct object function are not unknown in this area) and subsequently added an *-m* to the end of the word because he vaguely remembered that in direct object function a final *-m* should be written in accordance with traditional grammar. For the suggestion of a "rustic persistence of OLat. acc. -OM," cf. Elcock, 27.

[64] For the *-etis, -eti, -etem, -ete* inflection of Latin *cognomina* in *-ane* built on the pattern of Greek feminine names, cf. Hehl, 62 ff.

[65] E.g., *annis XXIIII et meses X dies XXVI* (2817) (but *vixit cum viro suo annos V, mesis V et dies XXVII* in the same inscription!); *annos L et*

support to the ablative interpretation of *annu*.[66] And while we cannot disregard the form in *-u* as a potential accusative, this possibility should be kept in mind and the spelling *-u* for *-um* in these time expressions looked upon with a question mark.[67]

(c) *Southern*: Among deviations in dated material, two involve *annu unu* (1491 a. 392) in an expression of time duration. In the same epitaph we also read *annis tribus*,[68] which could indicate that the writer may have had an ablative in mind in the singular also.

The other deviations read

> *parentis posuerunt contra votu et dolo suo* (4181 a. 400)
> *bixit Hilara super virginiu an. VIII* (4599 a. 385)[69]

Except for another instance of *vixit annu unu* (3191), we may record the following few examples from non-dated inscriptions,

> *post annu* (1738); *emi mici locu a dzaconu* (= *Diacono*) (3763)
> *emerunt locu bisomu a Gaudentiu fossore* (3811B)

---

uno (V830 a. 544); *annis XXIII mense uno dies XXVIIII* (3204); *annos cinque et meses set. et diebus dece* (4580); and *passim*.

[66] On the interchangeability of accusative and ablative "ad spatium temporis designandum," cf. Konjetzny, 330-331. Cf. also Pirson: "Dans les inscriptions de la Gaule, à quelque époque qu'elles appartiennent, l'ablatif a été complètement assimilé à l'accusatif pour exprimer la durée" (183). Similarly, and with specific reference to inscriptions found in Spain, Martin states that "it is not at all rare to find the Accusative and Ablative side by side in the same expression of time, thus confirming their practical identity to express duration of time" (23).

[67] This, of course, may also be said of forms in *-u* other than *annu*, especially those preceded by a preposition where there is always the likelihood of a syntactic substitution of ablative for accusative. *V. infra*, our discussion of apparent ablative forms in *-u* for the expected *-o*, p. 99 ff.

[68] This epitaph is concerned with the *depositio* of two brothers, one of whom lived one year and two months (*menses duo*) and the other three years.

[69] Hilara survived her *virginius* (i.e., her husband who had been a virgin before marriage) by 8 years. Cf. *vixit super virginium suum an. V* (4600) (*Aquileia*); *vicsit super nunum suum* (4602) (*Rome*). While the compound verb *supervixit* also occurs sporadically, e.g., *supervixit annum et menses quinque* (4597 a. 407, *Rome*), it is of interest to note that whenever the survivor is mentioned, the construction becomes *vixit super*.... generally followed by the noun in the classical accusative. The interesting construction *supervixit super maritum* (4428, *Rome*) may well give us an indication as to the possible genesis of this novel way of expressing the idea of 'surviving someone.'

The difficulty of deciding whether forms in -*u* represent accusatives or ablatives is further compounded by the fact that in some instances, like the above-quoted example *contra votu et dolo suo*, -*u* and -*o* endings occur concurrently in the same inscription in identical syntactic function. Is this to be taken as *prima facie* evidence that the form in -*u* reflects an accusative? That is, in essence, what Prinz (121 ff.) suggests when he claims that the frequent forms spelled with -*u* occurring side by side with classical ablatives in -*o* are to be interpreted as -*m*-less accusative forms. Further on this *v. infra*, 2.15, p. 92 ff.

D. *Rome*

Instances of -*u* spelling for the expected accusative in -*um* are attested in both dated and non-dated inscriptions, some of them involving also the forms *annu* and *annu unu* (e.g., 694 a. 522, 2557ad., 2572, 2616ad., 2692Aad., 2697B, 2799B, 2952Cad., 4002Gad., and *passim*). In view of what has been said already, these could also represent ablatives to express time duration (hence the question mark in our table under 6th-7th cent. material). Here are a few examples of deviations from the classical norm,

> *in mente habete Bassu*[...]*torem* (= *peccatorem?*) (2325 ca. 4th cent.)
> *sibi et filio dulcissimo locu ficerunt* (3503 a. 392)
> *est de regione VIII a lacu* (= *ad lacum*) *cunicli* (775 a. 375)[70]
> *post tertiu kal. Mai.* (1539 a. 338)[71]
> *paraverunt sibi locu a Ippolitu super arcosoliu* (2135)
> *in mente habeas Marcellinu peccatore et Iobinu* (2327)

---

[70] For the use of *ad* in this context, i.e., with the meaning of *apud*, cf. Stolz-Hofmann: "Als adnominales Begleitwort bedeutet *ad* neben Richtungsverben 'zu,' neben Verben der Ortsruhe 'bei'; beide Bedeutungen sind gleich alt und in den Dialekten belegt.... Die Verwendung neben Verben der Ortsruhe ist vor allem volks- und sondersprachlich" (219).

For the use of *de* "statt des Abl. originis," and the enroachment of this preposition upon *ab* and *ex* to show provenience and origin, cf. *ibid.*, 261/263.

[71] In the same inscription we also find an ablative spelled with -*u*.

> *ut quisque legerit roget deu* (2376ᵃ) [72]
> *fossor.... ne fodias! deus magnu oclu abet* (3877), [73] etc.

Here are also a few instances where the classical accusative occurs side by side with a form in *-u,*

> *locum quadricsomu (sic) emi* (3821 a. 381)
> *ad domnu meu Viventium* (1904)
> *se vivu comparabit locum vescandente ad domnu Laurentium* (2129) [74]
> *sepulchrum istu fieri regabimus ... si aliquis sepulchru istum violare bolueri* (= *voluerit*) (3855)
> *fecerunt sibi locum trisomu* (3816), etc.

There are many more examples of the apparent omission of final *-m* in the accusative in non-dated material but there are also a great number of correct occurrences. To further illustrate this phenomenon and to get an idea of a possible ratio of omission versus retention of final *-m,* we have selected a sampling taken from Chapter XXVI of Diehl's collection (*ILCV* Vol. II, 279ff), which includes 55 inscriptions from this area concerned with "Tituli ad locos bisomos biscandentes tercandentes quadrisomos eorumque emptionem et pretia pertinentes." Out of a total of 74 occurrences of the direct object (the usual formula being *emit* or *fecit (fecerunt) sibi locum bisomum (trisomum)*, or simply *locum, bisomum,* or *trisomum,* we found 36 occurrences spelled with *-u* and 38 with final *-m*. On six inscriptions, furthermore, we noted the concurrent use of accusatives in *-um* and forms in *-u,* as in *emit sibi et Maxentiae locum bisomu* (3810A). It is also interesting to observe that in five out of seven cases where the

---

[72] But *meruit titulum inscribi* and *ad deum suscipiatur* in the same epitaph. The word *deu* occurs at the end of a line, but so does *titulum,* thus weakening the argument for omitting final *-m* "margine urgente." Why omit the letter *m* in one place and not the other? If the stonecutter was, indeed, conscious of the use of *-m* in the accusative, why did he not make use of the convention of using a dash over the last vowel (the *u* in this case) to mark the missing letter?

[73] Proskauer has interpreted the form *magnu* as an *-s*-less nominative agreeing with *deus* (163). We rather think that this adjective modifies the direct object *oclu(m)*. Would the writer not have meant 'God has a large eye' (and, consequently, nothing escapes Him) rather than 'the great God has an eye' (with which He sees everything)?

[74] Concerning the construction *se vivo,* v. *infra,* our note #88, p. 89.

expected accusative appears with an -*u* ending, the ablative preceded by the preposition *a(b)* is also spelled with -*u*. [75]

Although the percentage of retention of orthographic final -*m* happens to be very high in dated material, a sampling like this one would seem to indicate a considerable hesitation between forms in -*um* and -*u* to signal direct object function, even in formulaic expressions where one might expect greater orthographic tradition. Such a hesitation on the level of orthography surely must reflect new spoken language habits. An attempt will be made to interpret them in a subsequent comparison of accusative and ablative cases, *v. infra,* p. 99 ff.

Before passing on to the discussion of the ablative, let us briefly consider what appears to be a morphological substitution of the classical accusative in -*um* by a form in -*o*.

(b) -*o* for -*um*: Instances of an -*o* spelling for the expected accusative in -*um* occur as follows: [76]

A. *Iberian Peninsula*

Examples of this phenomenon have been found on an epitaph from *Tarraconensis* which reads, in part,

> *siquis temtaverit isto monumento* (V262, 7th cent.)

In the areas of *Baetica* and *Lusitania* the direct object always appears spelled with final -*m*.

B. *Gaul*

(a) *Narbonensis*: On one and the same epitaph we twice read

> *Rusticus voto suo fecit* (1927[a/b] a. 470)

The same phrase also appears on a non-dated inscription: *Eufrasius pbr* (= *presbyter*) *in onore sci Petri apostolo voto suo fecet* (1928), but cf. *votum fecit Menas* (1926[a]) from this same area.

---

[75] Nos. 3811A, 3811B, 3811D, 3811E, 3811F.
[76] The reasons for omitting the form *anno* for *annum* from our discussion have been given above under 2.14, p. 77.

84   NOMINAL INFLECTION IN LATIN INSCRIPTIONS

(b) *Lugdunensis*: Instances of an apparent ablative for the expected accusative in direct object function are as follows:

> *semper deo temens* (1340 a. 486)
> *gesisti sacrum prbr* (= *presbyter*) *officio* (1075 a. 630)
> *pater titolo posuit* (3584D ad.)
> *filio dulcissimo titulo posuerunt* (4160 ad.)

Although in the last example one might also envisage the possibility of an influence of the dative forms *filio* and *dulcissimo* that precede *titulo*, formulae like *filio carissimo titulum posuit* (3582) or *titulum posuit dulcissimo filio suo* (3583B) found in the very same place (*Augusta Treverorum*, the present-day *Trier*) would indicate that this is not necessarily the case. In any event, we believe that the examples showing *titulo* in the direct object function are significant because they come from a group of 38 inscriptions (all from *Trier*) which all contain this formula, where the word *titulum* appears correctly spelled 33 times, the deviations being, in addition to the above, two occurrences of final -*u* (*titulu*) and one instance of a final -*n* (*titulun*). Indeed, the occurrence of forms in -*o* in such a stereotyped formula which a stonecutter would be least likely to misspell would seem to lend support to B. Löfstedt's claim that in the spoken language of this period (ca. 6th-7th cent.) "die Akkusativendung -*um* als -*o* ausgresprochen wurde" (224). [77] This view is further confirmed, it seems to us, by the concurrent use of a form in -*um* (*sacrum*) and one in -*o* (*officio*) in the accusative function (*v. supra*, #1075). [78]

In this particular area were also found two occurrences of the preposition *ad* followed by the apparent ablative in -*o*: *ad dei officio paratus* (1169 a. 557? 626?) and *ad domino* (3490), showing the

---

[77] Sittl (*Mittellatein*, 565) claims that the form *oblatum(est)* on an inscription from *Neretum* (*Calabria*) (CIL IX 10, a. 341) was already pronounced [oblato]. This [o] pronunciation is also reflected in the spelling of the verb form, e.g., (*Iulia*) *bocata so* (1537, *Rome*). Elcock (28) cites a pagan inscription from Naples that reads: *Antipatra dulcis tua hic so et non so* (CIL X 2070).

[78] In the text of the Salic Law composed in the fifth, sixth, and seventh centuries under the Merovingian kings — re-written under Charlemagne, although "not made grammatically correct, evidently so as not to disturb the people or make the document less intelligible to them" (Muller-Taylor, 180) — both -*o* and -*um* serve to indicate direct object function, e.g., *Si quis aut caballo vel jumentum furaverit*.... (cf. Elcock, 309).

confusion in the correct use of cases after prepositions which is considered to be a hallmark of Late Latin syntax. [79]

C. *Italy*

(a) *Northern*: Deviations from the classical norm occur only after prepositions which, in accordance with Latin grammar, require an accusative complement, for instance,

> *parent(es) contra voto posuerunt* (338ª a. 546)
> (but *sposus contra votum posuet* (338ᵇ a. 552) from the same place)
> *contra votum suo fecerunt* (756)

as well as four occurrences of *dabit in fisco auri (tot)* (464, 472, 497, 516) found on several epitaphs at *Concordia* (4th-5th cent.). [80]

The comment just made in connection with the form *titulo* in a highly stereotyped formula is also applicable in the case of *contra voto*, since the formula *contra votum* also frequently occurs in inscriptions from this area (*v. supra, -u* for *-um*, p. 78). The *contra votum/voto* dualism in #338a/b and the form *suo* immediately following the correct *-um* accusative ending in #756 would also suggest that the latter represents a residual orthographic form and that it does not in any way reflect actual pronunciation.

For the use of the preposition *in* with the ablative, despite the idea of motion involved, *v. supra*, 1.14, p. 40. Cf. also *in eo loco cum*

---

[79] Pirson states, in effect: "C'est un trait bien connu de la langue vulgaire et même de la langue littéraire de la décadence que l'emploi facultatif de l'accusatif ou de l'ablatif après les prépositions qui, selon la grammaire classique, régissent exclusivement un des deux cas" (200). Cf. also Stolz-Hofmann, 215. As will become evident from our subsequent discussion, particularly our comparison of accusative and ablative cases (*v. infra*, p. 99 ff.), we believe that we are simply faced with an oblique form in *-o* serving various syntactic functions. Particularly with prepositions it seems to have mattered little whether the noun complement ended in *-o* or *-um* (also *-a* or *-am*, and *-e* or *-em* in other declensions) since the preposition had become the semantic carrier. Thus, Ernout-Thomas conclude: "La préposition finissait ainsi par marquer plus que le cas lui-même la fonction du nom dans la phrase. L'élément flexionnel subsistait; mais il tendait à devenir un signe superflu..." (10).

[80] Uddholm interprets *in fisco* as an indirect object, presumably as an alternative to *fisco* without the preceding preposition, e.g., *dabit fisco auri libram unam* (493). He states, in fact: "Cet emploi de *in* doit être originaire du style juridique où il est extrêmement fréquent" (125).

venitur.... (*Peregrinatio*, I, 22, excerpted in Väänänen, *Lat. vulg.*, 245). Notice that in none of our examples given does *dabit in fiscum* (like *in manum dat*) ever occur.

(b) *Central*: A single example of an apparent ablative for an expected accusative in a non-dated epitaph,

> *contra boto bisosmum (sic) fecit* (3806)

suggesting, as in similar examples cited where both a form in *-o* and one in *-um* occur in direct object function, a purely formal rather than grammatical opposition between these two cases; the writer is still conscious, in a vague sort of way, of a form with final *-m* to mark the direct object without, however, following through consistently.

(c) *Southern*: The substitution of a form in *-o* for the accusative occurs in

> $\overline{p.\ c.}$ (= *post consulatum*) *secundo* $\overline{d.\ n.}$ (= *domini nostri*) *Iustini* (622 a. 575)

although the abbreviation might also stand for *post consulatu* (e.g., *post consulatu Limeni et Catulini* (2940A^a a. 350)) and even *post consulato*, attested as early as a. 386 (323), in which case we could logically expect *secundo*, although still a deviation in terms of Latin grammar.

On an epitaph attributed to the 7th and possibly even 8th century we find the preposition *ad* followed by an apparent ablative (but cf. our footnote #79): *ad populo urbis Ro[mae...]* (3851).

Here also belongs the example *contra... dolo suo* (4181 a. 400) already mentioned in connection with the concurrent use of forms in *-u* and *-o* as complements of the same preposition (*v. supra*, p. 80).

D. *Rome*

The earliest example of a form in *-o* in direct object function is found on an epitaph which Rossi believes to have been composed not later than the early 3rd century, namely

> *ne quis (h)un(c) titulo moles[tet]* (3872) [81]

---

[81] Cf. Diehl's *adnotatio* to this particular epitaph, *ILCV*, II, 297.

Other examples of apparent ablatives in accusative function are:

Alexandro Delicatus voto [posu]it (1923 ca. 5th cent.)
Victorina tumulavit Eraclio marito (362)
fecimus nobis.... arcosolio (3646)

The occurrence of forms in *-o* following a preposition which, in accordance with Latin grammar, would require an accusative in *-um* may be illustrated by the following few examples:

revoca me in foro Martis (712ª ca. early 4th cent.) [82]
benit in cimiterio (2119)
per cibo aut per potu tulita est de saeculo (2767) [83]
... l]ocu paravi secus eo (3736 ad.) [84]

It may be of interest to note at this point that the preposition *per*, although it occurs rather infrequently in our material from this area, is always followed by the classical ablative case. (Cf. also 1.14 and 3.14, pp. 42 and 143). The preposition *secus* occurs only once.

There is little doubt that the forms in *-o* reflect a morphological substitution of what appears to be the classical ablative for the accusative in *-um*. The problem we must address ourselves to is to determine how forms in *-u* fit into this picture, that is to say, whether they should be interpreted as classical accusative forms with the omission of final *-m* or as an "intermediate stage" in the emergence of a general oblique form in *-o*, which is neither accusative nor ablative but a kind of "Universalkasus" which fulfils the functions of dative, accusative, ablative, and, in some cases, also genitive.

Let us now turn to the discussion of the ablative and see if it can suggest a reasonable answer to this problem.

---

[82] The whole inscription found on a slave- or dog-collar reads: *tene me et revoca me in foro Martis ad Maximianum antiquarium*. The formula *revoca me in....* occurs on three more such inscriptions (Nos. 712, 767, 774) with the preposition invariably followed by the classical ablative, despite the idea of motion involved. Notice, however, that the prepositional phrase introduced by *ad* is in the accusative. Cf. also *revoca me in foro Traiani in purpuretica* [i.e., *in porticum porphyreticam*] *ad Pascasium dominum meum* (774). (Re *purpuretica* cf. *porphyreticum marmor non purpureticum marmur* in the *Appendix Probi*).

[83] In the same inscription we also read: *per innocentia sua*, v. supra 1.14, p. 42 and our note #62 re the form *tulita*.

[84] For the use of *secus* as a preposition governing the accusative case, cf. Lewis-Short, 1657.

2.15 Ablative

A glance at our table will show that the ablative in -*o* is, on the whole, quite stable. The following deviations, however, should be noted:

(a) -*u* for -*o*: This orthographic change may be observed in almost all areas under study.

A. Iberian Peninsula

No examples were found in either *Baetica* or *Lusitania*.

The three dated examples from the *Tarraconensis* come from epitaphs found at the *Tarragona* necropolis,

> *depositus est d. quintu k̄l Ianuari* (V192 a. 459)[85]
> ... *Vol]osianu [... con]sule* (V194 a. 503)
> *recess(it) consulatum Eugeni Augusti primu* (V189 a. 393)

In the last example one would expect the form *consulatu* (e.g., *consulatu Honori* (1315) 'in the consulship of ....') but it is also possible that the stonecutter had the formula *consulatum*.... *primum* in mind by analogy of the frequent *post consulatum*... formula.

In a non-dated epitaph we read *decessit*.... *tertiu idus Feb* (V261) found in the southern part of this region.

B. Gaul

(a) *Narbonensis*: A few instances of the -*u* spelling for the expected -*o* in 6th-7th cent. material and non-dated inscriptions, as follows,

> *LXVII aetatis anu de haec* (sic) *luce megravit* (1687[a] a. 527)
> *in hoc titolu requiescit* ... (3580 ad. ca. 6th-7th cent.)
> *recessit die septimu idus Maias* (2831 ad.)
> *obui[t] die quartu kal Aug* (2897)

---

[85] For a discussion of forms like *tertiu, quartu, quintu*, etc., v. infra, p. 92. This is also one of the earliest dated examples of an appositional genitive to denote the name of the month which, in classical Latin, appears as an adjective in agreement with *Kalendae, Nonae,* or *Idus* (Allen-Greenough, 429). This use of the genitive, which is not limited to a particular area (cf. Diehl, *ILCV*, III, 303), most likely "émane de la langue vulgaire" as Pirson puts it (182).

The form *titolu* could also represent a classical accusative with final *-m* omitted, especially since the word occurs at the end of a line. As a matter of fact, phrases introduced by *in hoc* and followed by an accusative form are quite frequent throughout our corpus, e.g., *in hoc tumolum* (1648) from this area.

For the accusative interpretation of the form *anu* denoting time *during* or *within which*, v. *infra*, p. 92.

(b) *Lugdunensis*: Examples of this orthographic deviation are also few in this area.

> *Boetio vero* (= *viro*) *clarissimu consule* (1749 a. 487)
> *prbr.... ordene que rictu* (= *recto*) (1075 a. 630)
> (but two ablative forms in *-o* also on the same stone)
> *annu XVI regno dmi Theodebert* (2916 a. 612)

In a rather garbled inscription, furthermore, we read *obiit quintu decmeu* (= *decimu*) (1687 ad.).

C. *Italy*

(a) *Northern*: in addition to a few examples in expressions of date such as

> *nonu k. Agust* (3527C ad. a. 434); *die tertiu kal Februar* (560)
> *qintu kal Gen* (= *Ienuarias*) (2841B); [86] *dodecimu k Iunias* (1361), [87] etc.

the *-u* spelling also occurs in *se vibu* (= *se vivo*) (1337), [88] *in fescu* (= *in fisco*) (811[b]), as well as in

> *de numeru Mattiacoru seniorum* (553, ca. early 5th cent.)

---

[86] Cf. It. *gennaio*. Is the letter G an attempt to render a palatal sound?
[87] Cf. It. *dodici*.
[88] According to the tenets of Latin grammar, the ablative absolute is not dependent on any word in the sentence (Allen-Greenough, 263). Hence, a phrase like *se vivo sibi et suis paravit* (310[b]) would be ungrammatical and, therefore, avoided by good writers: "optimus scriptor dicebat 'vivus fecit aliquid' et si dativus 'sibi' adiungebatur, recte 'vivus sibi fecit,' vel 'vivo sibi fecit,' ubi 'vivus' ad subiectum, 'vivo' ad dativum 'sibi' referri poterat" (Konjetzny, 322). It has been pointed out, however, that "cette prescription

(but *de numero Matiacorum iuniorum,* in 555 and 556), a formula that appears with some frequency on soldiers' epitaphs in the *Concordia* cemetery. (For the use of *de* in preference to *ex* to show origin or provenience, cf. our note #70, p. 81.)

(b) *Central*: In addition to *deposita est sextu decimu kalendas Februarias* (256 a. 469) (but *positus titulus a Virgilio* in the same epitaph), the -*u* spelling is found only in the following three examples:

> *vixit in seculu* (2277)
> *excepto Ursu et muliere sua* (3852)

and, on a garbled inscription, *in coniugiu* (4294 ad.).

(c) *Southern*: Examples of forms in -*u* for an expected -*o* are slightly more frequent in this area, even though the material is not substantially more abundant than in the two Italian areas just discussed. However, the percentage of deviations is still quite low (never more than 5 %) and there is no clear indication in the direction of a general -*u* ending for -*o*, which is characteristic of some present-day Southern Italian dialects. [89]

Here are a few examples of this phenomenon:

> *exsivit in pace die septimu kal Iunias* (2883 ad. a. 380)
> (but cf. the ablative *cum filio* in a subsequent line)
> *perit septimu calendas Agustas* (2792 a. 404)
> (two ablatives in -*o*, but also *vixit anum*. Final -*m*'s are omitted in *undeci* and *dece et nove*) [90]

---

a été plus d'une fois enfreinte par les écrivains de la meilleure époque" (Pirson, 185). (Cf. also Draeger, II, 808 ff.; Ernout-Thomas, 89.) As a matter of fact, constructions like *sibi vivo fecit* (4146 ad. a. 370), *vibi sibi fecerunt* (3236C), *vivus sibi et uxori suae* (quoted by Konjetzny, *loc. cit.*) are the rare exceptions in both pagan and Christian inscriptions, having given way to absolute constructions like *se viva, se vivo,* and *me vivo* in the singular, in addition to *se vivus*. In the plural, however, the expected *se vivis* is almost totally absent (only two instances were found in Italy, Nos. 850 and 3502 a. 392), being replaced by *se vivi* (nom. pl., *v. infra* our note #173) and *se vivos* (feminine *se vivas*), respectively. For the genesis of the ablative absolute construction of the *se vivo (fecit)* type, cf. also Rönsch, 419.

[89] Cf. Rohlf, *Grammatik*, I, 243-244.

[90] For the omission of final -*m* in invariable numerals as "fair phonological evidence of the possible disappearance of the *m* in pronunciation," cf. Pei, *Texts*, 106.

SECOND DECLENSION

> *depositus sub die nonu k̄al Iunias* (4416 a. 570)
> (but several ablatives in *-o*, e.g., *anno quarto*)
> *Ellu v̄.c.* (= *viro clarissimo*) *con(sule)* (1029A a. 478)
> *c* (= *cum*) *maritu fec ann XV* (260 a. 538)
> *si bibu* (= *vivo*) *cunparab[it*....] (3759A)
> *emerunt locu bisomu a Gaudentiu fossore* (3811B), etc.

The last example seems of interest to us because it suggests that the forms in *-u* must have sounded identical to the writer, despite the different functions that *locu bisomu* and *Gaudentiu* fulfil in the sentence.

D. Rome

Examples of the deviation under discussion are fairly numerous; yet, despite the greater abundance of inscriptional material than in any other area, the percentage of forms in *-u* for those in *-o* never exceeds 5.7 % (5th cent.). Here also, about one half of all instances of an *-u* spelling involve ordinal numbers in expressions of date, e.g.,

> *quintu kal Dec* [...*de*]*cessit* (4578 a. 291)
> *deposeta quartu īd Aprilis* (3115D a. 550) (but *con filio suo*)
> *depositus*... *octabu decimu kalendas Decembres* (3515C)
> *ottabu calendas Iulias*.... (4036), [91] etc.

Examples of this phenomenon involving other words are as follows:

> *vixit annis X mense unu* (2945A ad. a. 380)
> *locu bisomu emtu ab Ursu fossore* (3811A a. 403) [92]
> *locus lectoris de Belabru* (= *Velabro*) (1271 a. 461/482) [93]
> *Herculanu c̄os* (= *consule*) (3506 a. 452)

---

[91] Note the assimilation of the Latin *-ct-* consonant group. Cf. It. *ottavo* (Pei, *It. Lang.*, 56).

[92] Cf. our comments re: *locu bisomu a Gaudentiu* under "southern Italian area." It is of interest to observe that whenever, as a rule, *locu* or *bisomu*, or both, precede the prepositional complement the name of the individual from whom the burial place was bought is written with *-u* (e.g., *a Leontiu* (3811D), *a Alexandru* (3811E), *a Safargiu* (3755A), etc.), otherwise with *-o*, e.g., *emit a Celerino fos.* (3754D).

[93] For the genitive relationship expressed by *de* followed by an oblique form, v. infra, 2.12, p. 73.

se bibu (= *se vivo*) *fecit* (4146F ad. a. 405) [94]
cum maritu (3508 adn. a. 530-533) [95]
in hoc locu depositus est (467); *exsiut de seculu* (3053A) [96]
abea anathema da patre et filiu (3855) [97]
Lucida in deu (3366A); *in eternu dolore* (4355a), etc.

According to the tenets of Latin grammar, "time *during which* or *within which* could be expressed by the Accusative or Ablative of a noun in the singular, with an ordinal numeral" (Allen-Greenough, 266). Accordingly, both *vixit annum* and *vixit anno* would be acceptable, so that we are really left in the dark as to whether *annu* is to be interpreted as a classical accusative without final *-m* or an ablative in *-u* for an expected *-o*, possibly as a result of phonetic similarity between second and fourth declension singular endings, as has been suggested.[98] Similarly, in phrases expressing dates the construction *ante diem* (a.d.) was used with an ordinal in the accusative, followed, in turn, by an accusative, e.g., *a.d. quintum kal Maias* 'the fifth day before the calends of May,' or the ordinal alone in the ablative, e.g., *quinto die ante kal Maias* (Allen-Greenough, 267). There is a great deal of confusion in the use of the proper case, in that both forms in *-um* and *-o* appear in identical context, e.g., *depositus tertium idus Febb* (2115 a. 401) versus *tertio idus Februā* (1999), within the same area.

The problem of the *-u* spelling for the Latin /ō/ in declensional endings has been discussed at great length by Prinz (120 ff.). More especially, this scholar has attempted to ascertain whether this spelling, in what appears to be the ablative singular, is due to a *permutatio*

---

[94] *Se vivo* (spelled with *v* or *b* in a rather haphazard fashion) is, of course, by far the more frequent form. Note that in another epitaph from this area (3830) both *se bivo* and *se vivu* occur in consecutive lines.

[95] Occurring as the sole ablative form on half a dozen more inscriptions (Nos. 634, 2792C, 4220A, 4223B, 4224B, 4314A).

[96] The ending *-iu* (*-io*) (e.g., Sicil. *muriu, partiu*) presupposes a Vulgar Latin perfect indicative form in *-iut*, cf. Pei, *It. Lang.* 98.

[97] It. *da* from Lat. *de ab* or *de ad* "is a growth peculiar to Italian soil and does service for many functions in which the modern descendants of *de* and *per* must be used by other Romance tongues" (Pei, *It. Lang.*, 116).

[98] Indeed, Carnoy ascribes these apparent ablatives in *-u* to hypercorrections of a semi-literate stonecutter who is vaguely conscious of the difference in the ablative endings of second and fourth declension nouns, but no longer remembers which noun belongs to which class (220). Cf. also Prinz (120) and B. Löfstedt (116) for somewhat similar views.

vocalium or whether it reflects a morphological confusion, that is, the use of the classical accusative (minus final *-m*) for the ablative. On the strength of forms like *tertiu idus, se vivu, vixit annu*, and others, Prinz set out to show that in inscriptions from *Gaul* and the *Italian* area (including *Rome*), the *-u* spelling reflects a classical accusative case, the final *-m* having been omitted by the stonecutter for reasons of contraction, haplology (when the following word begins with *-m*), and lack of space (*margine urgente*), while in the *Iberian Peninsula* and in *Africa* the *-u* spelling seems to stand for the classical ablative. His line of reasoning runs something like this: Whenever the *-o* spelling occurs in the ablative, almost to the exclusion of *-u* or *-um* (the latter being an inverse spelling), the occasional orthographic *-u* is to be interpreted as representing the ablative case. On the other hand, where frequent *-u* and *-um* spellings occur beside the normal ablative forms in *-o* (particularly when found in the same inscription side by side), the orthographic *-u* would rather reflect a classical accusative form with the final *-m* omitted (121 ff.). It is perfectly true that in many instances forms in *-u* and *-o* (and also forms in *-um*) occur on one and the same inscription in what appears to be the ablative case; by the same token, there are just as many, and in some cases even more (e.g., *Rome*) instances where the ablative is represented by a form in *-u* exclusively. The fact that Prinz himself seems to throw up his hands in desperation when he admits "Dificillimum est iudicare, utrum in U terminatione accusativus an ablativus subsit" (130) would suggest that there is hardly any point in trying to decide when the *-u* spelling stands for final Lat. /ō/ in the classical ablative ending or a final *m*-less accusative form. B. Löfstedt certainly hits the nail on the head when he says

> M.E. ist es, wenn es sich um spätere Inschriften handelt [and, surely, he must have had Christian inscriptions in mind], grundsätzlich verfehlt, in jedem Falle mit Bestimmtheit entscheiden zu wollem, welches *-u* ein Akk. und welches ein Abl. ist: die Steinmetzen hätten es oft selbst nicht sagen können. Der Akkusativ and der Ablativ hatten sich frühzeitig einander syntaktisch angenähert.... (116)

Before we attempt to draw our own conclusions regarding the accusative-ablative relationship on the basis of the evidence presented in the foregoing pages, it will be well to illustrate another kind of deviation from the classical ablative ending, namely the occurrences of substitute forms in *-um,* both in absolute constructions and after prepositions.

(b) *-um* for *-o*: On the surface, examples of forms ending in *-um* for the expected *-o* ending in the ablative function would appear to be morphosyntactic substitutions of the accusative case for the ablative. In our epigraphic material this phenomenon is reflected as follows:

A. *Iberian Peninsula*

(a) *Baetica*: Examples of forms in *-um* for the expected ablative in *-o* occur only after the preposition *in,* denoting relation of place *where,*

> *in hunc tumulum requiescit* (V157 a. 662)
> (but *vixit in hoc sclo in pace*)
> *honor pellet.... in aeternum* (V313 a. 636/641)
> *in oc locum celsum aspice* (V135)
> *recondite in fundum Valles suburbio Obolconense* (V323)[99]

(b) *Lusitania*: The apparent accusative-ablative confusion is only found in one non-dated example: *in hoc locum requiesset* (V184).

(c) *Tarraconensis*: No example.

B. *Gaul*

(a) *Narbonensis*: The few examples from this area include forms in *-um* in expressions of date (where we would expect an ablative

---

[99] Sc. *reliquiae sanctorum. Valles* or *Vallis* is presumably the name of the estate which is located in a suburb of *Obulco* (*Cordubensis*). We believe that *suburbio Obulconense* is to be interpreted as a locative ablative, even though the preposition *in* is not repeated. (Note the concurrent use of a form in *-um* and one in *-o* to express the same relation of place.) Pirson notes the occurrence of several such constructions in his material (191-192), and sees in the anomalous omission of the preposition *in* "un trait particulier à la langue postclassique, qui tendait à augmenter le nombre des substantifs qui pouvaient à la question *ubi?* se mettre à l'ablatif sans préposition" (192). Other such examples from the Spanish area are: *mater filio loco peregrino memor[iam posuit]* (V22, 4th-5th cent.); *huic* (for *hoc*) *tumulo iacens* (V86 a. 632), both from *Lusitania,* and *sepulta est tumulo* (V159 a. 658) from *Baetica.*

in -*o*), as well as those following the preposition *in* to express place *where*,

> *obiit e saeculo die tertium nonas Iunias* (3437)
> *sub diae tercium kal Maias* (212 ad.)
> *in hoc tomulum requiescit* (3550 a. 511)

The formula *in hoc tumulo* appears in a group of 14 epitaphs found in the region of *Vienna* (present-day *Vienne*, south of *Lyon*), with *tumulum* appearing five times. In one instance the preposition *in* is also omitted: *hoc tomolom requescet* (4426).[100]

(b) *Lugdunensis*: No examples from dated material. There are two occurrences of this deviation in non-dated epitaphs,

> *clauditur oc gremium Sperendeus* (3649)
> *sub hunc titulum requiescit* (3487)[101]

C. *Italy*

(a) *Northern*: Instead of the expected forms in -*o* in absolute constructions we read

> *Symmacum v.c.cs.* (2738A a. 485) (for *Symmaco viro clarissimo consule*)
> *se vivum* (1263ª/b) (twice on the same stone); *se vibum fecit* (4156Bᶜ)

Other examples of forms in -*um* for -*o* occur mainly after prepositions:

> *vixit cum virginium suum* (1263ª) (but *cum birginio suo* in 1263ᵇ)[102]
> *depositus die tertium kalendas* (4504)

---

[100] For an interpretation of the -*om* ending, *v. supra*, our note #63. For the omission of the preposition *in* cf. our preceding note.

[101] The fact that *titulum* is preceded by the classical accusative form *hunc* is irrelevant, since both *hunc* and *hoc* are found in the same function followed by forms in both -*o* and -*um*, without regard as to classical grammar, e.g., *in hoc tumolum* (1648) versus *in hunc tetolo* (3597).

[102] No. 1263ª commemorates a deceased wife, while No. 1263ᵇ (written on the same stone) is dedicated to her daughter. Each epitaph appears to be written by the respective husband. Notice that in both we find *se vivum* for the expected *se vivo*, but in one instance this phrase is preceded by (*vixit*) *cum virginium suum* while in the other by *cum virginio suo*. It would

voluerit in hunc locum poni (508, 4th-5th cent.) [103]
in sequlum annus militavit XLV (811ᵇ)
centenarius de numerum equitum catafractariorum (504, 4th-5th cent.) [104]
de donum dei fecerunt (121), also in 1906B ad. [105]
cum suum sunbirgino (= *sum birginio?*) *bicxit* (4252) [106]

(b) *Central*: There are very few deviations in this area. In a time expression we read: *depositio Exuperiae die quintum kal. Iuliarum* (4813), while forms in *-um* after the preposition *in* occur in the following two examples:

requiescit Sabastianus in Cristum (3294 a. 400/405)
vixet in hunc seculum (1153)

(c) *Southern*: The apparent accusative in *-um* is found in the following ablative absolute construction, side by side with forms in *-o*,

regnancte domino nos[tr]o Hiesum Cristum (4677 a. 529) [107]

Deviations after prepositions are as follows,

recessit in somnum paces (3181, 5th cent.) [108]
positi sunt in cimiterium (2000, 7th cent.) [109]
sub imperium domni Eracli imperatoris (3860 a. 612)

---

seem unlikely that the hypercorrect form with *-um* should have sounded any different from that in *-o. V. infra*, our note #117.

[103] "Verbs of *placing*, though implying motion, take the construction of the place *where*" (Allen-Greenough, 273).

[104] On *catafractarii* 'armored horsemen' cf. Pauly-Wissowa, III, 1783. We consider the hypercorrect *numerum* to be quite significant because it occurs in a frequently used formula that indicates the military status of the deceased. In this particular group of epitaphs with similar phraseology (all of them from the military cemetery at *Concordia*), the correct construction *de numero* occurs 15 times and *ex numero* 5 times. Again, it is unlikely that *numerum* should have reflected a pronunciation that was different from *numero*.

[105] For the increased use of *de* for *ex* in Late Latin, cf. Stolz-Hofmann, 262-263.

[106] It would seem that the stonecutter inadvertently repeated the possessive. Note the unstressed short form *sun* (cf. Fr. *son*, Väänänen, *Lat. vulg.*, 133) and the possessive forms *mi, tu, su* in some *northern Italian* dialects (Rohlfs, *Grammatik*, II, 147).

[107] Note the hypercorrect spelling in *regnancte*.

[108] Occurring also in #4183 a. 563. In 17 other epitaphs from this general *Teanum-Capua-Aeclanum* region the correct *in somno pacis* is found.

[109] Cf. It. *cimitero*, Fr. *cimetière* (REW #2023, 192).

SECOND DECLENSION 97

In this latter inscription there is also an occurrence of a plural ablative preceded by *cum,* side by side with two apparent accusative forms: *cum filiis suis Proclanum et Gemmulum.*

An example of the concurrent use of a form in *-o* and *-um* may be seen in

fideli in Xρo Ihesum Hireni (= *Ireni*) (649)

D. *Rome*

Occurrences of forms in *-um* for the expected ablative in *-o* in both absolute constructions and after prepositions are attested in both dated and non-dated material. However, as may be seen in our table #3, they are far from being overwhelming in number.

In *vixit annis VIII die unum* (2972) we would expect the form *uno* because of the preceding ablative *die*. In other phrases that express dates, for instance,

depositus tertium idus Febb (2115 a. 401)
depositus diem quartum nonas Augustas (748 a. 348)
depositus ... septimum kalendas Septembris (4400B a. 399)

it is always possible that *ante diem* is understood (*v. supra,* p. 92) and that, therefore, these forms in *-um* are not really deviations from the classical norm, cf. *depositus.... ante XVIII kal* (2972 ad. ca. 4th cent.). Hence, these instances are not recorded in our table.

The classical accusative is used in the following absolute constructions instead of the ablative:

c̄ostatinos (= *constat nos*) *emisse locum... auri solidum* (2137 a. 426) [110]
cons. Theodosio Aug primum et Romorido (2757 a. 403)
emptum locum ab Artaemisium... et pretium datum fossori (3813) [111]

---

[110] Here we would expect a so-called "ablative of price" (Allen-Greenough, 261). It is of interest to note that *solidum* occurs in two more such constructions (3779 a. 543; 3779ad.) (instead of *solido*) and that in the plural we find *solidos* rather than *solidis,* e.g., *se vivos comparaverunt auri solidos....* (3784), except for one instance of an apparent nom. pl. in *auri solidi tres* (3782 a. 465) (for the expected *solidis tribus*).

[111] Reminiscent of the "accusative absolute" construction found in Late Latin authors, cf. Charles H. Beeson, *A Primer of Medieval Latin* (Chicago, 1963), 17.

The construction *se vivo* shows up as *se vivum* (also spelled *se vibum, se bivum,* and *se bibum*) with some frequency, particularly when preceded or followed by a direct object complement, e.g.,

> *locus quem se vivum emit* (702 ad.)
> *emit sibi locum... se vibum* (2143)
> *se vibum fecit locum bisomum* (3801A)
> *se bibum cum coniugem suam fecit sibi locum* (3512), etc. [112]

These examples (and others of this type) suggest that whenever the direct object was expressed by a form in *-um* (or by the relative *quem*) the ablative *vivo* would be written *vivum*, probably as a result of orthographic analogy.[113] This view seems to be supported by the fact that in the absence of such a complement the construction invariably appears as *se vivu* or *se vivo,* as in *se vivo sibi et suis paravit* (310^b) or *Ursus se bibu fecit* (4148).

Forms in *-um* for *-o* occur more frequently after *in* and *cum* than any other preposition. Here are a few examples:

> *in hunc locum posita... simul cum Martinum [ma]ritum suum* (3503 a. 404)
> *Bonifatius... positus in bisomum in pace* (3798)
> *fuit in saeculum annos XXXII* (1603 a. 369) (but *in aevo*)
> *cum eum vixit annis X* (3763 a. 317/330) (but *de saeculo exibit*) [114]
> *Emisina... c]um virginum suum* (4461B a. 423)
> *pro hunc unum ora subolem* (1464 a. 380)
> *sepulchrum fieri rogabimus pro remedium anime* (D3855)
> *fecit cum maritum annos III* (4219B a. 392)
> *de locum istum... iactaverint* (1273), etc.

---

[112] Of the three occurrences of the *me vivo* construction in our material, one is spelled *me vivum*: *hunc locum me vivum paravi* (1615 a. 483), for which orthographic influence of *locum* might be responsible; but cf. *ego F. Victor me vibo conparasse.... locum* (3754B).

[113] In the feminine, however, the rule is *se viva* even when directly preceded or followed by a direct object in *-um*, e.g., *Lucia se viva locum sibi emit* (3739E). We found only one occurrence of *se vivam, v. supra,* 1.15, p. 45.

[114] The two examples of *de* followed by a form in *-um* were found in *decesset de saeculum* (1296 a. 367) and *recessit de seculum* (2759 ad.). For the use of *de* after verbs of motion in epigraphic material, cf. Pirson, 195.

An example of the concurrent use of the classical ablative and accusative occurs in *emisse locum ... a fossoribus Burdone et Micinum* (2137 a. 426).[115]

The picture that seems to emerge from the foregoing analysis of accusative and ablative cases would suggest that

(a) while orthographic *-um* and *-o* are still generally kept apart to signal the respective cases they represent, there exists, nevertheless, a confusion concerning their correct use in all areas under investigation; and,

(b) it is pointless to try to determine whether orthographic *-u* represents a classical accusative less final *-m* or an ablative form.

Concerning the first observation, the following two questions come to mind: (1) Is the interchange of *-um* and *-o* that was noted in both absolute constructions and after prepositions to be attributed to an uncertainty in correct case use on the part of the speaker (or writer), i.e., to a *syntactic confusion,* or (2) Should we rather assume that both forms represent a single *oblique* case and the reflex of a phonetic identity, as suggested by B. Löfstedt (*v. supra*, p. 93), indicating that on the level of content the opposition between accusative and ablative has been obliterated while differences on the formal level are still observed, especially in the written language? As far as our material is concerned, we are inclined to answer the *second* question in the affirmative without, however, negating the first one, if we assume that the concept of accusative and ablative may still have been alive in the mind of the average speaker of, say, the fourth century, an assumption that, in our opinion, is very much open to question. The argument for favoring the second hypothesis is the following: With the fall of final *-m,* forms like *muru* (acc.) and *muro* (abl.) fell together in pronunciation as /muro/,[116] possibly with an allophonic [u], later phonemicized in some southern Italian dialects.[117] The

---

[115] We counted a total of 24 occurrences of the formula *emit (emerunt)* or *comparavit (comparaverunt) a* [name of person] *fossore* in which the name of the *fossor* is spelled twice with *-um,* 9 times with *-u* and 13 times with *-o.*

[116] On this point authorities seem to be in agreement, cf. Lausberg, I, 150-151.

[117] Speaking of the orthographic *-um* ending for the expected ablative in *-o,* Schuchardt remarks: "Häufig finden wir auch Ablativ in *-um.* Man pflegt zu sagen, der Akkusativ sei für den Ablativ gesetzt. Es ist dies ein etwas

morphological distinction between accusative and ablative having thus collapsed, it mattered little whether a direct object function was signalled by the innovative form in -*o* or the residual form in -*um* (preserved for a time by conservative speakers influenced by traditional orthography), e.g., *fecit titulo* versus *fecit titulum,* the more so since forms in -*um* and -*o* had never been in opposition in this particular function anyway. By the same token, a hypercorrect use of, say, *maritum* preceded by *cum* did not impair communication either, since the speakers' attention was now focused on the preposition rather than on the ending of the noun complement.[118] Furthermore, it is a well-known fact that a linguistic change is not reflected in writing until long after the change is implemented, while retaining, nevertheless, residuals forms (such as high-frequency words and formulaic expressions) which may or may not eventually be brought into line with the innovation.

As was seen (*supra*, p. 86), the earliest attestation of a direct object form in -*o* is found on a *Roman* epitaph said to go back to the early

---

schiefer Ausdruck, der am ersten noch auf solche Schreibungen wie *a virum, de meum,* aber durchaus nicht auf solche wie *se vivum,* anwendbar ist. Das *m* wurde nicht mehr gehört; es bestand kein lautlicher Unterschied zwischen *in locum* and *in loco.* [*V. supra,* our notes Nos. 102 and 104, pp. 95-96. What Schuchardt says merely confirms our hypothesis.].... Wenn wir nun anderseits -*os,* -*om,* -*o* in Nominativ und Akkusativ geschrieben sehen [*v. supra,* 2.11, p. 59 ff. and 2.14, p. 79 ff.], so geht daraus noch nicht hervor, dass im Vulgärlatein der Stammauslaut der 2. Dekl. in den verschiedenen Kasus verschieden geklungen habe, in diesem *o,* in jenem *u*; sondern er klang in allen gleich und zwar ursprünglich als ein *u*-ähnliches *o* oder *o*-ähnliches *u*.... Für diesen Mittellaut haben die meisten romanischen Idiome *o*; in wenigen aber, die überhaupt *u* begunstigen, ist *u* an seine Stelle getreten. So im Walachischen: *teatru, lucru, ochiu, domnu(l), vinu(l).* Ferner in fast allen südit. Mundarten; im Kalabr., Sizil., Calar., Logud. Es ist sehr wahrscheinlich, dass dergleichen dialektische Differenzen schon sehr früh bestanden" (II, 94-95).

For the survival of acc. sing. /-ŭm/ as /u/, cf. Lausberg, *loc. cit.* and our note #89, p. 90. Some scholars seem to believe that /u/ in the accusative ending may have become [ų] by analogy with the nom. sing. /-ųs/, cf. Battisti, 109.

[118] Of interest in this connection are the comments by Ernout-Thomas: "Il n'y avait pas toujours de relation sémantique entre le cas et les prépositions utilisées.... La préposition finissait par marquer plus que le cas lui-même la fonction de nom dans la phrase. L'élément flexionnel subsistait; mais il tendait à devenir un signe superflu, dont il serait facile de se passer, lorsque les désinences sous l'effet d'actions analogiques et phonétiques, se seraient confondues ou effacées" (10).

3rd century. Other attestations to the south and to the north are found around the 5th and 6th centuries (not until the 7th century in the Spanish area). This does not mean, of course, that the change in question had not taken place at an earlier date in those areas also (cf. instances of reverse spelling, i.e., *-um* for *-o*, in *northern Italy* around the 4th-5th century). As Lehmann once said, "Scribes generally indicate contrasts which distinguish meaning" (149), so that once the opposition between accusative and ablative became obliterated on the content level — an opposition that even in classical times was more apparent than real — the stonecutters, while striving to observe traditional patterns on the level of form, thought nothing of occasionally using *-um* and *-o* interchangeably, since both endings could serve as devices to signal the same grammatical relationship.

A final word concerning forms in *-u*. As stated before, we feel that it is entirely futile to try to ascertain whether the *-u* spelling in *votu fecit* or *vixit annu* represents a classical ablative or an accusative form with final *-m* omitted. It may well stand for both. It may either be an attempt on the part of the stonecutter to render a classical accusative as, for instance, in *tertiu idus Maias* (following the formula *ante diem tertium idus Maias*) or, indeed, reflect a [u]-colored pronunciation of final /o/ of a merged accusative and ablative form, particularly in those areas in which it occurs with the greatest frequency, namely *Rome* and *southern Italy,* indicating that this pronunciation may have covered a greater area of the southern part of the Peninsula than today. [119]

In the context of the latter possibility, we believe that forms in final *-u* merely represent a transitional spelling and, maybe, a pronunciation stage in the process of gradually restructuring the singular oblique system by eliminating a formal category (the accusative in *-um*) and, thus, simplifying Latin inflectional morphology.

2.2 Plural

2.21 *Nominative*

The occurrence of this case is quite infrequent, as may be seen in our table #4 of the Appendix. The only deviations involve an

---

[119] *V. supra,* our note #117, p. 99.

occasional form *fili* for *filii*, e.g., *hi fuerunt fili Hilari et Dalmatiae* (2760, *Narbonensis*), that is, the merger of stem vowel and ending, a phenomenon already observed in connection with the genitive singular, *v. supra*, 2.12, p. 66.

In addition to the masculine *-i* ending, sporadic occurrences of the neuter nominative in *-a* have also been found. Some of these neuters, however, appear to be used as singular feminine. Thus, on a 7th cent. epitaph from *Baetica* we read: *haec cava saxa Oppilani continet membra* (V287 a. 642), where we wonder whether the writer meant, indeed, 'hollow rock,' as used by Virgil, [120] or rather 'rocky hollow (cavity),' taking *cava* as the noun and *saxa* (for *saxea?*) as the adjective. [121]

On another epitaph from *León* (*Tarraconensis*), dedicated to a certain abbot *Vincentius* who died a martyr's death, we read, in part

caeleste regnum mutasti in melius cum gaudia vitae (V285 a. 630)

although there is some doubt as to the interpretation of *gaudia* as a feminine singular form, since the preposition *cum* is often found with a plural accusative form, *v. infra*, 2.25, p. 114 ff.

The form *lustra* in

ter denus (= *denos*) *et lustra sic gesserat annus* (= *annos*) (1218 a. 584/621)

found on an inscription from *Lugdunensis* may also be interpreted as a feminine singular rather than a neuter plural, cf. Fr. *lustre*.

An interesting example of the use of a neuter plural in *-a* as a feminine singular form occurs on a 4th cent. epitaph from *Rome*, which, in part, reads

depositus opera eorum (4248 a. 384)

where one would expect the ablative *opere* 'as a result of (their) labor,' as in *haec cub(icula) suis sumtibus et suis operibus perfecerunt* (2330). [122]

---

[120] *Ter scopulī inter cava saxa dedēre* (*Aeneid*, 3, 566-567).

[121] Cf. It. *cava*, Fr. *cave*. These forms, however, may also represent the substantivized feminine form of the adjective *cavus*, cf. REW 1796.

[122] Cf. also *hic reliquie defuncti Xpi famuli requiescunt opere dicno* (114 ad. ca. 6th cent.).

Except for this latter example, it will be noted that all instances involving an apparent gender shift from neutral plural to feminine singular are of a relatively late date.

2.22 *Genitive*

The plural genitive *-orum* ending is sometimes spelled *-oru* or *-oro*, particularly in the *Italian* area. No deviation from the classical spelling was found in *Gaul* [123] and only one instance of an apparent omission of final *-m* in the *Iberian* area on an epitaph from *Lusitania*, which reads *Cunde Marcianus famulo Dei annoru XXI*. (V64ᵇ 4th-6th cent.?). [124]

(a) *-oro* for *-orum*: The earliest attestation of the genitive plural in *-oro* for *-orum* is found on a third century *Roman* epitaph which records the form *misoro* (4578 a. 291) for *mensorum* (as in #4570, for example). This seems to be an analogical genitive plural formation, probably under the influence of *annorum* with which it is frequently used side by side, as in *depositus puer Maurus annorum quinquae mensorum tres...* (1527). [125]

---

[123] Sas (172) notes that in his Merovingian documents the ending in *-orum* is the most frequent genitive ending. Pai states that "In the genitive the ending *-orum* shows a fairly strong tendency to survive" (*Texts*, 143). For the survival of forms in *-or* (< *-orum*) in Old French, e.g., *gent paienour*, *temps ancienour*, cf. Meyer-Lubke, *Grammatik*, II, 11. Concerning OFr. *lor*, mod. Fr. *leur*, consult Brunot-Bruneau, 237-238.

[124] For the use of *famulo* in subject function, v. supra, 2.11, p. 62.
This genitive plural form *annorum* followed by a numeral to mark the age of the deceased seems to be an extension of the classical genitive of quality used with numerals to define measures of length, depth, etc. (Allen-Greenough, 213). This particular use of the genitive is not limited to a specific region and is frequently found with *defunctus, obitus, decessit*, and even *esse* (e.g., *annorum triu(m) fuit*, #3439). Nor is it restricted to *annorum*, as can be seen in *defunctu annoru duoru mesoru III dieru VI* (3574E), or in *mesoro duoro.... et diero XXX* (4575). For more detailed discussion of this use of the genitive, cf. Konjetzny, 312-313, and Pirson, 177-179.

[125] Pirson states: "*Orum* semble avoir été la désinence préférée de la langue populaire au génitif pluriel" (125). The analogical genitive *mensorum* does not, of course, imply that *mensis* has undergone a declensional shift; the accusative plural appears always as *menses* or *mensis* (often spelled *meses* or *mesis*) never as **mensos*, while the acc./abl. sing. forms read *mensem* (*mesem*) and *mense* (*mese*), respectively. The analogical nature of *mensorum* is also borne out by the form *meserum* (in *fecit filie anniclae et meserum quinque*, (4576), *Rome*) created, no doubt, on the pattern of *dierum*. For a discussion of the forms *mensorum, mesoro*, etc., v. infra, 3.22, p. 159 ff.

The most frequently found genitive in *-oro* is the form *annoro* (or *anoro*), the only one to occur also in *northern* (3197C; 3240) and *central Italy* (2993; 4118D), besides *Rome*. Leaving inflectional morphology aside for a moment, the use of this genitive plural with the verb *vivere* is worthy of note, as in *vixit annoro III et menses VII dies V* (2976B a. 372), because it is equivalent to the more usual accusative or ablative to express time duration. Notice also the concurrent use of genitive and accusative to show duration of time. Concerning this usage, which does not seem to be limited to the area of *Rome*,[126] Pirson makes the following comment:

> Cet emploi suppose que le génitif a perdu toute trace de sa signification première pour devenir l'équivalent de l'accusatif ou de l'ablatif de temps. C'est là sans doute le point extrême de son développement dans la langue populaire. (178-179) [127]

Other examples of genitive forms in *-oro* from the area of *Rome* are as follows:

> *amicus amicoro* (4622 a. 402?); *quoro sun nominae* (2133) *per man* (= *manos*) *eoro* (1948ᶜ); *XVI kal Octob marturoro*... (1999A),[128] etc.

Prinz (115) interprets this *-oro* ending for *-orum* as an assimilation of the unstressed final vowel to the stressed vowel and supports this contention by the fact that the genitive plural of first declension nouns never shows up as *aro. But is such an explanation really necessary? To begin with, it does not account for forms like *diero* (= *dierum*) (4575) and *mesero* (= *menserum*) (CIL VI 2662), the latter reported by Prinz himself (116) from a pagan epitaph (cf. the form *meserum* reported in our note #125). Also, it would be most unusual to find an *-o* ending with an *-a* stem noun; indeed, Romance forms like *candelora, feminoro,* and *loro* seem to point to a substitution of the

---

[126] We found *vix anorum XXXI* in an African epitaph also (4027B), while Pirson (179) adduces a couple of examples from pagan inscriptions.

[127] For the beginnings of the use of the genitive in these constructions, cf. also Martin, 15.

[128] Sc. *marturorum* for *martyrum*. Again, this analogical genitive, probably patterned after the genitive form *sanctorum*, with which it is often used together, should not be taken as implying a declensional shift. Other declensional forms are quite in accordance with traditional grammar, e.g., *martyri*

masculine *-orum* (*-oro*) ending for *-arum*.[129] We wonder, therefore, whether the *-o* ending in *-oro* is not simply an orthographic reflection of the [o] pronunciation of written *-um*, as in the case of the accusative singular (see in this connection our reference to B. Löfstedt, *supra*, p. 93). Let us recall that the earliest example of an *-o* spelling for *-um* in the accusative singular was also found in a third century *Roman* epitaph (*supra*, p. 86), so that it seems both reasonable and logical to connect the two phenomena.[130] Furthermore, as in the case of the accusative singular, we find the concurrent use of genitive forms in *-o* and *-um* (i.e., *-oro* and *-orum*) in the very same inscription, as in *decessit Quintus annoro octo mensorum dece* (2817C) or *annoro VI. ... annorum* (3727H ad.) in an otherwise garbled epitaph also from the *Roman* area. And just as the alternation of orthographic *-um* and *-o* in the accusative, this concurrent use of *-oro* and *-orum* also suggests a formal variation on the expression level.

(b) *-oru* for *-orum*: Except for the single occurrence of *annoru* on an *Iberian* epitaph cited above, the genitive plural is frequently spelled *-oru* in those areas where the *-oro* spelling is also attested. Here are a few examples:

(a) *Northern Italy: de numero equitum bracchiatoru* (493)
de numero Mattiacoru seniorum (553)

both found at *Concordia* (ca. 5th cent.).

(b) *Central Italy: fecit filie ... annoru ses dieru* (4128C)
(c) *Rome; d.p.* (=*depositus*) *postera die marturoro* (2119)
defuntus annoro II mensoru X (2797B)
quievit dece anoru (3096A),[131] etc.

(*martiri, marturi*) and *martyribus* (*marturibus*) (datives), and *martyres* (*martires, martures*) (nom. pl.).

Just as in Pompeian inscriptions where, as Väänänen reports, "les deux succédanés de /y/, *u* et *i*, sont en balance" (*Lat. vulg.*, 38), we find both spellings, though forms with *-u* are decidedly more frequent in *Roman* and *African* inscriptions. For OIt. *martore*, cf. REW #5385. For Prov. *martror* "La Toussaint" < *dies martyrorum*, cf. Uddho'm, 60.

[129] Rohlfs, *Grammatik*, II, 23-24. It is likely, as a matter of fact, that the feminine form in *-arum*, though continued to be written, was replaced by [-oro] in the spoken language at the time the *-um* ending came to be pronounced as [o].

[130] In this connection one could envisage an analogical equation such as *annum* : *anno* :: *annorum* : *annoro*.

[131] The past tense of *quiescere* or *requiescere* with the meaning of 'was

Parallelling the situation we found in the accusative-ablative singular (*v. supra*, p. 101), the final *-u* would also seem to represent a transitional stage between *-um* and *-o*.

On the basis of the evidence it seems that the genitive plural in *-oro* (less frequently *-oru*) is characteristic of an extensive area of *Italy*, as shown by the survival of *lingua angeloro, peccatoro, mortuoro* in Old Italian, in addition to the pronoun-adjective *loro* which has survived to this day (cf. our note #129).

(c) *Prepositional constructions*:

In the famous inscription from *Briord* (*Lugdunensis*) (150), discussed already under 2.12, p. 67 in another connection, the expected *membra duorum fratrum* is expressed by a periphrasis with *ad: membra ad duus* (= *duos*) *fratres*. This construction with the force of a possessive genitive [132] is sporadically attested in Merovingian Latin, but it was probably far more widespread in the spoken language than written documents would suggest. [133] The origin of this periphrasis "est à rapprocher de l'usage resté tojours vivant, que la langue populaire fait depuis l'époque ancienne du datif pour exprimer le rapport de possession" (Väänänen, *Lat. vulg.*, 122). The expression of possession by *à*, as an alternative to *de*, was quite usual in Old French and survives in the modern language (e.g., *fils à papa*), although expressions like *la voiture à Monsieur* have been condemned by grammarians as vulgarisms. [134]

In the phrase *Maximus conditarius de castris praetoribus* (624), [135] found on a *Roman* epitaph, a replacement of the expected genitive *conditarius castrorum* by an analytic construction might also be envisaged. However, as a so-called "ablative of origin," along the lines of *ducenarius de Batavis* (498) or *centenarius de equitum comitis* (506), indicating the military branch to which the deceased soldier had

---

put to rest' is quite unusual in this area. It is a characteristic feature of epitaphs from *Lusitania*.

[132] Cf. Bourciez: "praepositio *ad* inter duo nomina posita possessionis relationem perspicuam signat et vim proper habet genetivi coniunctivi" (*De praepositione* "*ad*," 45).

[133] "Creberrimos dumtaxat fuisse usus in vulgari sermone suspicari licet, sed prodeunt.... rarius apud scripta documenta" (Bourciez, *De praepositione* '*ad*,' loc. cit.).

[134] Brunot-Bruneau, 423.

[135] Maximus was probably a cook at the *Castra Praetoria*.

belonged (*v. supra*, Chapter 1, note #44, p. 35), this construction is quite acceptable in terms of traditional grammar.

2.23 *Dative*

The occurrence of this case is extremely rare in our material. When it does occur, it is generally spelled with -*is*. However, the following exceptions should be noted.

In a non-dated inscription from *Sorrento* (*So. Italy*) we read: *nam quit profuit miseros* (3861) for the expected *miseris* (since *prodesse* takes the dative case in Latin grammar). (Although rare in the classical language, the accusative is only permissible when preceded by the prepositions *ad* or *in*.) In the absence of more occurrences of this case it is hard to say whether an example like this would be indicative of a trend toward substituting the classical accusative for the dative, perceptible in connection with the ablative, *v. infra*, 2.25, p. 114 ff.

The form *filibus* is found on a *central Italian* and a *Roman* epigraph, respectively,[136] that at first glance might appear to be a shift of declension. However, it is more likely due to analogy with the frequent first declension form *filiabus*, *v. supra*, 1.23, p. 52.

2.24 *Accusative*

(a) The -*os* ending of the masculine [137] is frequently replaced by -*us*, particularly in the areas of *Gaul* and *Italy* (including, of course, *Rome*).[138] Instances of this orthographic change in the *Iberian* area are quite rare.[139]

---

[136] *Mater filibus suis fecit* (3601, *Beneventum*); *fecit filibus duobus* (4487, *Rome*).

[137] There are a total of 14 occurrences of the neuter accusative in -*a* which is always correctly spelled.

[138] Grandgent states that "*os* and *us* were interchanged from the third century on" (*V. L.*, 64) (which is confirmed by our data from *southern Italy* and *Rome*) and that "The accusative plural in -*us* was particularly common in Gaul" (*loc. cit.*). The latter statement is clearly not in accord with inscriptional evidence.

[139] Carnoy (50) reports a single example, *anus* (= *annus*). Cooper (51-52) reports *solidus* (= *solidos*) in Book VIII of his Visigothic *Forum Judicum* and only two -*us* occurrences in Books I and II, while Jennings (94 ff.) makes no mention of this phenomenon at all.

By far the most frequent -*us* spelling occurs with the form *annus*, although in areas where this orthographic deviation occurs with some frequency other words are also affected. Examples of this phenomenon are as follows:

A. *Iberian Peninsula*

The sporadic -*us* spelling occurs only in *annus*, e.g.

(a) *Baetica: Flavianus vixit annus in Crixto plus minus Lta* (V142 a. 636)

(b) *Lusitania: Serenianus famulus Di vixit anus IIII* (V70 a. 541)
    Allius Bebius famulus Dei annus XXVII (V64ª)

(c) *Tarraconensis: Lupa infas.... q. vissit annus XV* (V200) [140]

B. *Gaul*

(a) *Narbonensis: ... qui vixit annus ...* (1216 a. 496) and *passim*
    vixit annus duus et mensis III (3552 a. 597)
    sivi vius (= *vivus*) *elegir* (= *elegerunt*) (3580)

(b) *Lugdunensis: qui vix. annus....* (306 a. 488) and *passim*
    ad duus fratres (150)
    reliquit libertus (= *libertos*) (1749 a. 487)
    ter denus gesserat annus (1218 a. 548/621)
    dignit (= *dignet*) *orare pro parentis suus* (2340 ca. 7th) [141]

C. *Italy*

(a) *Northern: .... qui vixit annus....* (250 a. 474) and *passim*.

There are at least two instances in which both *annus* and *annos* occur on the same inscription, namely

vixit anus XLII et cum compare fecit annos XX (4203 a.)

and No. 4252 with a similar formula.

---

[140] Notice the orthographic $x > ss$ change in *vissit*, reflecting, it would seem, a /ks/ > /s/ development, which is rather typical of inscriptions from the *Italian* area.

[141] *Parentis suus* = *parentes suos* for the expected *parentibus suis*. Cf. *roga pro fratres et sodales tuos* (2343) on a Roman inscription.

SECOND DECLENSION 109

On a sarcophagus we read, in part: *quid facis ad superus, homo, qui nescis vivere* (4725). [142]

(b) *Central*: The accusative plural in *-us* was only found with the form *annus*, e.g., *Mavarata qui vixit annus* XXVI (1359 a. 417). Here, too, the concurrent use of *annus* and *annos* was noted on one and the same inscription, *Ienuarius qui vixit annos.... et inter se fecerunt annus....* (4279).

(c) *Southern*: Except for *cuius anema inter iustus sit* (3350) (but *qui vixit annos* three lines above!), all instances of an *-us* spelling involve the form *annus*.

D. *Rome*

With the exception of *hunc locum... se vibus* (= *vivos*) *comparaverunt* (also *qui vixit annus*) (1137 a. 521),[143] all *-us* accusative plural endings found in dated material are restricted to *annus* (earliest occurrence in 3315 a. 268). However, in non-dated epitaphs the following forms were also found:

in crupta noba retro sanctus (2153)[144]
in pace cum santus (3558); *de filius ipseius* (2372)[145]

---

[142] Cf. *hic multum fleti ad superos....* (*Aeneid*, VI, 481), with the meaning of 'those living on earth.' For the use of *ad* with the force of *apud* 'among,' cf. Stolz-Hofmann, 219.

[143] Also *se vivus emerunt* in #3757 from this area.

[144] Note the use of the adverb *retro* 'backwards, behind' with the force of a preposition. Cf. It. *dietro*, Fr. *derrière* < *dē retro*, REW # 2582.

[145] This new feminine formation *ipseius* is also attested in Nos. 1525 (*Rome*) and 4008 (*Naples*). It seems, however, that this form was not limited to the *Italian* area. Diehl (*V.I.*, 17) reports *ipsaius* from a Dalmatian inscription (CIL III 14014) and two occurrences of *ipseius* from *Lugdunensis* (CIL XIII 7028; 8249). A dative form *ipsei* is also attested in our material, Nos. 3702A (*Ostia*) and 4556 a. 393/4 (*Rome*). Cf. also *amator illeius* (CIL VI 14484) and [*fecit*] *sibi et ilei* (4554) on a pagan and Christian inscription from this area, respectively. Rohlfs claims that these new feminines in *-eius, -ei* (*illeius, ipseius, ipsei, illei*) "nach den klassisch-lateinischen Formen e i u s und e i gebildet sind" (*Vulgärlatein*, 62). But once the *cuius : queius, cui : quei* pairs had been established (*v. supra*, our note #61 (chapter 1), p. 61), may we not assume that analogy would have taken care of the creation of new feminine forms within the *ille* and *ipse* pronominal pattern also, quite independently of the cl. Lat. *eius* and *ei* forms? Since it is generally held that V.L. *illuius* and *illui* were patterned after the Cl. Lat. *cuius, cui* forms, why not make the same assumption concerning *ipseius, illeius, ipsei*, and *illei* (by analogy of *queius* and *quei*)?

The concurrent use of the accusative in *-os* and *-us* may be seen in the following examples:

> [*vixit*] *annus duos* (2553)
> *se bibos* [*fecerunt*] ... *qui vixit annus* (3506 ad. a. 452)
> *vixit annus* ... *fecit con maritu annos* ... *et demisit filius duo* (sic) (4566)
> *que filius suus acerbos remiset* ... *bixet annos* (4569)

The interchangeability and practical identity of accusative and ablative in expressions of time duration has already been pointed out (*v. supra,* our note #66, p. 80). The use of *annis* to show duration (*vixit annis*) is just as frequent as that of *annos* in the same function (parallelling that of *annum* and *anno* in the singular) and the concurrent use of both forms in the same inscription (e.g., *vixit annis p̄l minus annos XXXV* (4169A)) is good evidence of this syntactic identity.[146] On occasion, the accusative form in *-us* also occurs side by side with *annis,* as in *bixit annis plm* (= *plus minus*) *XXV*.... *fecit cum marito annus p.m. septe....* (808B a. 408).

Several explanations have been offered to account for the *-us* accusative form. Thus, Sas (181) sees in the orthographic substitution of *-us* for *-os* a purely phonetic phenomenon and attributes only minor importance to it.[147] For his part, Pirson states that "Dans les inscriptions chrétiennes, *annus* est pour ainsi dire devenu la forme régulière de l'accusatif pluriel" (42) (which seems to be confirmed by our figures from the area of *Gaul* that Pirson is referring to), and ascribes the phenomenon to the merger of unstressed /ō/ and /ŭ/ "dans un même son fermé représenté par *u*" (41).[148] In his monumental study of the Latin of Gregory of Tours (a work that goes well beyond the

---

For *illeius, illei, ipseius, ipsei* as being a crossing between V.L. *illuius, illui, ipsuius, ipsui* and the old dative forms *illae* and *ipsae,* cf. Tekavčić, II, 238.

[146] Further proof of this syntactic identity is the fact that more often than not *annus* is followed by *menses* (also *mensis*) and *dies.* Cf. also Pirson, 183-184.

[147] Pei, who considers this phenomenon to be of a morphological order, also feels that "From the standpoint of later developments, the phenomenon is not significant, save insofar as it shows the process of weakening of all final vowels which were later destined to disappear" (*Texts,* 55).

[148] In the same vein, Bonnet had stated already before him that "*o* long est rendu par *u* très souvent dans les syllabes ouvertes de toute position, et dans les finales fermées" (126).

scope of its title in the analysis of Late Latin), Max Bonnet also considers the plural accusative in -*us* as "sans doute principalement affaire de phonétique" (337). He recognizes, however, that "l'*u* dans cet accusatif est relativement plus fréquent que dans d'autres situations" (*ibid.*) (meaning non-morphological endings, no doubt) and this leads him to conclude that "peut-être que dans la langue parlée *u* était le son reconnu de l'accusatif, et qu'on ne cherchait même pas à réagir contre cette prononciation" (237-238).

Carnoy (50) combines a phonetic and an analogical explanation for the accusative in -*us* which, he believes, arose out of a merger of final /ō/ and /ŭ/ and an equation like *rosa(m)* : *rosa* :: *annu(m)* : *annus*. Diehl suggests a similar analogy but leaves phonological considerations out of account, [149] while his pupil, Otto Prinz, who otherwise follows suit, further specifies that the -*us* ending may have spread from the *Italian* area under Greek influence. [150] (The chronology of our dated examples would seem to strengthen the hypothesis that the phenomenon did, indeed, spread from this area, specifically *southern Italy* and *Rome*.)

Rejecting the analogical explanation advanced by Carnoy, Diehl, and Prinz, respectively, that takes the accusative singular as its *point de repère*, Bengt Löfstedt has recently argued in favor of a phonetic explanation of this phenomenon. [151] According to this scholar, the -*us*

---

[149] Diehl suggests the following analogy: "vocalis *u* orta est ex numero singulari ad analogiam 'horam horas, diem dies, mensem menses, manum manus,' potius quam ex vocali *o* mutata in *u*" (*ILCV*, III, 485).

[150] "US terminationem vi analogiae ortam esse puto" says Prinz and specifies his analogy in the following terms: "U ex accusativo singulari in pluralem translata est, ut in declinatione altera eodem modo quo in ceteris declinationibus accusativi singularis et pluralis vocalis par redderetur" (135). His argument for an alleged Greek influence that may have favored the extension of an accusative plural in -*us* is that "in titulis vetustissimis, qui US exhibent, vestigia linguae Graecae occurrunt et haec terminatio in Italia, ubi vis linguae Graecae maxima erat, orta est" (136).

[151] Löfstedt argues, in fact, that since the accusative singular was probably pronounced [o] in Late Latin anyway (as evidenced by the frequent -*o* spelling of this case side by side with classical -*um*), the analogy suggested by Carnoy et al. would have rather resulted in the preservation of the accusative in -*os* (87). If one is to look for an analogy at all, it would seem more logical to see it in the orthographic influence of the -*us* nominative singular ending "die selten mit *o* geschrieben wird und in der sich die Aussprache *u* vielleicht länger als im Akk. erhalten hat" (*loc. cit.*), thus the Swedish scholar reasons. In support of his theory, Löfstedt finds that the -*us* spelling for -*os* in the acc. pl. seldom occurs in words whose nom. sing. does not end in -*us*. For

accusative plural ending would be the reflex of a "closing influence" of final [s] on the preceding [o], [152] very much the way frequent -*is* spelling for -*es* in third declension nominative and accusative plurals found in texts from *Gaul* and *Italy* reflects a closing of [e] (v. infra, note #88, p. 157). [153] There is a clear implication, then, of an [u]-colored pronunciation of the accusative ending, "ein *u*-ähnliches *o*" as Hugo Schuchardt once put it (II, p. 95), brought about, we believe, by the general merger of Latin /ō/ and /ŭ/ in unstressed syllable rather than an alleged closing influence of final [s], paralleling the situation found in connection with the accusative and ablative singular where the -*o* and -*u(m)* spelling frequently alternates. And just as the frequent -*u* spelling for classical Latin /ō/ in the singular ablative, for instance, the -*us* ending for classical /-ōs/ appears also only in morphological endings; thus, the -*us*/-*os* alternation becomes primarily a phenomenon of a morphological order, that is a free variation on the formal level; [154] however, the -*us* accusative

---

the suggestion that *annus* actually represents a nominative singular form, "une dénomination stéréotypée de catégorie d'années dans les calculs de date," cf. Henrico Zilliacus (ed.), *Sylloge Inscriptionum Christianarum Musei Vaticani* (Helsinki, 1963), II, 30, and, more recently, Veikko Vaananen, "Autour du problème de la division du latin: appoint des sources écrites, en particulier des inscriptions," *Travaux de linguistique et de littérature* (Centre de Philologie et de Littératures Romanes, Strasbourg), VI, 1 (1968), 141-148. The fact, however, that both *annus* and *annos* may occur on the same inscription (as in #4566) and that accusative plural forms other than *annus* are also spelled with -*us* (e.g., *cum santus, de filius, inter iustus*, where a "frozen" nom. sing. is unlikely) would seem to weaken this theory.

[152] "... schliessende Einwirkung durch -*s*" (88). The suggestion of such a closing influence on the preceding vowel has also been advanced by Politzer (*Rom. Trends*, 28), albeit less forcefully.

[153] It is particularly noteworthy, Löfstedt says, that in those texts in which the -*us* spelling occurs for the expected -*os*, one also finds -*is* for -*es*. Inscriptional evidence, however, does not support this contention. As a matter of fact, a close study of inscriptions reveals that the form *annus*, for instance, is just as likely to be followed by *menses, Septembres* and other forms in -*es* (not to speak of *dies*, which is hardly ever spelled *diis*) as it is by *mensis, Octobris, parentis*, etc. This suggests that the two phenomena are not connected. Löfstedt's argument seems to be weakened by the fact that the classical form *annos* is, on occasion, also followed by forms in -*is* (e.g., Nos. 2690, 4146F ad., 1341, 3246 and *passim*). Cf. also our discussion of third declension nom./acc. plural nouns and adjectives, 3.21 and 3.24, pp. 152 and 162 ff.

[154] "La haute fréquence d'une certaine graphie pourra, sinon prouver, du moins soutenir que nous avons affaire à un phénomène morphologique" — Uddholm says (53).

ending is of no significance for the later developments of the Vulgar Latin of either French or Italian. [155]

(b) The accusative in -*os* (-*us*) preceded by a preposition is replaced by the classical ablative in -*is* in the following epitaphs:

Lugdunensis: *vitam transportavit in caelis* (1078, 6th-7th cent.) [156]
Narbonensis: *pax tecum inter sanctis* (2257)
So. Italy: *Callistus vix XX per annis* (753) [157]
 a (= *ad*) *superis munda transiit* (3350)
Rome: *vibas inter sanctis* (3315 a. 268)

The use of the classical ablative with prepositions that traditionally require the accusative case is also reported by Sas (188), Pei (*Texts*, 143), and Politzer (*Lomb. Docs.*, 77; *Rom. Trends*, 27), from their respective documents. However, the reverse trend (that is, the use of the classical accusative with prepositions that would require the ablative) is better attested in our material, particularly for what concerns the *Italian* area. [158]

---

[155] For the use of acc. pl. -*us* for -*os* in Gaul, v. supra, our note #147 p. 110. As to developments in Italian, let us recall that the Latin form *murōs* does not survive in this language since, with the fall of final /s/, it would have been confused with the generalized singular form *muro* (Pei, *It. Lang.*, 72).

[156] Showing the use of the preposition *in* with both accusative and ablative without regard as to motion or state, v. supra, 1.14, p. 40.

[157] Let us recall the frequent alternation of *annos* and *annis* to express time duration, e.g., *vixit annis VI*, etc.

[158] It seems that this trend later reversed itself on Italian soil. Politzer reports that "in the accusative the -*os*, -*us* ending appears to be giving way to -*is*, -*i*" (*Rom. Trends*, 27), particularly in *central Italian* documents, and that this tendency to replace -*os* (-*us*) in the accusative is definitely broken in the region north of the Po. As the -*is* and -*i* endings occurred more and more frequently in the accusative and ablative functions, "the -*i*, -*is* ending was becoming generalized in order to maintain plural connotation" — thus Politzer argues (*loc. cit.*). This evidence then leads him to see in the second declension masculine plural the result of a merger of the nominative, dative and ablative (after the fall of -*s* in the latter two cases). Cf. also his *Lomb. Docs.*, 80.

Politzer subsequently modified his stand in that he claimed derivation of the second declension plural in Italian only from the dative/ablative in -*is*, cf. his "On the Origin of Italian Plurals," *The Romanic Review*, XLIII (1952), 277 ff. For omitting the Latin -*i* nom. pl. as a source of the Italian *o*-declension plural he was criticized by B. Löfstedt who, otherwise, has upheld Politzer's earlier theory of the possibility of a nominative and dative/ablative merger as "ein Produkt aus dem durch den Wegfall von -*s* bedingten

2.25 Ablative

The frequent occurrences of the form *annis* in expressions of extent of time (as in *vixit annis tot, v. supra,* note #66, p. 80) was not included in our count because of its interchangeable use with *annos* to express the same concept and the fact that the substitution of *annos* for *annis* would not be a deviation anyway. Hence, table #4 shows only occurrences of the ablative in *-is* in absolute constructions (including ablatives traditionally required by a preceding verb) and after prepositions. Although these ablatives are rather infrequent (except for non-dated material in some *Italian* areas, particularly *Rome*), sporadic replacements of the expected ablative by the classical accusative in *-os* (also *-us*) and *-a* (in the case of neuters) are, nevertheless, found in virtually all areas under study. Our analysis reveals, however, that these substitutions occur mainly after prepositions.

A. Iberian Peninsula

(a) *Baetica*: Except for occurrences of *annis*, the ablative in *-is* is attested only once in a dated epitaph and three times in non-dated inscriptions, e.g., *Diona cum filiis* (V405); *vivas cum tuis* (V406). An expected ablative governed by *cum* is replaced by the classical accusative in *tabernacula aedificata sunt ... cum operarios vernolos* (V303 a. 594).[159]

(b) *Lusitania*: No occurrences of this case in either dated or non-dated material (except a few instances of *annis*), and no example of any deviation.

(c) *Tarraconensis*: The ablative in *-is*, besides *annis*, is not attested in our material from this region either. The classical accusative is found in *vibas cum beatos* (V189 a. 393) and *in os tumulos requiescit* (V267).[160]

Zusammenfall der lat. Dat.-Abl. Endung *-is* mit der Nominativendung *-i*" (238).

[159] The adjective *vernulus* 'indigenous, native' which does not seem to be attested in classical Latin literature, appears to be a crossing between *vernus* and *vernaculus*. Blaise (843) records it in his dictionary as an alternative to *vernaculus*.

[160] The use of the plural for the singular occurs also elsewhere, e.g., *his tumulis quiescit* (3555 a. 508), *Narbonensis*; *condita oc tumulis* (3567), *Lugdunensis*; *conditur his tumulis* (244), No. Italy, and *passim*. For the omission of the preposition *in* in these constructions cf. our note #99, p. 94.

B. Gaul

(a) *Narbonensis*: The replacement of an expected ablative by a classical accusative occurs only in a non-dated epitaph: *cum filios* (2366A ad.). The ablative is correctly used in *his tumulis requiescit* (3555 a. 508). (For the use of the plural rather than the singular and the omission of the expected preposition, cf. our note #160.)

(b) *Lugdunensis*: Besides *annis*, there are few examples of the ablative. It is correctly used a total of five times after prepositions that require this case and is replaced by the accusative once in *pro parentis* (= *parentes*) *suus* (= *suos*) (2340 ca. 7th cent.).

Two ablatives of time *within which* are replaced by accusative forms in *transiit in annos XXXXV* (2911) and *transiit in annos sexaginta* (2915) (presumably with the meaning of 'in his 45th (60th) year').[161] This deviation, however, may be accounted for by the fact that *annis* and *annos* are interchangeable and practically identical in expressions of *extent of time*.

C. Italy

(a) *Northern*: The correct use of the ablative in -*is* is attested in both dated and non-dated inscriptions, particularly after prepositions. Thus, in a group of about twenty non-dated epitaphs from the general area around *Aquileia* the phrases *cum suis* and *cum filiis suis* (Diehl, *ILCV*, I, 367 ff.) consistently show the use of this case.

Only the neuter accusative in -*a* is substituted for the expected ablative in the expression *de data dei* (1942; 1942 ad.).[162] (But cf. *de donis dei* in 1880.)

---

[161] *V. infra*, p. 168, the occurrence of *in annibus* on an *Iberian* epitaph with the same meaning.

[162] It may be of some interest to note that in a number of *central* and *northern Italian* documents Politzer finds a slightly higher percentage of the -*is* ablative replacement by neuter accusatives in -*a* than by masculine accusatives in -*os* (*Rom. Trends*, 29 and 31). B. Löfstedt's comment is also worth noting in this connection: "Dieses Vordringen von -*a* auf Kosten von -*is* bei den Neutra war sicher volkstumlich; die Endung -*a* der Neutra lebt ja noch im Romanischen als Kollektivendung weiter, während die mask. Pluralendung -*os* u. a. im Italienischen nicht fortgeführt wurde" (237).

(b) *Central*: No deviations have been noted in dated material. In non-dated epitaphs we recorded eight correct occurrences of the ablative after prepositions and two accusative substitutions in

> *puer Taurinus ... de invictos sen(iores)* (531) [163]
> *pax tibi cum sanctos* (2261 ad.) (but *cum sanctis* in 2261)

Diehl notes in connection with the last two epitaphs found at *Bolsena*: "pax tibi cum sanctis legebatur in multis eiusdem coemeterii titulis scariphatis" (*ILCV*, I, 439). Clearly then, the phrase *cum sanctis* (like the *cum suis* mentioned under *No. Italy*) must have been a frequently recurring fixed formula that the stonecutter was not likely to misspell, so that the deviation *cum sanctos* may be quite significant in betraying the trend to replace the ablative by the accusative in the spoken language.

(c) *Southern*: The ablative in *-is*, which occurs after prepositions in both dated and non-dated epitaphs (five times in the latter) is replaced by the neuter accusative in

> *queius de vitae documenta* (615); *de dona dei* (1936)
> *ex loca dua concessa* (3776) (occurring twice)

No example of the replacement of the ablative by an accusative in *-os* was found.

D. *Rome*

In addition to the great number of *annis* forms to express time duration, the classical ablative occurs with some frequency in both dated and non-dated epitaphs, particularly after prepositions that traditionally govern this case. Deviations from the classical norm, while not overwhelmingly numerous, are nevertheless frequent enough to be somewhat significant, amounting to about 15 % of all ablative occurrences after prepositions, that is, not counting ablative absolutes. Here is a fairly complete list of examples:

---

[163] *Taurinus* was apparently a member of the "invicti seniores" division. Cf. *centenarius de equitum comitis seniorum* (5c6). For the use of *de* for *ex* (e.g., *de numero* rather than *ex* (or *e*) *numero*), cf. Stolz-Hofmann, 262-263.

SECOND DECLENSION

[... *pro tanta*] *merita accepit* (2148ª a. 382) [164]
ab eos (129 ca. 3rd cent.); *pro eos* (2346)
pete pro parentes tuos (2337); [165] *de filius ipseius* (2372) [166]
anathema abeas ... da sca Xρi evangelia (3856), [167]
cum malificia sua (1558 ad.); *cum sanctos* (1524)
cum tuos omnes (2192D), etc.

A reliable example of the use of an accusative for a so-called "ablative of means" was also found in this area: *locus ... quem se vibo comparavit solidos V* 93786). [168] (But cf. *loc. quem comparavit ... solidis* (3787 ad.)).

The few occurrences of the ablative in *-is* in the area of *Gaul* and the *Iberian Peninsula* make it very difficult to draw any conclusions as to the stability of this form in the Latin spoken there. The occasional substitution of the classical accusative for the ablative after prepositions has also been noted by Carnoy (269) (who, in addition to *cum operarios vernolos* (*v. supra*) also records *cum filios* from a pagan epitaph (CIL II, 736)), as well as Pirson (201-202), although neither of these scholars suggest that the ablative in *-is* was seriously threatened by the accusative. Nevertheless, a situation like the one encountered in *Tarraconensis* where both occurrences of an expected ablative show up as accusatives in *-os* would seem to suggest at least a trend toward the syntactic replacement of forms in *-is* by what is eventually to become the *casus universalis* in the plural of second declension nouns in Spanish. [169] For the persistent conflict between forms in *-is* and *-os* in Merovingian texts and Late Latin documents from Spain, cf. Pei, *Texts*, 143-144; Sas, 199; Jennings, 96. [170]

---

[164] The editor's reconstruction is based on the occurrence of the phrase *pro meritis* which occurs in similar epitaphs concerned with "depositiones ad martyres" (e.g., #2156 a. 390).

[165] Cf. also *pete pro nos* (2335) and *roga pro nos* (2315) for the expected *nobis*.

[166] *Filius* for *filios*. Concerning the form *ipseius*, v. *supra*, our note #145, p. 1c9.

[167] Concerning the preposition *da*, v. *supra*, our note #97, p. 92.

[168] On a garbled inscription we read, in part, *e*]*mptu lo*[.... *soli*]*dos sex au*[*ri*] (3786A) which also seems to attest the use of the accusative in this function.

[169] Cf. Menéndez Pidal, *Gramática*, 206.

[170] While Pei reports that "the balance of gain seems to be in favor of *-os*" (*Texts*, 143), Jennings finds that in the *Cartulario* (i.e., as late as the 11th century) the classical ablative in *-is* still seems to be in the lead which, he says, is surprising "in view of later results in Spanish" (96).

The material from the whole *Italian* area also seems to indicate such a trend towards replacing the ablative in *-is* by the classical accusative. It is of interest to note, however, that in both the *northern* and *southern Italian* areas only the neuter accusative form in *-a* is substituted for the expected *-is* ending. As was seen (*v. supra*, our note #162, p. 115), B. Löfstedt has particularly underscored the fact that in some 7th-8th cent. *central* and *northern Italian* documents this *-a* is a more frequent substitute for *-is* than is the masculine form in *-os*, and explains this encroachment upon the expected *-is* ablative of neuter nouns as a popular feature still reflected in a small number of Romance plurals taken in pairs or with a general collective sense.[171] In our material from *southern Italy* the classical neuter in *-a* replaces the *-is* ending in about 25 % of all cases.

The masculine ending in *-os* as a substitute for the ablative in *-is* is only attested in the *central Italian* area and in *Rome*. (In the latter area, if we subtract the two occurrences of *-a* for *-is* in neuter nouns, we are still left with a 13 % *-os* substitution after prepositions.) It seems, however, that this accusative ending in *-os* never really became a serious competitor of the ablative in *-is*, if we are to judge from later Latin documents from Italy.[172] This is no doubt due to the fact that when the *-os* ending was threatened with the loss of final *-s*, the remaining *-o* would have become ambiguous. To the extent then that our evidence from this area allows us to draw any conclusions, it would seem fair to state that the classical ablative is quite stable in the period covered by our inscriptions and that, in the plural, accusative and ablative are still fairly well kept apart; yet, there is also an undeniable trend for the accusative to encroach upon the ablative after prepositions, particularly for the neuter form in *-a*.

The substitution of accusative for ablative is particularly evident in the construction *se vivos*, (corresponding to the singular *se vivo*, cf. our note #88, p. 89) for the expected ablative *se vivis*. (For the feminine *se vivas*, *v. supra*, 1.25, p. 53.) In the area of *Rome*, for

---

[171] Cf. Elcock, 56-58. For the survival of neuter plurals in Italian specifically, cf. also Rohlfs, *Grammatik*, II, 81-82; Tekavčić, II, 93-96.

[172] Politzer finds that in Lombardic documents "in the ablative, the most frequently used ending is *-is*" (*Lomb. Docs.*, 87), followed by *-i*, while *-os* (*-us*) occurs only in approximately 10 % of all cases (cf. also his *Rom. Trends*, 27). For his theory of the alleged survival of the classical ablative (and dative) in *-is* in the Italian masculine plural of the (*i*) *muri* type, *v. supra*, our note #158, p. 113.

instance, where this construction occurs most frequently, we counted 16 occurrences of *se vivos* (also spelled *se bivos, se bibos, se vivus, se bivus*), as against one single occurrence of *se vivis*.[173] While Diehl explains *se vivos* as being due to a " 'se' male intellecta" (*De m finali*, 205), Konjetzny (323) prefers to see an "accusative absolute" construction. We have no quarrel with the latter view, of course, but wonder whether the average stonecutter may have been conscious of a shift in construction in the plural with respect to the singular *se vivo*. As the opposition between ablative and accusative collapsed in the singular and there emerged an oblique form which in pronunciation was realized as an [o] (with a possible [u] coloring in some areas), is it not possible that the form *vivos* merely reflects a popular trend to tack on to the singular an *-s* plural marker by analogy of first (*-a* vs. *-as*) and third (*-e* vs. *-es*) declension nouns? This same trend would then also explain the forms in *-os* used with prepositions that according to traditional grammar would call for the ablative.

2.3 Summary

Our findings concerning the second declension may be briefly summarized as follows.

2.31 Singular

2.311 *Nominative*

Masculine nouns show the *-us* ending rather consistently. Orthographic deviations involve the replacement of *-us* by *-os, -u,* and *-o,* respectively.

---

[173] In addition to the *se vivos* construction, *se vivi* (also spelled *vibi, bivi,* and *bibi*) occurs with considerable frequency also. Besides *Rome*, where we counted 45 occurrences, it is attested in other *Italian* areas and twice in epitaphs from *Dalmatia* (Nos. 821 ad. and 3835). There is no reason to believe that *vivi* represents an *s*-less ablative form. For one thing, the omission of this consonant is quite exceptional in epigraphic material (cf. Proskauer, 175); in the second place, the plural nominative is also found without a preceding *se*, as in *Leo et Statia vivi fecerunt* (4150C) and, in a few instances, one even finds nominative and ablative cases used side by side, e.g., *fecerunt se vivi locum cum suis* (3503A a. 403). Also, final *-i* was the normal nom-

(a) The nominative singular in -*os* occurs mainly in proper names, although an occasional -*os* spelling was also found in common nouns and adjectives, such as *iustos, parvos, tuos*, etc. While this substitution in proper names may be due to the influence of Greek names, the -*os* spelling could also reflect the phonetic merger of /ŏ/ and /ŭ/ in the unstressed syllable especially in those areas (*Gaul* and *No. Italy*, in particular) where the -*us* > -*os* orthographic change may also be observed in other than morphological endings.

As to nouns and adjectives in -*os* found in those areas where this change occurs only in morphological endings (*Spain* and rest of *Italy*), one might also envisage the use of an oblique form like *iusto, parvo*, and *tuo* in a subject function to which the stonemason subsequently added an -*s* as an "afterthought" as a reminiscence of the classical nominative case. Such forms in -*os* could, then, reflect an incipient conflict between nominative and oblique cases, a conflict which was eventually resolved by the use of a single form in -*o* in the singular of *o*-stem nouns in Italian and Spanish.

(b) The apparent omission of final -*s* in the nominative singular ending resulting in a form in -*u* is sporadically attested throughout our inscriptional material. In cases where the word involved occurs at the end of a line, the omission of this letter *margine urgente* is not unlikely, but in cases where it does not, the -*u* ending may indeed reflect, as has been suggested, "a compromise between the popular oblique in -*o* and the learned form in -*us*" (Jennings, 94). This view seems to be supported by the occasional substitution of a form in -*o* for -*us*, i.e., the use of an oblique form in the nominative function (*v. infra* (c)). In the area of *Rome* forms in -*u* are particularly frequent with proper names.

(c) It is undeniable that the -*o* spelling for nominative -*us* reflects a morphological substitution. Sporadic examples of this phenomenon are attested in almost all areas, though examples illustrating this phenomenon (like those of -*u* for -*us*) seem to be somewhat more frequent in the *Italian* area. While a conclusion to the effect that the nominative was being usurped by the oblique would not be justified on the

---

inative plural ending anyway (*v. supra*, 2.21, p. 101), corresponding to the singular in -*us*, e.g., *Leo se vibus fecit sibi et*.... *Marcellinae* (4146 a. 376/378) versus *Iovinianus et Proba se bibi fecerunt* (4146F a. 399). The nominative plural interpretation of *vivi* is implicit in Konjetzny, 323.

basis of the evidence, the occasional extension of a form in -o would, nevertheless, indicate that on the level of *parole*, at least, there is a trend toward an "Universalkasus" in the singular.

The nominative singular of neuter nouns occurs very infrequently. The apparent omission of final -m as well as the morphological substitution of the oblique in -o for -um were observed in a few instances in *Roman* epitaphs. (*v. infra* our interpretation of forms in -u showing the apparent omission of this consonant).

2.312 *Genitive*

On the whole, the -i ending is quite stable. The expected -ii ending of proper names and adjectives in -ius is often reduced to -i.

(a) Noteworthy is the use of a form in -o in the genitive function, notably in *Gaul* and the *Italian* area, although in the latter it frequently occurs in expressions indicating consular years, as in *sub consulatu Modesto* (2976B), where the apparent genitive in -o could be the result of a confusion with the ablative absolute construction of the *consule Titiano* (2805) type. The most innovative region in regard to this phenomenon is *Lugdunensis* where in the sixth century we find a better than 30 % replacement of the classical genitive by the oblique form in -o.

(b) Of interest are also the analogical genitives *Mercuris* and *Saturnis* found on several *Roman* epitaphs.

(c) An example each of the periphrastic construction with *de* followed by the classical ablative was found in epitaphs from *Tarraconensis* (7th cent.) and *Narbonensis* (5th cent.). In the area of *Rome* three such examples were found, with *de* followed by forms in -u in two instances. The earliest examples dates back to the fourth century. (The earliest written attestation of this "analytic" genitive involving first declension nouns was also found in a *Roman* epitaph dating back to the middle of the 4th century.)

2.313 *Dative*

The occurrence of this case is quite sporadic but when it does appear it is generally spelled with -o. We noted a few examples of an apparent genitive in -i for the dative, particularly in the *northern Italian* area, which seems to illustrate what Dag Norberg has referred to as "dativische Funktion des Genitivs," also attested in other Late Latin texts.

2.314 *Accusative*

The expected accusative in *-um* is quite frequently replaced by forms in *-u* (the apparent omission of final *-m*) and *-o*, except for *Baetica* and *Lusitania* where this case is always spelled with *-um*, in both dated and non-dated epitaphs.

(a) Except for a few examples in *Lugdunensis*, the orthographic change from *-um* to *-u* is limited to the *Italian* area where, in addition to direct object complements (as in *votu fecit*) it is also quite frequent in time expressions (as in *vixit annu unu*). Because of the interchangeability and practical identity of accusative and ablative in expressions of time duration, the form *annu* may also be interpreted as an ablative, especially in view of the frequent *-u* spelling for the expected ablative in *-o*.

Although some regions show a greater orthographic retention of final *-m* than do others (e.g., the *northern* and *central Italian* regions as against the *southern Italian* region and *Rome*) there is, nevertheless, enough of a hesitation in the use of forms in *-um* and *-u* (even disregarding the frequent occurrence of *annu*), so that final *-m* as an accusative marker would appear to be a matter of traditional orthography and no longer an inflectional morpheme on the level of *parole*.

(b) Examples of the morphological replacement of the classical accusative in *-m* by a form in *-o* (the apparent ablative) are found in almost every area (*Baetica* and *Lusitania* being the exceptions). It is significant that forms in *-o* for *-um* also occur in highly formulaic expressions (such as *titulo posuit*) and that occasionally both forms may appear on the same epitaph, either as direct object or as prepositional complements. Indeed, such examples would seem to suggest a purely formal rather than a grammatical opposition between the classical accusative in *-um* and the ablative in *-o*, pointing to the emergence of a general oblique form capable of fulfilling several syntactic functions.

2.315 *Ablative*

In the overwhelming majority of instances the ablative ends in *-o*; in some cases, however, this ending is replaced by forms in *-u* and *-um* (the apparent accusative), the latter occurring particularly after prepositions.

(a) Except for seemingly conservative *Baetica* and *Lusitania*, the *-o* > *-u* orthographic change was observed in all areas under investigation, occurring with greater frequency in *southern Italy* and *Rome* than elsewhere. Since many cases of an *-u* spelling involve ordinal numerals in phrases expressing time duration (as in *vixit annu VIII*) or dates (as in *deposita quartu id. Aprilis*), these forms could stand for either a classical accusative without final *-m* or an ablative in *-u* (for the expected *-o*), seeing that according to Latin grammar the use of both accusative and ablative is permissible in these constructions. The fact that both forms in *-um* and *-o* appear in identical context (as in *deposita tertium idus Feb.* versus *dep. tertio idus Feb.*) further adds to this uncertainty of interpretation. Attempts to determine whether these instances of *-u* spelling reflect an accusative or an ablative have not been wanting with the inevitable conclusion, however, that it is impossible, and even futile to try to decide which *-u* spelling stands for a classical accusative and which one for an ablative.

(b) The apparent morpho-syntactic substitution of the accusative case for the ablative, as reflected in the orthographic replacement of ablatives in *-o* by forms in *-um*, occurs in virtually all areas (no example from *Tarraconensis*), particularly after prepositions, and in the ablative construction *se vivo* (the latter limited, as far as our material goes, to the *Italian* area). Examples of the concurrent use of forms in *-o* and *-um* in the same epitaph, and even governed by the same preposition, have also been found.

A comparison of accusative and ablative cases seems to show that (a) although orthographic *-um* and *-o* are still generally kept apart to signal the respective cases they stand for, there is a great deal of confusion concerning their correct use in almost all areas under study and (b) that it is pointless to attempt to determine whether orthographic *-u* represents a classical accusative form with the final *-m* omitted or an ablative. With the fall of final *-m*, forms like *muru* (acc.) and *muro* (abl.) fell together in pronunciation as [muro] (possibly, as Schuchardt (II, 95) has suggested, as a "Mittellaut" at first with an [u]-colored [o] or an [o]-colored [u], most Western Romance languages in which the final vowel survived having eventually developed an [o], except for those dialects in which a stronger [u]-coloring resulted in [u]), bringing about a morphological collapse of accusative/ablative distinction, although, in terms of flexional elements, still observed in traditional orthography in accordance with the stonemason's level of instruction. Thus, we see emerging a single *oblique* case form on the level of content in which semantic relationship is no longer bound to morphological distinction, the same form (innovative *-o*, or residual *-um*) serving to express both classical accusative and ablative functions.

Within this framework, then, forms in *-u* would be neither ablatives nor accusatives but rather represent a "transitional" spelling in the overall process of restructuring the system of *casus obliqui* in the singular, as a result of eliminating the formal category of the accusative in *-um* from the language.

2.32   Plural

2.321   *Nominative*

The few masculine nominatives found in our material end in *-i*.

Of the still fewer occurrences of the neuter in *-a* some appear to be used as feminine singulars, e.g., *cava*. Except for one example found on a 4th century epitaph from Rome (*opera*), instances of this shift of gender (observed in *Baetica*, *Tarraconensis*, and *Lugdunensis*) are of a relatively late date (7th cent.).

2.322   *Genitive*

(a) The *-orum* ending is occasionally spelled *-oru*, or it is replaced by *-oro*. Except for one example of the *-oru* spelling in a *Lusitanian* epitaph, this change seems to be characteristic of inscriptions from *Italy*, particularly *Rome*. The final *-u* in *-oru* would seem to represent the same kind of "compromise" spelling between *-orum* and *-oro* (reflecting a final [u]-colored [o](?)) discussed in connection with the accusative and ablative.

(b) Noteworthy is the use of *annorum* (*annoru, annoro*) to mark the age of the deceased. This usage, however, is not limited to a particular area.

SECOND DECLENSION

(c) The expected possessive genitive *duorum fratrum* is expressed by a periphrasis with *ad* in an oft-quoted inscription from *Lugdunensis*: *membra ad duus fratres*. The epitaph in question probably does not antedate the 7th century.

2.323 Dative

The occurrence of this case is extremely rare. In one instance (*southern Italy*) the expected *-is* ending is replaced by the accusative in *-os*.

2.324 Accusative

(a) In the areas of *Gaul* and *Italy* the *-os* ending is frequently replaced by *-us*. The form *annus* is particularly frequent and occasionally we find it side by side with the correct *annos* in the same epitaph, although the concurrent use of forms in *-us* and *-os* occur in other words also.

Scholars have attempted to account for the *-us* spelling in the accusative by invoking phonetic reasons (such as the alleged "closing" influence of final *-s* on the preceding [o]), analogical reasons (such as the transfer of the final *-u* of the singular accusative *-um* ending to the plural), as well as Greek influence. Some have also seen a "fossilized" nominative singular in the frequent *annus* form. Considering, however, that the *-os/-us* alternation appears only in this morphological ending, the phenomenon should be looked upon as a morphological variation on the formal level. As to the *-us* spelling itself, it probably also reflects an [u]-colored pronunciation of the final [o], parallelling the situation in the singular where the *-o* and *-u(m)* spellings also frequently alternate.

(b) In a few cases (*Gaul, southern Italy, Rome*) the ablative in *-is* is used for the accusative after the prepositions that traditionally govern the latter case. These hypercorrect forms further serve to support what has already been suggested (*v. supra*, note #79, p. 85), namely that it is the preposition which marks the function of the noun in the sentence and that the flectional ending that it governs has become of secondary importance. For the trend, however, to use the classical accusative with prepositions that require the ablative in Latin grammar, *v. infra*, 2.325.

2.325 Ablative

Except for the frequent occurrence of the form *annis* to show extent of time (as an acceptable alternative to *annos*), the plural ablative is not widely attested and, in fact, quite poorly in some areas, particularly *Gaul* and the *Iberian Peninsula*. Consequently, it is impossible to draw specific conclusions as to its stability in these areas, although sporadic replacement of this case by the classical accusative in *-os* seems to suggest a trend toward the extension of the latter as the *casus universalis* in the oblique. The fact that in the *Tarraconensis*, for example, the two occurrences of the expected ablative show an accusative form in *-os* may be more than just a coincidence.

As to the *Italian* area, including *Rome*, where the occurrence of the ablative is more frequent, it is of interest to note that in both the *northern* and *southern* regions the replacement of the ablative by the accusative only involves neuter nouns, that is, a form in *-a* for *-is* (about 25 % replacement in *southern Italy*), while the occasional substitution of the accusative in *-os* for the ablative in *-is* is attested only in the *central Italian* region and in *Rome*. (A 13 % substitution of *-os* for *-is* in the latter area.) The use of the accusative for the expected ablative occurs almost without exception after prepositions. Despite the detectable trend to replace the ablative as a prepositional complement by the accusative, it may, nevertheless, be said that contrary to the situation noted in the singular, in the plural, due to their distinctive endings, accusative and ablative are still fairly well kept apart.

In the *Italian* area, particularly in *Rome*, furthermore, the trend toward substituting accusative for ablative is rather evident in the *se vivos* for the expected *se vivis* construction. Since in the singular this construction reads *se vivo* (and the orthographic alternate *se vivum*), it is conceivable, and even likely, that the plural form *vivos* (as well as other accusatives in *-os* or *-us* used after prepositions that govern the ablative case) reflects a popular trend to add the plural *-s* marker to the singular oblique form, by analogy of first and third declension nouns where the vowel in the ending is identical in singular and plural, namely *-a* vs. *-as* and *-e* (*-i*) vs. *-es* (*-is*).

Chapter 3

THIRD DECLENSION

3.1 Singular

For a summary of morphological endings, see table #5 in the Appendix.

3.11 *Nominative*

The nominative singular is represented by masculine and feminine nouns and adjectives ending mainly in *-as, -es, -is, -ix, -er, -o, -or, -os,* and neuters in *-e* and *-us,* those in *-is, -o,* and *-or* being in the majority. However, our table shows only those deviations that seem to have morphological implications, notably the *-is* > *-es* orthographic change in parisyllabics, which is sporadically attested in all areas. Occasionally changes like *felix* > *feles* (oblique *felice(m)*) or *lector* > *lectur* — basically also due to phonetic causes (merger of unstressed /ĕ/ and /ĭ/ and /ŏ/ and /ŭ/)[1] but, as far as we are concerned, without morphological significance — as well as the consistent *nepus* spelling for *nepos* (attested in *Gaul* and *Italy*) which seems to be an analogical formation patterned after second declension masculine nouns,[2] have not been included in our count.

Concentrating, then, on the *-es* spelling for *-is* we find the following situation in the various areas under study.

---

[1] Cf. our *Local Variations,* 164 and 192.
[2] *Ibid.,* 193.

A. *Iberian Peninsula*

(a) *Baetica*: Only one deviation in *Licinia dulces anima* (V115 a. 485). All other parisyllabics in *-is* are correctly spelled.

(b) *Lusitania*: No example.

(c) *Tarraconensis*: Two examples from the Tarragona cemetery (4th-6th cent.)

> ...*fideles in pace* (V197)
> *quod dedit heu tristes tibi... coniunx* (V295)

B. *Gaul*

Examples of *-es* spelling for *-is* are as follows:

(a) *Narbonensis*: [*hic*] *requiiscit... f*]*edeles famula* [*dei*] (1432 ad. a. 514)
in pace requiescit... Apriles (2891A a. 530)
hic requiescet... Matrona scemuniales (1677)[3]

(b) *Lugdunensis*: *hic iacent Maria... et eius Eugenia neptes* (1676 a. 552)
hic in pace quiescit Dicnissima fideles (1371)
ic pausat Amabeles in Cristo (3301)
hic iacet Apronius principales (373)

It might be noted that none of the dated examples occur earlier than the sixth century. The contrary phenomenon, i.e., the orthographic change of *-es* to *-is* (e.g., *comes* > *comis*) is once attested in the latter area, the expected *miles* form being spelled *milix* (with a hypercorrect *x*, *v. infra*, note #12).[4]

C. *Italy*

The *-es* spelling for *-is* is attested in all areas. However, the *Central Italian* area seems to be most conservative in this regard. Examples are as follows:

---

[3] *Sc. sanctimonialis* 'pious, religious.'

[4] *Iohannis* (an acceptable alternative for *Ioannes*, cf. Lewis-Short, 1013), which is given by Pirson (31) to illustrate the orthographic change of *-es* > *-is* in the nom. sing., is not really an appropriate example. Conversely, this scholar adduces a number of instances of *-es* spelling for *-is* (35-36).

(a) *Northern:* *Ursicinus cives Tarrisianus* (4440 a. 424)
Dacco ... vixet in pace fedeles (1360)
quem omnes eclesia diligebat (1741)
in die iudicii inmones (= *immunis*) *a penes ebadas* (2879, 6th-7th cent.) [5]

An example of an apparent morphological replacement of the nominative by an oblique form was found in

in hoc loco depositum Vitale (3527) [6]

where the omission of final *-s* (i.e., *Vitales*) because of lack of space (the name happens to occur at the end of a line) seems unlikely, though of course not impossible, in view of forms like *plus, menus, Septembres, defuntus,* and even *diae Lunis*! (the latter also occurring at the end of a line).

There is also one example of the reverse phenomenon, the spelling *-is* for *-es,* namely *Laurentius milis de numero Tarvisiano* (559). In dated inscriptions we counted a total of four occurrences of the nominative in *-es,* always correctly spelled.

(b) *Central:* Only two non-dated examples were found in this area,

F. Mauricius ... cives Gallus pelegrinus (1474C) [7]
fideles in omnibus fuisti (2312)

(c) *Southern:* It so happens that all available examples are dated;

hic est positus Dianeses (= *Dianensis*) *innocens* (2932 a. 397)
Lucianus ... mansuetus, mites, letus (3114 a. 469)
hic requiescit Domitia cives Romana (4430 a. 551)

The reverse phenomenon (*-es* > *-is*) was recorded in

Petrus $\overline{vc}$ (= *vir clarissimus*) *comis* (114 a. 549)

---

[5] *A penes* for *a poenis*.

[6] One wonders whether *depositum* (for an expected *depositus*) is a spelling error or whether it represents an oblique singular form — in accord with the following *Vitale* — reflecting, however, the orthographic hesitation between written forms in *-um* and *-o* to mark this case. V. supra, 2.14, p. 76 ff.

[7] Note the dissimilation in *pelegrinus,* cf. It. *pellegrino,* Fr. *pélèrin* (REW #6406), also Eng. *pilgrim*.

as well as in the proper name *Monsis* (*Moses?*) (1150). [8]

D. *Rome*

Examples of *-es* spelling for *-is* in both dated and non-dated epitaphs are as follows:

> *Leontia con[iux] incomparaviles* (= *incomparabilis*) (2732 a. 368)
> *Megetio ... cibes Eliopolitanus* (4461 a. 345) [9]
> *hic posita est anima dulces* (4623 a. 388)
> *Labinia virgo dei inimitabiles* (1722 a. 409)
> *depositus Zosimus fideles annorum octoginta* (1353C) [10]
> *martyribus ... quorum natales est XVIII kal. Maias* (2124), [11]
> etc.

Two examples of the *-is* spelling for *-es* in the nominative singular were also found: *milix* (529; 414 ad.) for *miles*. [12]

In order to evaluate the morphological significance of the *-is* > *-es* orthographic change in noun and adjective endings, it may be well to compare it with the reverse phenomenon, namely the *-is* spelling for nominatives that end in *-es*. Although the occurrence of these nom-

---

[8] The name *Mosses* is attested on a Roman epitaph (#1150). *Monsis*, apart from the *-es* > *-is* orthographic change, would also appear to be a hypercorrection, cf. *formosus non formunsus* in the *Appendix Probi*.

[9] The form *Megetio* could be an oblique form in nominative function (*v. supra*, 2.11, p. 62 ff.) or the classical dative of *Megethius* (#4504 and *passim*), in which case *cibes Eliopolitanus* would simply be an incorrect apposition. The adjective *Heliopolitanus* is formed on *Heliopolis*.

The form *cives* is also attested in Nos. 411 (a. 408), 465 and 4456.

[10] For the use of the genitive plural to show the age of the deceased, *v. supra*, our note #124, p. 103.

[11] In connection with epitaphs commemorating the *natales sanctorum*, it may be of interest to mention the occurrence of *natale* in the nominative function on a few *African* inscriptions (e.g., *natale domini Cristi VII kalendas Ianuarias*, #2114) and on an epitaph from *Salonis* (*natale Septimi martyris*, #2116) (for other examples from the *Dalmatian* area, cf. Diehl, *AI*, 34). Diehl's comment in connection with the form *natale* is that "natale ceterum idem quod depositio" (*ICLV*, I, 415), where the loss of *-s* may be due to analogy with an *s*-less nominative (*sc. depositio*), although the final vowel would seem to indicate that, morphologically, it is an oblique form. For the meaning of *natale*, *v. supra*, our note #14, p. 29.

[12] Notice the hypercorrection, probably indicating that the [ks] cluster has been assimilated to [s], as in Lat. $d\bar{\imath}x\bar{\imath}$ > It. *dissi*, cf. Pei, *It. Lang.*, 35.

inatives is quite infrequent, [13] it would seem, nevertheless, that the trend is in the direction of a general *-es* ending for *-is,* suggesting the extension of the thematic /e/ of accusative/ablative endings that was to become the characteristic vowel of third declension singular nouns in Italian and Spanish. [14]

3.12 *Genitive*

The classical genitive singular of Latin third declension nouns invariably ends in *-is*. [15] This spelling is most frequently replaced by *-es*; in some instances we noted a replacement by a form in *-e* (the oblique form) and by what would appear to be the second declension genitive *-i* ending.

(a) *-es* for *-is*: The *-es* spelling for the expected *-is* closely parallels the situation already encountered in connection with the nominative. Therefore, except for giving a few examples from those areas in which this orthographic change occurs (all except *Baetica* and *Lusitania*), it need not be further commented upon.

Here then are a few random examples from both dated and non-dated inscriptions:

---

[13] In dated material, for instance, we counted only one occurrence in *Lusitania* and a total of eight in the *Italian* area.

[14] Scholars have generally attributed the *-es* spelling for *-is* (and vice versa) to a merger of Latin /ĕ/ and /ĭ/ in the unstressed syllable, and the resulting "incertezza -es/-is nella finale" (Pisani, *Testi,* 121). Cf. also Battisti, 206. Carnoy refers to the nominative singular in *-es* as "n'intéressant que la phonétique" since "ils montrent le passage de *ĭ* en syllabe finale à *e*" (217). (Note that he gives no example of the reverse phenomenon.) Pirson, as already pointed out in our note #4 (*infra,* p. 128), gives many more examples of *-es* spellings for *-is* in the nominative singular than *-is* for *-es* and clearly implies the morphological importance of this change when he says: "Cette substitution de *e* à *i* atone.... n'a pas laissé de modifier dans une large mesure le domaine de la morphologie. Elle a contribué à simplifier considérablement le système de la déclinaison en unifiant les désinences casuelles en *is* et en *es*" (36). Our findings, which confirm those of the French scholar, seem to be also entirely in accord with Sittl's conclusions: "Beim Nominativ der dritten Deklination [referring to the singular only] lassen sich sämtliche neutrale einerseits und geschlechtliche Formen andererseits unter die zwei Endungen *e* und *es*.... zusammen bringen" (*Mittellatein,* 559). The morphological significance of the *-es* spelling for *-is* thus seems clearly established.

[15] Cf. Allen-Greenough, 24 ff.

A. *Iberian Peninsula*

   (c) *Tarraconensis: tetulum Victoes* (= *Victoris*) (V239)

B. *Gaul*

   (a) *Narbonensis:*   *iuniores* (1808 a. 530; 2909 a. 537);
Orestes (2891A ad. a. 531); *consoles* (3279 a. 565)
cruces, fontes (1512), etc.

   (b) *Lugdunensis:*   *recordaciones* (1463 a. 643); *reges* (2919A a. 546/606?) [16]
curator civitates (1919), etc.

C. *Italy*

   (a) *Northern:*   *Filia comites ... p.c. Felices* (116 a. 512); *p.c. Iohannes* (848 a. 539)
in somno paces (305); *marteres* (= *martyris*) Χρι (2015 ad.)

   (b) *Central:*   *in somnum paces* (3181 a. 443); *die Veneres* (4402A)

   (c) *Southern:*   *depossio infates* (= *infantis*) (3029 a. 401)
in somno paces; iuniores (248 a. 508)
die Martes (2777A), [17] etc.

D. *Rome*

   honeste recordationes vir (301 a. 396)
Orestes (2139 a. 531); *die Veneres* (2372)
die acceptiones sue (1535); *locus Filicitates* (3511C), etc.

Note that in the last example despite all the *i*'s (*i* for *e* in unstressed initial syllable) the vowel of the ending is *e*.

(b) *-e* for *is*: This apparent extension of the oblique form to the genitive was observed in two areas;

---

[16] Note that just as in the case of the nominative no dated example occurs before the sixth century.

[17] Cf. It. *martedì*, Sp. *martes*.

(a) *Narbonensis:* $\overline{ann}$ X $\overline{regn}$ $\overline{dom}$ $\overline{nos}$ *Teude re[gis]* (2892 a. 541) [18]
$\overline{pcs}$ *Pau iuniore* (3038 a. 536)

(b) *Rome:* $\overline{pc}$ *Lampadi et Oreste* (318 a. 531)
relictis tuis iaces in pace sopore (3459)
consulatu . . . Valinte et Valentiniano iuniore (4219 a. 376)

Although in the last example we would expect genitives, since the construction is introduced by *consulatu* rather than *consulibus*, in which case the proper names would be part of an ablative absolute construction, it will be recalled that hybrid constructions (the crossing of an ablative absolute with a construction introduced by *consulatu* or *post consulatum*) in expressions showing consular year are quite common, particularly at this time (*v. supra*, 2.12, p. 71 ff.). Thus the validity of *Valinte* and *iuniore* (*iuniore* also in #3038), like that of *Valentiniano*, is somewhat weakened, although these forms cannot be dismissed as potential oblique forms in a genitive function.

(c) *-i* for *-is*: This orthographic change was recorded in a number of instances, as follows:

A. *Iberian Peninsula*

(a) *Baetica*: There are six occurrences of the genitive in *-i* for *-is* in dated material and a couple of examples in a non-dated inscription, generally involving proper names:

> *requiescit corpus Belesari famuli Xpi conditori* (V157 a. 662?)
> *reliquie scorum id Ioanni Babtiste, Eulalie*
> *Iuste, Rufine et Felici martirum* (V306 a. 648)
> $\overline{reliq}$ $\overline{scorum}$ *Vincenti, Felici, Iuliani martirum* (V305 a. 644),
> etc.

---

[18] For the name of the Visigothic king *Theudis* (and its spelling variants) cf. Schönfeld, 234-235. Since the form *regis* is reconstructed by the editor (the last syllable being no longer legible on the stone), it is not unlikely that the original reads *rege*, i.e., also an oblique form to accord with the preceding *Teude*. For the frequent use of *rege* in the genitive function in Merovingian documents (e.g., *annum nono VIIII Childerio rege*, Tardif, 53, 18), cf. Sas, 207 ff.; Taylor, 75-76.

If we look at the forms *conditori, Ioanni,* and *Felici* in the context in which they occur, it will be noticed that in most cases they are surrounded by genitives that normally end in *-i*, since they belong to the second declensional class. It would appear, therefore, that the *-i* spelling for the expected *-is* is to be attributed to the influence of these second declension genitives rather than the omission of a final *-s*. The analogical pull in the case of proper names seems to have been strong enough for those that traditionally followed the inflectional pattern of third declension nouns to be treated as though they belonged to the second declension. *Ioanni* and *Felici* in V333[b], for instance, are the only masculine nouns in an enumeration of martyrs.

(b) *Lusitania: Eolalii clerici confessori abtus est locus* (V47).

The *-i* in *confessori* (like the above *conditori*) is no doubt due to the preceding genitives in *-i*.

(c) *Tarraconensis*: In an enumeration of saints' relics we read the forms *Felici* (V307[b]) and *Pastori* (307[c]), showing the kind of analogical extension of the second declension genitive ending already observed on *Baetica*. The inscription in question comes, incidentally, from the southern part of this region, precisely where it borders on Baetica where these analogical genitives have been found. Note, however, that on an inscription from the northern part (*Asturias*) we read *sci Ioannis* (V330), despite the occurrence of several other names that follow the second declension.

B. *Gaul*

There is only one example of the *-i* spelling for the expected *-is* found in an inscription from *Lugdunensis*, namely

> *Lupa ... transiit VII k Dec $\overline{indic}$ IIII $\overline{dn}$ Teobaldi regi* (2914 a. 515)

Here, too, the influence of the preceding genitive in *-i* may be envisaged.

C. *Italy*

We have also recorded a few instances of the *-i* spelling for *-is* in this area. In some cases the influence of a preceding second declension genitive in -*i* is most likely. In others, the reason for the omission of final -*s* is not as obvious.

(a) *Northern: Alexandro* (dat.) ... *singulari innocentiae* (711, 4th-5th cent.).

In this "genitive of quality" we would expect *singularis*.[19] However, note that the word occurs at the end of a line, so that the omission of the final consonant for lack of space is also possible.

The replacement of -*is* by -*i* occurs in another, similar construction: *bone memorie et perpetue sanctitati* (2101 ad.), where the incorrect form, however, does not occur at the end of a line.

(b) *Central*: The analogical factor seems to be responsible for the orthographic change in these two examples from this region,

post consulato Arcadi et Bautoni (323 a. 386)
pos col (= *consulatum/-o*) *Lampadi et Horesti* (= *Orestis*) (3166A a. 531)

(c) *Southern*: The -*i* spelling occurs in a "genitive of quality" similar to the one found in the Northern area: *Desiderio* (dat.) ... *dulcedini supremae* (297 a. 360).

In what Diehl believes to be "vetustissimum fort. exemplum dierum mensis numerandorum" (*ILCV*, I, 71), we read *dp. die VI mnsi Iunii* (4422 a. 345).

Is the incorrect genitive in *mensi* influenced by the following *Iunii?*

D. *Rome*

In three dated epitaphs the expected genitive form *urbis* appears as *urbi*:

in ipsa praefectura urbi (90 a. 359)
pre(fectus) urbi (94A ad. a. 315)
exceptor praef. urbi (451[a] a. 482)

---

[19] The syntactic mingling of the "genitive of quality" and the "ablative of specification" is interesting to observe in this particular epitaph; Alexander is *mirae verecundiae* and *singulari(s) innocentiae*, but *castitate integrus* and *notarum litteris eruditus*. For the concepts of "genitive of quality" and "ablative of specification," cf. Allen-Greenough, 213 and 262.

"Die Form *praefectura urbi* überwiegt weitaus zu allen Zeiten; selbst *praefectus urbi* findet sich..." the great German historian, Theodor Mommsen, states [20] and he himself uses this expression to designate the Prefect of the city of Rome.[21] In this particular context, therefore, the form *urbi* (possibly by analogy of *vici*, in the title *magister vici?*)[22] must be considered as an acceptable alternative rather than an orthographic deviation.

The -*i* spelling for -*is* is also attested in the following "genitives of quality":

> *miri* (= *mirae*) *bonitatis atq. sanctitati* (4326 a. 348)
> *innocentie et dulcitudini filio* (dat.) *fecerunt* (4337A)

These may be instances of the omission of final -*s*.

On the basis of the evidence just presented it would seem that in the majority of cases where the -*i* spelling appears for the expected -*is* genitive ending, there is an analogical influence of the preceding or following word at play. In the few examples, particularly from the *Italian* area, where such an analogical extension of the second declension genitive ending is not immediately apparent, it must be assumed that the stonecutter erroneously omitted final -*s,* although the analogical factor should not be dismissed either.

(d) *Prepositional Replacement*: The practical equivalence of the *de* construction and the classical genitive is well illustrated in the following inscriptions from *Acci* (*Tarraconensis*) and *Narbo* (*Narbonensis*), respectively

---

[20] *Römisches Staatsrecht*. Dritte Auflage. (Leipzig, 1887), Vol. II², 1059.

[21] Originally (in Republican times) appointed as deputy to an absentee chief magistrate (viz. consul) of the city of Rome, the office of the *praefectus urbi* became a permanent institution under the Empire with the primary responsibility of assuring peace and order in the eternal city and its vicinity. Hence, the occasional reference to the Prefect as *custos urbis*. The *praefecti*, in addition, also exercised criminal and civil jurisdiction. Cf. Mommsen, *ibid.*, 1059 ff. While, according to the German scholar, the genitive form *urbis* occurs only sporadically when used with *praefectus*, it is the more usual form in conjunction with *praefectura*. In our material, the expression *praefectus urbis* is attested four times (70a/b; 92; 714). In re *praefectus urbi*, cf. also Proskauer, 145.

[22] Re *magistri vici*, cf. Joachim Marquardt, *Römische Staatsverwaltung*. Zweite Auflage. (Leipzig, 1881), Vol. I, 9.

reliq[uie de] cruore $\overline{Dni}$, $\overline{sci}$ Babile... [de] pane $\overline{Dni}$
$\overline{sce}$ Paule... [de] cruore $\overline{Dni}$... [de v]este $\overline{Dni}$, $\overline{sce}$ Crucis, (V307^{b} a. 652?)

$\overline{epi}$ Aratoris de sorore nepus (1806 a. 441?)

Of interest is the fact that in the latter we have an example of the possessive idea expressed by a periphrastic construction ('the bishop sister's nephew'), but it is also noteworthy that personal names appear in the classical genitive.

3.13 *Dative*

(a) The *-e* spelling for *-i* (cl. Lat. *-ī*) is sporadically attested in both dated and non-dated inscriptions, particularly in the *Italian* area, including *Rome*. No deviations were found in the *Iberian* area [23] and only one instance of an *-e* spelling in *Gaul*, in the phrase *Olebrio* (= *Olybrio*)... *et Nepote* (1191, *Lugdunensis*). [24]

Examples of datives in *-e* from the *Italian* area are as follows:

(a) *Northern: arca Manioni milete* (545 a. 394-402) [25]

Anastasio innocenti... petente in Cristo (1507)

---

[23] Carnoy, however, reports a few examples of datives in *-e* from pagan inscriptions (47). Cooper finds the dative *-i* ending "firmly intact" (53), while Jennings lists a number of examples of datives in *-e* (99).

[24] Pirson gives a few dative forms in *-e* from both pagan and Christian inscriptions e.g., *fidele* (XIII 2115) on an epitaph not included in the Diehl volumes. Curiously, the French scholar offers different explanations for the *-e* spelling in the dative according to whether it occurs on a pagan or Christian inscription. As to the former, he states: "La désinence *e* du datif des substantifs.... et des adjectifs.... peut être le résultat de la réduction du suffixe primitif *ei* en *ē*, dont on retrouve encore mainte trace dans les inscriptions de l'époque impériale" (120). His comment on the same phenomenon in Christian inscriptions, on the other hand, is that *e* "peut résulter de l'affaiblissement de l'*ī* atone" (121). For the frequent dative forms in *-e* in Merovingian documents, cf. Sas, 221.

[25] In other epitaphs from this place (the *Concordia* cemetery) we find the proper name in the classical genitive case, e.g., *arca Ursicini lapedario* (654) (for *lapedario*, v. supra, 2.12, our comments under *No. Italy*, p. 69) and *arca Numeriani prencepalis* (370). Is it not also possible, that instead of a so-called "dative of possession," *Manioni* and *milete* represent oblique forms used in genitive function? Cf. oblique forms in *-o* of the second declension used in the genitive function also.

(b) *Central:* *salvo domno papa Victore* (1840A a. 539-546) [26]
              maritus benemerente Cassanete ... fecit (2851C) [27]

(c) *Southern:* Only a single example: *Mirurianete filiae dulcissime* (2948A) [28]

(d) *Rome:*   *Cassie ... coniuge benemerenti* (158 ca. 3rd. cent.)
              Aureliae Anianeti ben.m. coiuge (2232) [29]
              benemerente filio Asello (2942 a. 366), and *passim*

In an otherwise correctly written non-dated epitaph we read: *maritus uxori optime quiescente* (2452A), in addition to the datives *fratre meo* (4104) and *patre nostro* (4651) found on two inscriptions form this area.

Battisti states that the substitution of *-e* for cl. Lat. *-ī* in the dative case is "comune nelle iscrizioni" and believes that this ending is a reflex of the "incertezze" between the original *i*-stem and consonant-stem ablatives in *-ī* and *-e*, a hesitation which eventually "si chiude colla vittoria di *-e*" (205). [30] Our material seems to show that where the dative occurs with some frequency (particularly in *Italy*) it is generally spelled with *-i*. [31] Yet, we believe that examples that show an *-e* spelling cannot be dismissed as occasional errors without significance; rather, they point in the direction of a trend to extend a

---

[26] For the use of *papa* (= *episcopus*) as an invariable noun, cf. also *salvo an papa n̄ Petro* (1907), and *passim*.

[27] Nom. form *Cassane*. Concerning the *-etis, -eti* inflectional pattern of feminine nouns in *-ane*, v. supra, our note #64 (chapter 2), p. 79.

[28] A garbled form for *Mercurianete*.

[29] Notice the concurrent use of a dative in *-i* (*Anianeti*) and in *-e* (*coiuge*). (In the next line we read *quem coiuge habui an VIIII*, also showing the *-e* oblique ending in direct object function. But note the correct accusative form *quem*.) Further examples of *coniuge* in the classical dative function in Nos. 2727A and 4619. In the latter we find both *coniugi suae* and *coniugae dulcissimae* in succeeding lines.

[30] B. Löfstedt objects to any connection of this sort and explains the *-e* spelling for *-i* in the dative (which, however, he finds only sporadically attested in his documents) through an analogical extension: "Da die Nomina der 3. Dekl. im Akk. und Abl. Sing. auf *-e* endeten und diese Formen die häufigsten, in der Volkssprache des 7.-8. Jhs. vielleicht die allein lebendigen waren, ist es natürlich, dass bisweilen dies *-e* auch im Dat. für *-i* eintreten konnte" (68-69). This view supports our contention that the *-e* spelling in the dative reflects a morphological phenomenon.

[31] In his 7th and 8th cent. documents, Politzer finds a comparable stability of the *-i* ending with only an occasional replacement, mainly by *-e* (*Rom. Trends.*, 22; *Lomb. Docs.*, 61).

single ending to all *casus obliqui*, thus reflecting a morphological rather than phonological phenomenon.

(b) *Periphrastic Construction with "ad"*: This construction as a substitute for the synthetic dative would appear to be used in an epitaph from *Lugdunensis*, where we read

>hic ad innocentem et peregrinum Ursicinum (1475)

for the expected *innocenti* and *peregrino Ursicino*.

The following two examples may be reported from the *Italian* area,

>ad fratre et sorore (3749), Milan
>iunctus virgo ad virgine (2159), Rome

for the expected *fratri, sorori*, and *virgini* (cf. *iuncta marito*, 3446). However, this last example may not actually be a deviation from the classical standard, seeing that *iunctus* with the meaning of 'yoked to' could also be constructed with *ad*, followed by the accusative case, cf. Lewis-Short, 1617.

3.14 *Accusative*

The anticipated *-em* ending of masculine and feminine nouns sometimes appears as *-e*. Details of this orthographic deviation according to area are as follows.

A. *Iberian Area*

There are relatively few occurrences of this case in this area.

(a) *Baetica*: The *-e* ending for the expected *-em* in a direct object function is seen in: *dedicavit hanc aede d̄m̄s̄* (= *dominus*) *Bacanda* (V308ᶜ a. 660).

Since the form *aede* seems to occur at the end of a line, the argument may be advanced that the final *-m* was omitted for lack of space. While this possibility cannot be disregarded, such an argument is likely to conceal the true state of affairs, namely a reflection of actual pronunciation, as already suggested in connection with the accusative of first declension nouns (*v. supra*, 1.14, p. 38 ff., particularly note #57). The fact that no omission of final *-m* was found in the accusative of second declension nouns and that inscriptions from this area are in general carefully written (i.e., in accordance with the tenets of traditional grammar) suggests the emergence of an oblique case which, on the plane of expression, may be represented by forms in *-em* and *-e*.[32] This hypothesis seems to be strengthened by the use of *nomine* and *funere* instead of the expected classical accusative *nomen* and *funus* in

> *pos nomine Xρi* (V159 a. 658),[33] and
> *tumulo procumbit Servande post funere corpus* (V286 a. 660)

giving rather clear evidence of the collapse of the classical accusative/ ablative opposition on the plane of content.

(b) *Lusitania*: Whenever the classical accusative appears either in direct object function or after a preposition, it is always spelled with *-em*.

(c) *Tarraconensis*: Of the few occurrences of this case, two are spelled with *-e*,

> *Froila requivit* (= *requievit*) *per bona confessione* (V259 a. 562)
> *abeat parte com Iuda* (V262, 7th cent.)

While we realize that this material is rather scanty to justify definite conclusions, we believe that the comments made in connection

---

[32] The use of *hanc* side by side with *aede* is, of course, no proof that the writer is conscious of a case distinction. Cf. the use of *hunc* in the classical ablative function on an epitaph from this area (V157). The apparently interchangeable use of *hanc* and *hac* is reflected in Fr. *encore* and It. *ancora* (both from *hanc hora*) versus Sp. and Port. *agora* (< *hac hora*). Cf. Pei, *It. Lang.*, 82; Bourciez, *Phonétique*, 11 (where, however, *encore* < *in qua hora* is also suggested); Menéndez Pidal, *Gramática*, 337.

[33] While in cl. Latin it is customary simply to use the ablative form of *nomen* to express the idea in whose name an action is performed (e.g., *Antonio tuo nomine gratias egi*, Cic. *Att.*, 1, 16, 16), in Late Latin, particularly in ecclesiastical style, the "delegated power" is reinforced by the preposition *in*, e.g., *locuti sunt in nomine Domini*, Vulg. *Jacob* 5, 10. In Christian inscriptions this analytic construction is the rule. In two inscriptions from the *Iberian* area, however, the preposition *in* is replaced by *post* (cf. the example listed under *Baetica*) and *per*, as in *Ursicinus in pace dormit per nomen Dei* (V258, *Tarraconensis*). This latter usage is not unknown in oaths, entreaties, and asseverations by a god (e.g., *per Iovem*), by men, or by inanimate or abstract things (e.g., *per salutem meam*), cf. Lewis-Short, 1332.

THIRD DECLENSION

with our findings in *Baetica,* i.e., an indication as to the creation of an oblique form in *-e* in both classical accusative and ablative functions, are also pertinent to this region.

B. *Gaul*

(a) *Narbonensis*: The *-e* spelling for *-em* appears only after a preposition that traditionally would call for the classical accusative: *vivens post morte* (3487B), as well as in the adverbial expression: *in onore sci Petri apostoli voto suo fecet* (1928).[34]

(b) *Lugdunensis*: We recorded several instances of an *-e* spelling both after verbs and prepositions,

> *dismisit grande crudelitate uxsori et filis* (554)
> *reliquit libertus Scupilione.... Ildelone* (1759 a. 487)
> (also *Leuvera, Orovelda,* but *Gerontium, Balderedum*)[35]
> *frater propter caritate tetulu fecit* (4162)[36]

C. *Italy*

Examples of the *-e* spelling for *-em* in this general area occur both after verbs and prepositions.

(a) *Northern: arcam corporale ... comparaverunt* (833, 4th-5th cent.)

---

[34] But cf. Einar Löfstedt's comment: "Abgesehen von dem altbekannten Schwanken zwischen Akk. und Abl. bei *in* im Spätlatein ist die Verbindung *in honore alicuius* bemerkenswert, da sie bei verschiedenen Schriftstellern sowie in Inschriften dieser Zeit vorkommt, und wie es scheint, eine gewisse Festigkeit erhalten hat" (*Peregrinatio,* 182).

[35] Väänänen cites a *graffito* (#5380) from his Pompeian material in which accusatives of first-and third-declension nouns are written with *-a* and *-e*, respectively (*halica, bubilla, pane*), while those belonging to the second declension show the expected *-um* ending (*botillum, casium, pisciculum*). This evidence leads him to the conclusion that "l'*m* final aurait été plus résistant après *u* qu'ailleurs, ou que, plus exactement peut-être, après *u* il y a eu facultativement réduction ou amuïssement total, tandis qu'après n'importe quelle autre voyelle l'amuïssement était à peu près définitif" (76). Bonnet, indeed, claims that, as late as Gregory of Tours, final *-m* was probably pronounced after *u,* while in connection with first and third declension nouns, *-a* and *-e* appear regularly for *-am* and *-em* (154-155).

[36] For our interpretation of forms in *-u, v. supra,* 2.14 and 2.15, pp. 77-83, and 89-101.

> *venit ut istam urbe videret* (4812A, 4th-5th cent.) [37]
> *adiuro ... et te custude beati Iuliani* (3863)
> *ad fratre et sorore* (3748) [38]

In the following epitaph a classical accusative in *-em* and a form in *-e* appear side by side in the same function: *grandeque caritatem* (4340).

(b) *Central*: The direct object is spelled with *-e* in the following instances:

> *abeat parte cum Iuda traditore* (3849, ca. 7th cent.)
> *maledictione dī avea* (= *habeat*) (3852)
> *ne quis velat aperire Iulianate vel Lucentiu* (820) [39]

Here are examples of an *-e* spelling after prepositions that traditionally would call for an accusative in *-em,*

> *in honore sancti ... martiris Stephani* (1797 a. 550) [40]
> *pos morte ipsius* (846, ca. 6th cent.)
> *pos depositione eius* (3859, ca. 6th or 7th cent.)

(c) *Southern*: The *-e* and *-em* spellings occur side by side in direct object functions in *abis ... pace perennem* (1356 a. 395).

The example *qui meum nomine miserit* (3851 ca. 7th cent.) [41] is the more interesting since the second declension accusative is signalled by *-m*, while instead of the expected accusative *nomen* we get an oblique form in *-e*. [42]

---

[37] Since this phrase is taken from a short verse epitaph, it may be that *urbe* is written for *urbem* for the sake of the meter, i.e., *metro urgente*, cf. Diehl, *De m finali*, 220.

[38] For the use of the "periphrastic dative," v. *supra*, 3.13, p. 139.

[39] *Velat* presumably for *velit* or *vellet*. Cf. *ne aliquis velet alium super hoc ponere* (839a).

[40] Cf. our note #34, p. 141. Another occurrence of *in honore* in #1798b.

[41] The editors have interpreted *miserit* as a garbled form for *laeserit*.

[42] Cf. also *pos nomine* cited above under Baetica. It is well known that in Classical Latin already a number of neuters became masculine and that in Vulgar Latin this trend must have been quite strong. Thus, Grandgent assumes that besides *nomen* there must have been a masculine accusative form *nominem (V. L.,* 145), but cf. Pei, *Accusative*, 252 ff. for reasons why it is unnecessary to postulate such a hypothetical form.

Examples of an oblique form in -e for the anticipated -em with prepositions are as follows,

>   hic recuiescit per inditione Va (3119 a. 389/391)
>   per indictione quarta anno ... (4302 a. 570)
>   perfice usque in fine (2374)

D. *Rome*

Occurrences of forms in -e for the expected -em in both dated and non-dated inscriptions are quite numerous.[43] Here are some examples of deviations in direct object function:

>   feci nobis domum aeternale (3663 a. 356)
>   hic abet sede Leo prb (= presbyter) (1128A)
>   se viva conparabit locum vescandente (= biscandente) (2129)[44]
>   quem coniuge habui an. VIIII (2232)
>   se viva fecit eterna securitate (3701A)[45]
>   si quis alterum omine sup (= super) me posueri(t) (3856)[46]
>   accepit requie in deo (3298A), etc.

In the following example we find both a form in -em and forms in -e used in the same function: *queius fidelitatem et castitate et bonitate omnes vicinales experti sunt* (2157).[47]

The -e spelling for the anticipated -em after prepositions like *per*, *post*, *ante*, *super*, etc. occurs quite frequently. A few examples will suffice:

>   ad calice benimus (1568 a. 375)
>   vixit usque at die mortis sue (2805 a. 337)

---

[43] We have excluded the occasional occurrence of *mense unu* since, as was seen, the form *unu* does not necessarily reflect a classical accusative form, v. supra, 2.14, p. 79 ff. In one instance we read *mense unum* (4661) but the preceding hypercorrect *cum maritum* would seem to suggest that the apparent acc. form *unum* is also a hypercorrection.

[44] This formula, or a variant thereof, occurs in four more epitaphs from this area (Nos. 3815, 3815 adn., 3815A, 3815A adn.), with the expected *biscandentem* consistently spelled without -m, despite the preceding *locum*.

[45] The expression *securitas aeterna* is used here as a synonym for *domus aeternalis*, cf. #3663 listed here above.

[46] Note the use of *alter* in the sense of *alius* 'another' (out of many).

[47] Concerning the form *queius*, v. supra, note #61 (chapter 1), p. 41. Note the nominalization of the adjective *vicinales*, probably with the meaning of 'friends and neighbors.'

> *ante natale domni Asteri* (2124)
> *super omnem dulcitudine filiorum dulcior* (2733) [48]
> *post adceptione sua* (1536ᵃ)
> *iunctus mihi... virgo ad virgine* (2159)
> *fecit sibi... super coniuge sua* (3830A)
> *ad oblatione vel luminaria nostra* (3778ᵇ), [49] etc.

The usual confusion of the use of *in* followed by the apparent ablative, regardless of whether state or motion is involved, is seen in

> *regrediens in urbe* (3332 a. 217)
> *in luce domini susceptus est* (3444 a. 397)
> *vite redempta secessit in luce* (1718 a. 452)

In connection with his study of Merovingian documents, Sas (240) had stated that the use of *-e* as object of the verb (and he may have added "as object of the preposition" also) is too common to be due to the "ignorance" of a scribe, so that when he used the *-e* ending for *-em* he must have done so intentionally to record the new morphology of his own period. The feeling expressed by this scholar would also seem to be applicable to our material. Indeed, the *-e* ending, which is occasionally also encountered in the genitive and dative functions, clearly points to the creation of an "Universalkasus," in accordance with the changing morphology of the language.

3.15 *Ablative*

Because of the occurrence of *i*-stem nouns and adjectives whose ablative case traditionally ends in -*ī*, [50] this section is divided into two parts, namely (1) ablatives in *-e*, and (2) ablatives in *i*.

(1) Ablatives in *-e*

The overwhelming majority of nouns that appear in our material are consonant stems which regularly take this ending. Deviations

---

[48] For the use of *super* with the meaning of 'more than,' cf. Lewis-Short, 1804 (*dulciora sunt super mel et favum*, Psa. 18, 11). A similar construction occurs in *filio super omni caritate dulcissimo* (4683).

[49] *Vel = et* (cf. Lewis-Short, 1963). *Luminaria* seems to be used as a singular here, which means that this neuter has shifted to the first declension noun class, cf. Sp. *lumbrera* < *luminaria* (REW #5162).

[50] Allen-Greenough, 28-32; Ernout, *Morphologie*, 86.

therefore involve the spelling *-i* and *-em* both after verbs, prepositions, and in absolute construction.

(a) *-i* for *-e*: An occasional *-i* spelling for the expected *-e* occurs in almost all areas; this deviation is totally absent from the *Iberian Peninsula*.

B. *Gaul*

The orthographic change *-e* > *-i* is attested only in a few cases.

(a) *Narbonensis: p.c. Basili.... indexioni tesia* (3279 a. 565) [51]
requiebit in pace dominica (3289) [52]

(b) *Lugdunensis: requiivit in pace in mensi Iulio* (3129 ca. 6th cent.), [53]

where an ablative in *-e* and one in *-i* occur side by side.

C. *Italy*

There are very few examples of this orthographic deviation in this area also.

(a) *Northern*: No deviations to report.

(b) *Central*: A single deviation in the proper name *Constans*,

Constantio... et Constanti (consulibus) (3226 a. 339)
(but *Constante* in 4225; 2938 ad.; 2978) [54]

---

[51] For *indictione tertia*. Both the spelling with x = [ks] of *indexioni* and the *-si-* combination of *te(r)sia* would seem to be good evidence of the assibilation of the [-tį-] consonant group.

Ini (= *indictioni*), with an ablative in *-i*, also appears in #3552 (a. 597) from this region.

[52] The formula *requievit in pace*, with the likely meaning of 'was put to rest,' is rather typical of epitaphs from *Lusitania*, cf. Vives, 16.

Another occurrence of *in paci* in #3473 from this region.

[53] Noteworthy is the use of the preposition *in*, as if to say 'in the month of July.' In this case *Iulio* could also be taken as an oblique form in *-o* in the genitive functions. *V. supra*, 2.12, p. 68. A similar construction is found in *IIII° idus Iulii* (1071, ca. 6th cent.).

[54] Participles used as nouns generally have the ablative in *-e*, cf. Allen-Greenough, 53.

(c) *Southern:* *Arcadio et Bautoni conss.* (81 a. 385)
  (but *Bautone* in 4599; 488)
  Datiano et Ceriali conss (3911 a. 358)

in addition to two occurrences of *in paci* (2812; 1148).

D. Rome

The *-i* spelling for the anticipated *-e* occurs with some frequency in this area, in both dated and non-dated epitaphs. A few examples will suffice:

> *Tiberiano et Dioni coss* (2305 a. 291) (but *Dione* in 4366A; 4578)
> *Valenti et Valentiniano iuniori cons* (1328 a. 376)[55]
> *Aetio conli* (= *consuli*) (333 a. 432)
> *que mecum a virginitati sua vixit* (314); *pridie natali suo* (1524)
> *cum coiugi fecit menses VIIII* (4243A)[56]

In the following examples both the ablative in *-i* (for the expected *-e*) and the correct one in *-e* appear side by side,

> *cum Felicitate coiugi suam* (3697)
> *depositus in paci natale domnes Sitiretis* (2115 a. 401)[57]
> *filii fecerunt in pace qui in unu deu crededit in pace* (1596a)[58]

---

[55] The ablative form *Valenti* is also attested in Nos. 4393A and 2604. However, it is correctly spelled (i.e., *Valente*) in 23 other instances. Similarly, the name of the consul *Stillico* is spelled four times with *-i* (*Stilliconi*) (Nos. 1299, 159 adn., 2281 adn., and 4146F) but 12 times correctly with *-e*. Other proper names that are occasionally spelled with *-i* in the ablative are *Arbitio* (three times *-i* vs. three times *-e*), *Bauto* (once *-i* vs. twice *-e*), and *Victor* (once *-i* vs. twice *-e*). For the increased use of the *-i* ending in the ablative of comparatives in post-classical literature and its survival in formulae like *a priori, a posteriori*, etc., cf. Kieckers, II, 56-57.

[56] Since the dative forms *coniugi benemerenti* occur in the previous line, the possibility of an orthographic influence on the ablative cannot be excluded. The same kind of influence may also be responsible for the ablative in *-i* in *quam adfectioni coniugali tam industria morum suorum* (4709).

[57] For *dominae Soteridis*. For the orthographic substitution of *-es* for *-ae* in the genitive singular of feminine nouns, v. *supra*, 1.12, p. 27 ff.

[58] The very common adverbial phrase *in pace* is spelled with *-i* in three more instances (Nos. 2509, 2692A adn., and 3099C).

Speaking of these ablative forms in -*i* for the expected -*e*, Pirson makes the following observation:

> L'*i* des ablatifs *paci*.... *mensi*... trouve naturellement sa raison d'être dans l'équivalence des sons ĭ et ĕ *atones* (121).

Pei, on the other hand, who also records ablatives in -*i*, such as *abbati* for *abbate*, feels that this kind of change "is very frequently of a morphological rather than a phonetic character.... where the morphological factor of the development of a single oblique case looms large" (*Texts*, 42). The morphological factor reflected in this orthographic change is also implicit with B. Löfstedt (54), although this scholar specifically refers to the -*i* spelling for -*e* in the comparative form of adjectives, e.g., *maiori*, to which may be traced the survival of formulaic expressions of the *a fortiori* type. (Cf. also our note #55.)

Before drawing our own conclusions, let us examine the ablative of third declension *i*-stem nouns and adjectives in -*i* to determine whether they are just as likely to be spelled with -*e* as those traditionally ending in -*e* with -*i*.

(b) *-em for -e*: Instances of forms in *-em* for the anticipated ablative in *-e* occur as follows:

A. *Iberian Peninsula*

There are only a couple of occurrences of this deviation.

(a) *Baetica*: No examples.

(b) *Lusitania: a comunionem scm* (= *sanctam*) *seclusus* (V47 ca. 6th cent.).

(c) *Tarraconensis: vixit cum comparem suam Nonnitam* (V205 ca. 5th cent.).

Note also the form *crededit* for the Cl. Lat. *credidit*. This Vulgar Latin form presupposes a stress on the second syllable (*credédi*) rather than on the first (*crédidi*). It is the former that must be posited to explain the Italian form *credei*. For the problem of the derivation of Italian perfects in *-ei*, cf. Grandgent, *Italian*, 117; Pei, *It. Lang.*, 98-99. For It. *credetti* < V.L. *crededit*, cf. Rohlfs, *Grammatik*, II, 369.

B. *Gaul*

(a) *Narbonensis*: The *-em* spelling for *-e* occurs only in the frequent adverbial phrase *in pace; requiescit in pacem* (1648) (also a hypercorrect *in hoc tumulum* in the previous line), while in another epitaph we read both *hic in pacem* and *vicset in pace* (2909).

(b) *Lugdunensis*: In addition to a couple of occurrences of *in pacem* (1372, 3110B ad.), the *-em* spelling is found in the "ablative of means" construction *tum propia sepe levavit opem* (1075 a. 630), as well as after the preposition *pro* in

> *pro redemtionem animae suae* (1616[b] ca. 6th cent.)
> *pro caritatem* (1374; 2252; 4161)

(but cf. *pro caritate* in nos. 1374 ad. and 4161 ad. from the same place).

C. *Italy*

Examples of forms in *-em* are found mainly after the preposition *cum* and in the adverbial phrase *in pace*.

(a) *Northern:* *cum comparem suam* (4206; 4237)

(b) *Central:* *cum Iuda traditorem* (3850 after 6th cent.)
cum comparem suam (4231C)

(c) *Southern:* The adverbial phrase spelled *in pacem* occurs in five instances [59] and there are two deviations after the preposition *cum*, in *cum coiugem suum* (887A) and *cum neptem* (4550).

D. *Rome*

We found a single instance of an *-em* spelling for *-e* in the absolute construction: *F. Valentem et Vatentiniano* (*conss.*) (4146A[b] a. 378).

All other examples of this deviation occur with a preposition, in both dated and non-dated epitaphs. Here are some representative examples:

---

[59] Nos. 2345A, 2524 adn., 2973F, 3161, and 3220.

sub illa ... condicionem (841 a. 584)
orate p̄r me peccatorem (3865 ca. 7th cent.) [60]
vixit cum parem suo (4238); [61] *cum uxorem suam* (2883 a. 360; 4239)
vixit mecum cum omnem simplicitatem (3307) [62]
cum fratrem sum (1602A); *cum coniugem suam Hirenetem* (4112) [63]
sine animi lesionem (but *sine macula*) (3387)
pete pro Celsinianu coniugem (2347)
me comparasse locum a Laur. fossorem (3754B a. 380)
Victoria de regionem Admederensium (4454); [64] etc.

The adverbial expression *in pace* is quite frequently spelled *pacem* also; e.g., *ibet in pacem* (2875 a. 382) (but cf. *ibit in pace* (2874B); *ivit in pace* (4339 a. 392)), d. (= *depositus*) *in pacem* (2971 a. 391), and *passim* in both dated and non-dated epitaphs.

In comparing the accusative and ablative cases in the first declension singular, we stated that the *-a* spelling for *-am* occurs more frequently than the reverse phenomenon and that given the same number of occurrences of both cases the *-a* spelling for *-am* would still probably outweigh the hypercorrect *-am* forms for *-a* (v. *supra*, p. 45). This state of affairs seems to find a clear parallel in the singular of third declension nouns also. The ratio of a clearly predominating ablative occurrence with respect to the accusative is even more pronounced than in the first declension so that here, too, it would seem safe to assume that given a comparable number of classical accusatives and ablatives, the *-e* spelling for *-em* would have the upper hand. Under the circumstances one wonders whether the time-honored theory, namely that the single case of the modern Romance languages (the oblique cases of Old French and Old Provençal) is the direct descendant of the classical Latin accusative, is indeed

---

[60] This particular epitaph is of further interest because of the occurrence of the periphrastic future: *cod estis fui et quod sum essere abetis*.

[61] Note the use of *par* with the obvious meaning of *compar*.

[62] Cf. the similar formula: *cum omnem castitatem mecum vixit* (4271).

[63] For the declension of proper names of the *Irene, -etis* type, v. *supra*, note #64 (Chapter 2), p. 79. Other occurrences of *cum coniugem* in Nos. 628, 2132, and 3521, and *cum comparem* in Nos. 4460 (a. 385) and 4231. The correct forms *cum coniuge* and *cum compare*, of course, outweigh the incorrect ones.

[64] For the use of *de* to show provenience, v. *supra*, note #70 (Chapter 2), p. 81.

tenable.⁶⁵ While this is not the proper place to discuss this question in greater detail (*v. infra*, 3.25, p. 169 and our notes #120, p. *ibidem* and #2 in chapter 5, p. 198), suffice it to say at this point that the orthographic hesitation between forms in *-em* and *-e* in both accusative and ablative functions seems to indicate the speaker's loss of consciousness of this case distinction and the emergence of a single case signalled by *-e* that encompasses both classical case relationships.

(2) Ablatives in *-i*

The occurrence of ablatives of *i*-stem nouns and adjectives is quite infrequent in both dated and non-dated inscriptions. In some areas these ablatives are not attested at all, while in others the few occurrences make for a high ratio of forms in *-e* for the expected *-i*. The situation in the individual areas under study is the following:

A. *Iberian Peninsula*

Deviations from the classical norm (i.e., *-e for -i*) were found only in the *Baetica* region,⁶⁶ namely

> *aram in medio altare recondit* (V313 a. 637)
> *cum virginibus sacris nobile cetu* (V286 a. 649)
> *in fundum Valles suburbio Obolconense* (V323, 7th cent.)⁶⁷

In referring to the form *tale* found in his material, Carnoy states that

> l'ablatif *tale* [est] une preuve de la disparition progressive de l'ablatif en *i* dans la langue parlée. À l'époque chrétienne les ablatifs en *e* pour *i* ne font que se multiplier (218)

and cites the above forms *altare* and *nobile* to support his conclusion. Although our material is too scanty to subscribe to Carnoy's generalization regarding the whole Iberian area, his conclusion as far as

---

⁶⁵ Cf. Elcock: "... the accusative case alone was normally the source of the modern Romance substantive" (60).

⁶⁶ On a Jewish inscription from *Tarraconensis* included in a special section of the Vives collection we read *pauset anima eius in pace cum omne Israel* (V430).

⁶⁷ For the interpretation of *suburbio Obulconense* as a locative ablative, *v. supra*, note #99 (Chapter 2), p. 94.

Baetica goes is certainly valid. On the other hand, we have found no instance of the reverse phenomenon, i.e., the spelling *-i* for *-e*, so that the stability of ablatives in *-e* would seem to suggest that the latter ending had become general in the whole Iberian area.

B. *Gaul*

While a couple of ablatives in *-e* were found to be spelled with *-i*, the reverse was not encountered. It must be said, however, that the occurrence of classical ablatives in *-i* is extremely rare in our material from this area (none in dated material from the *Lugdunensis* region).

Pirson reports a few examples of deviant forms from pagan inscriptions (e.g., *animo forte*) with the comment that "certains adjectifs prennent *e* à l'ablatif contrairement au bon usage" (120), and that examples of this phenomenon are also sporadically attested in literature.

Pei reports, as being particularly noteworthy, the fact that in Merovingian documents "the ending *-i* of the ablative of adjectives of the third declension is regularly changed to *-e*" (*Texts*, 51) and sees in this phenomenon the reflection of a morphological rather than a phonological factor, namely the remodelling of these adjectives on the form of the ablative of the noun.[68]

C. *Italy*

Occurrences of the classical ablative in *-i* are very infrequent. Only two deviant forms were found, none in the *southern Italian* region.

(a) *Northern*: arca Numeriani de civitate Mursese (370, 4th-5th cent.).[69]

(b) *Central*: Caius Zobonis de lo(co) Kasense (4451B).[70]

---

[68] Cf. also B. Löfstedt: "Dies [i.e., the replacement of ablatives in *-i* by those in *-e*] erklärt sich natürlich durch analogische Beeinflussung durch die substantivischen Kons.-Stämme auf *-e*" (68).

[69] The adjective *Mursensis* built on *Mursa* (present-day *Eszeg*) in Lower Pannonia.

[70] On an inscription from the province of *Numidia* we read: ordo municipi Casensium (CIL VIII 4327).

D. Rome

Here, too, the ablative form in -*i* occurs very infrequently. All deviations in fourth century material occur in the proper name *Cerealis: Datiano et Cereale conss.* (2976; 2941 ad.; 2690 ad., a. 385), no doubt by analogy of other third declension proper names and common nouns, but cf. *Datiano et Ceriali conss.* (3911).

Another -*e* spelling for the expected -*i* occurs in *F. Iohanne orientale* (318 a. 538) (influenced by the preceding proper name?).

From a comparison of ablatives in -*e* which occasionally show up with an -*i* spelling and the -*e* spelling of the few ablatives that traditionally end in -*i*, it would seem fair to conclude that this "incertezza nell'ablativo" — as Battisti (205) has called it — is due to a morphological confusion resulting from the shift of all *i*-stem ablative forms to a generalized -*e* ending (except for a few "fossilized" survivals of the *a priori* type) which speakers must have come to regard as the regular pattern. The development of a single ablative ending in -*e* is, furthermore, quite in accord with the general trend that was observed throughout the singular of this declension to replace cl. Lat. /ĭ/ by /e/ in morphological endings.

3.2 Plural

A summary of morphological endings is given in table #6 in the Appendix.

3.21 *Nominative*

According to the tenets of Latin grammar, the third declension nominative plural of masculine and feminine nouns and adjectives always ends in -*ēs* (Sommer, 382). Nevertheless, instances in which an -*is* ending appears for the anticipated -*es* in this grammatical function are already attested in Republican times.[71]

Despite the few occurrences of this case form in our material (none in some regions), the -*is* spelling occasionally replaces the ex-

---

[71] Ferdinand Sommer records the forms (prai)TORIS, FINIS, among others and further notes that "*puppīs, restīs* sagte man zu Varros Zeit neben -*ēs*" (382).

pected -es. Examples of such deviant forms were found in the following areas:

B. *Gaul*

(a) *Narbonensis*: No example. The few nominatives occurring in non-dated inscriptions are spelled with -es.

(b) *Lugdunensis*: While no occurrences of this case ending was found in dated material, several instances of the form *patris* (with the meaning of *parentes*) [72] were found in a group of non-dated inscriptions from *Trier* (1371; 1682; 2455 ad., 3589; 3590A) (also *patres* in 3589; 3590; 3110A; 4374).

In addition to these examples, the form *innocentis* (3102) also shows a nominative in -*is*.

C. *Italy*

Examples of nominatives in -*is* were found both in dated and non-dated inscriptions.

(a) *Northern: parentis dolientis contra votu ficierunt* (847; 1366), in addition to several more occurrences of *parentis* (2963; 3361; 4725 ad.) and one occurrence of *patris* (1499) (usually followed by *titulum posuerunt* and the name of the child in the dative case, e.g., *Maxentiae filiae*).

(b) *Central*: The only deviation occurs in the form *parentis* (4813 a. 420).

(c) *Southern*: The form *parentis* for the expected *parentes* is attested twice (4181 a. 400; 4616).

---

[72] The use of the form *patres* with the meaning of *parentes*, although occurring most frequently on inscriptions from this region, must have been more widespread. It is found in other regions of *Gaul*, such as *Vienne* (*Narbonensis*) (1350) and *Baudobriga*, present-day *Boppard* (*Lugdunensis*) (1423), in the region of *Aquileia* (*No. Italy*) (283, 1499), as well as on an African inscription from *Mauretania* (*cum patribus suis*, 3269).

D. Rome

In addition to the rather frequent appearance of *parentis* in both dated and non-dated inscriptions, [73] outweighing the classical form *parentes*, [74] the nominative in *-is* also occurs in

>   *fratris se bibi... fecerunt* (4146F ad. a. 400)
>   *fratris dulcissimo ficeru* (2810E ad.); *fratris* (3992A)
>   *de filius ipseius qui superstitis sunt* (2372) [75]

In discussing deviant third declension plural forms found in inscriptions from *Gaul*, Pirson already pointed out that

>   Certains vocables à thème consonantique ou vocalique dont le génitif pluriel est en *ium*, prennent à l'accusatif pluriel la désinence *is* au lieu de *es*. Ce phénomène s'observe encore dans les inscriptions chrétiennes des VIᵉ et VIIᵉ siècles (118).

(Note, however, that no reference is made to forms in *-is* in the nominative function.)

This seemingly formal variation between *-es* and *-is* endings in the nominative is an obvious extension of the same kind of variation in the accusative (*v. infra*) which, in turn, is but an echo of the alternation between consonant and *i*-stem nouns in Classical Latin. [76] Indeed, from the evidence at our disposal it would appear that the *-is* ending, limited as it is in origin to a certain class of nouns, fell into competition with the more usual *-es* ending (*v. supra*, note #71), resulting in what seems to be a morphological variation that persists in later Latin documents from *Gaul* and *Italy*, in particular, both in

---

[73] Nos. 657 (a. 376) (twice), 2627 (a. 346), 2629 (a. 366), 3253 (a. 367), 2702 ad., 2711C, 2763 adn., 2816C adn., 2990C, 3399A, 3902, 4043, 4131, and 4279B. The frequency of occurrence of *parentis* as a nominative in this and other *Italian* areas clearly contradicts Battisti who claims that this form and others in *-is* for *-es* are quite rare in inscriptions (205).

[74] E.g., Nos. 2702, 2701, 2700, 2711C ad.

[75] Sc. *de filios* for the expected *de filiis*.

[76] Latin masculine and feminine *i*-stem nouns regularly take the *-īs* ending in the accusative plural, while consonant stems never do (Allen-Greenough, 31). For the opposition of nominative *-ēs* and accusative *-īs* of *i*-stems in archaic Latin, still well attested in Republican times, cf. Ernout, *Morphologie*, 87.

the nominative and accusative functions.[77] While of little or no consequence for the eventual outcome of final syllables in French, "inasmuch as the vowel of the termination eventually disappeared in French" (Pei, *Texts*, 45)[78] this free variation on the level of form is of considerable interest in connection with the problem of the genesis of third declension nouns in *Italian*, i.e., nouns of the sg. *cane* — pl. *cani* type.[79]

In his review of Carnoy's study on the Latin of Spanish incriptions, Edouard Bourciez[80] stated in connection with the *-is* ending attested here and there both in the nominative and accusative plural of non *i*-stem third declension nouns: "Je crois que cette flexion *-is* a pris pendant la période [sc. Vulgar Latin] une grande extension en

---

[77] Pei reports that in Merovingian documents he found "24 + 10 cases of *-is* for *-es* in the nominative, and 23 + 13 in the accusative, while *-es* appears 14 + 37 times in the nominative and 10 + 26 times in the accusative" (*Texts*, 147). This represents a ratio of 34 *-is* to 51 *-es* endings in the nominative, while in the accusative the *-es* ending is replaced in 50 % of all cases. The figures given by Sas (254-255) for documents of the same period amply confirm Pei's findings.

Politzer reports from his study of Lombardic documents that "in the nominative the uses of the endings *-es* and *-is* are about evenly matched, the former occurring in twenty-three cases and the latter in twenty-one" (*Lomb. Docs.*, 84), while in central Italian documents the occurrence of *-is* in the nominative plural exceeds that of the *-es* ending (79 *-is* to 62 *-es*) (*Rom. Trends*, 28). (Cf. also his article "On the Origin of the Italian Plurals," *Romanic Review*, XLIII (1952), 275.) A confirmation of Politzer's findings is given by B. Löfstedt: "Betreffs der Verwendung von *-is* statt *-ēs* im Edikt [viz. the *Edictus Rotharii*] ist ferner zu beachten, dass in den ältesten Hss. *-is* ebenso häufig im Nom. wie im Akk. *-es* ersetzt und ebensooft bei Kons. Stämmen wie bei *i*-Stämmen eintritt" (39).

[78] Some scholars have attempted to account for the *s*-less plural nominative outcome of third declension masculine nouns in *Old French* by positing an analogical remodeling after the pattern of the second decl. pl. nom. in *-ī*. Thus, Bourciez (*Éléments*, 229) states that the nominative plural became *cani by analogy of *muri* during the Merovingian period already — a claim supported by neither Pei (*Texts*, 150) nor Sas (255). A more cautious view has been advanced by Grandgent (*V. L.*, 154) who states that, although the process may have begun in the Vulgar Latin period, there is virtually no evidence that it started so early. This same analogical remodeling is also claimed for *Italian* and *Rumanian* (v. infra, our note #86, p. 156); however, few scholars are willing to admit the possibility that the morphological extension of the original *-is* ending of *i*-stems may have been the first step in this process.

[79] The problem in *Rumanian* is essentially the same. Here, too, the outcome of Lat. *-ēs* is *-i*, e.g., *câini* < *canes*.

[80] In *Revue critique d'histoire et de littérature*, XII (1907), 221-222.

Italie et en Gaule; c'est à cette circonstance que je rattacherai volontiers en partie la formation du pluriel italien...." [81] At one point, the eminent Italian scholar, F. D'Ovidio, had entertained the likelihood of a connection between an archaic FONTĪS and Italian *fonti*;[82] however, he soon abandoned this theory in favor of an analogical extension of the plural nominative of second declension masculine nouns to those of the third declension, [83] because he felt that there was no reason to assume a chronological continuity between archaic Latin and Italian. [84]

Subsequently, Sextil Pușcariu took up again the idea that Italian (and Rumanian) plurals of the *cani* type derived from a form in *-īs* rather than *-ēs*, i.e., *canīs* rather than *canēs*. [85] Struck by the frequent alternation of *-is* and *-es* in the nominative and accusative cases, the Rumanian professor argued that the old *-is* ending of *i*-stem nouns had persisted in the spoken language and that after the fall of the final *-s*, the *-i* ending prevailed as a morphological marker of all masculine nouns under the influence of second declension masculines where the *-i* plural morpheme is etymological. As to feminine nouns of the *(le) chiave* < Lat. *clavēs* type, which is quite widespread in medieval literary texts, the *-ē(s)* plural seems to have survived somewhat longer, due to analogy with first declension feminine nouns. And although Pușcariu is not explicit about the causes of the eventual change of *chiave* to *chiavi*, we may assume that it occurred under the influence of the masculine nouns, aided by the desire to keep singular and plural apart. [86]

---

[81] *Ibid.*, 221. Subsequently, Bourciez advanced the same theory in his *Éléments*: "Les pays de l'Est ont donc eu comme sujet et régime *canī(s)*" (229).

[82] In "Ricerche sui pronomi personali e possessivi neolatini," *Archivio Glottologico*, IX (1886), 89.

[83] "È fuor di dubbio che *cani* ecc. sono formati analogicamente su MULĪ, BONĪ, ecc." (*Ibid.*, 86).

[84] "Con un latino arc. faccio quel che con morti si deve fare: lo lascio in pace" (*Ibid.*, 96).

[85] "Une survivance du latin archaïque dans les langues roumaine et italienne," *Mélanges de philologie et d'histoire offerts à Antoine Thomas* (Paris, 1927), 359-365.

[86] Adherents of what may conveniently be called the theory of analogy, that is, those who hold with Grandgent that "the masculines of the third patterned themselves on the second, the great masculine declension" (*Italian*, 49), claim that the normal plural *cane* (< Lat. *canēs*) outcome eventually changed to *cani* in literary Italian as the result of the analogical pull exerted

As noted above, few scholars are willing to admit nowadays the possibility that the morphological extension of the original -*is* ending of old *i*-stem nouns may ultimately be at the root of the genesis of third declension nouns in Italian. In a study devoted specifically to this problem [87] (in which we also review the various alternative theories to account for the *cani* type plurals), [88] we have attempted to demonstrate, on the basis of the frequency of forms in -*is* in both nominative and accusative cases, and their alternation with those in -*es* (occasionally used concurrently on the same inscription), that there existed a free morphological variation between these two endings marking the same grammatical relationship and that phonetic considerations (such as a neutralization of front vowels) should not distort the essentially morphological nature of the phenomenon. At the same time, we also suggested that the origin of these Italian -*i* plurals may well be sought in the survival of the archaic -*is* ending of Old Latin *i*-stems [89] and that these variant endings existed side by side for a

---

by plurals of the *o*-declension masculine nouns (as in *gallo* versus *galli*). This force of analogy was further aided by the need to keep sing. *cane* and pl. *cani* apart by means of a distinctive plural ending. Thus also Rohlfs, *Grammatik*, II, 49. Tekavčić, who otherwise supports "la tesi del Rohlfs," is quick to point out, however, that "l'analogia non esclude necessariamente una evoluzione organica della desinenza /es/ in /i/" (II, 65-66) and that the possibility that Italian third declension plurals in -*i* may also derive from the old Latin *i*-stem plural in -*īs* "non è da escludere" (*loc. cit.*).

[87] "The Plural *i*-Ending of Third Declension Masculine Nouns in Italian," in John Fisher and Paul A. Gaeng (eds.), *Studies in Honor of Mario A. Pei* (Chapel Hill, 1972), 105-114.

[88] In addition to the theory of analogy (*v. supra*, note #86): (a) Meyer-Lübke's phonological "law" that states that Lat. -*ās* and -*ēs* become -*i* in *Italian* (cf. F. D'Ovidio and W. Meyer-Lübke, *Grammatica storica* (Milano, 1932), 90; (b) Mario Pei's explanation that the form *cani* is based on the fact that Latin *ē*, *ĕ*, *i* in unstressed final syllable frequently show a final -*i* rather than -*e* outcome in present-day Italian, e.g., *domani* (< *de manē*) but *pure* (< *purē*) ("Latin and Italian Front Vowels," *Modern Language Notes*, LVIII, No. 2 (1943), 116-120); and (c) the "phonological theory," according to which the -*is* spelling would reflect a closing of Lat. [ę] to [i], possibly under the influence of a following [s] (cf. B. Löfstedt, 45). What adherents of the latter do not seem to have sufficiently recognized is that the alternation of -*es* and -*is* occurs *only* in morphological endings, which tends to suggest that this is a phenomenon of a morphological nature (an allomorphic variation of -*es* and -*is*) and that the phonetic factor (such as the closing influence of final -*s*) is irrelevant.

[89] As Puşcariu has said: "Seule l'idée erronée, suivant laquelle il y aurait un abîme infranchissable entre le latin archaïque et les langues romanes pourrait nous empêcher de voir une continuité entre les pluriels latins ar-

long period of time, until the eventual choice of *-i* as the characteristic plural morpheme after the fall of final *-s,* a choice aided by the analogical pull of the second declension *i-* plural. Thus, the hypothesis of a chronological connection between the old *-is* ending and third declension plurals in *-i* (for which further evidence will be furnished in connection with the accusative, *v. infra*) and that of the analogical extension of "the great masculine declension" (cf note #86) come to complement each other, in that what speakers felt to be the plural pattern in *-i* eventually helped resolve the secular conflict between *-es* and *-is* (as well as *-e* and *-i* in early Italian, still reflecting this conflict after *-s* had disappeared) in favor of the *-i* plural marker in standard Italian.

Neuter forms in *-a* or *-ia* are extremely rare in our material and occur mainly in the accusative function. The two deviations noted involve a shift of gender, as in *in qua.... nominis sui conscribi iussit* (849, 4-5th cent.) from *Concordia (No. Italy)*, with the accusative form in *-is* for *-es,* and both a gender and declensional shift in *ad... luminaria nostra (sc. luminariam nostram)* (3778[b], 6th cent.) found on a *Roman* epitaph.

---

chaïques en *-īs* et les pluriels italiens et roumains en *-i*. Mais un tel abîme n'existe pas en réalité, car "archaïque," "vulgaire," "rustique," "urbain," et "littéraire" ou "classique," sont des termes qui ne doivent pas être mis en opposition les uns avec les autres, mais qui expriment seulement, au point de vue historique et social, des aspects différents de la même langue" (*Art. cit.*, 363). Cf. also Tagliavini: "al plurale, specialmente all'accusativo, troviamo larghe tracce di *-is* per *-es,* ciò che dimostra la continuazione di una tendenza sviluppatasi nel Latino arcaico" (208). (Despite his recognition of this chronological continuity Tagliavini discards the *-is* ending as the possible original factor in the development of Italian (and Rumanian) third declension plurals in *-i*.) Is there any reason to assume that this archaic *-is* ending may not have persisted in the spoken language just as, say, the *-as* feminine plural has, which has been traced back to the second century B.C. and is said to be a reflex of the old Indo-European *-as* nominative preserved in some Italic dialects? On this question cf. also Paul Aebischer, "La finale *-i* des pluriels italiens et ses origines," *Studi linguistici italiani*, II, No. 2 (1961), 73-111; also Francesco Sabatini, "Sull'origine dei plurali italiani: il tipo in *-i*," *Studi linguistici italiani*, V (1965), 5-39.

3.22 Genitive

The genitive plural endings *-um* and *-ium*[90] do not occur frequently. Deviations involve the replacement of the expected third declension endings by the second declension *-orum* ending.

Except for the entire *Iberian* area where this phenomenon is not attested, the *-orum* ending for *-um* (*-ium*) occurs in almost every region under study. Here is a list of examples:

> *pater pauperorum* (3553), *Lugdunensis*
> *comites martyrorum* (2019), No. Italy
> *pro foribus martyrorum* (1549), So. Italy
> *amator pauperorum* (2816 a. 341),[91] Rome
> *inter manos parentor.* (2797B),[92] Rome
> *postera die marturoru* (2119),[93] Rome

By far the most frequent substitution of the ending *-orum* (also *-oro* and *-oru*) for the expected *-um* (*-ium*) in the latter area involves the word *mensis*, e.g., *anniclu mensoro duoro* (4575). In fact, the analogical new formation *mensorum*, *mensoru*, *mensoro*, and even *misoro* (attested as early as a. 291, 4578),[94] patterned after the genitive *annorum* and *annoro* (v. supra, 2.22, p. 103 ff., particularly note #125, *ibidem*) heavily outweighs the classical *mensum* (*mensium*), the ratio

---

[90] *I*-stem nouns and adjectives generally have the genitive plural in *-ium*. (Allen-Greenough, 31). The genitive form *mensium* (Nos. 1475A and 3040), whose underlying consonant stem is *mens-* (cf. the more usual classical genitive form *mensum*, also found on inscriptions), seems to be built on the analogy of *i*-stems, cf. Kieckers, II, 54. On the analogical transfer of the gen. *-ium* ending to consonant stems (e.g., *parentium*, *fratrium*, *civitatium*), cf. also Sommer, 382.

[91] Also *amatrix pauperorum* in the same epitaph. This genitive occurs furthermore in Nos. 2148 (a. 383) and 2138B, while *pauperum* is only found once (#2169 a. 377). The adaptation of some third declension adjectives to the first and second declensional pattern is, of course, attested in the *Appendix Probi: tristis non tristus* (cf. It. *tristo*); *pauper mulier non paupera mulier* (which presupposes a masculine *pauperus* form also), Cf. Elcock, 31.

[92] Also *amatrix parentorum* (#4187).

[93] Concerning the gender of *dies* in Latin and the Romance languages, cf. Meyer-Lübke, *Grammatik*, II, 428.

The form *marturoro* is attested in #1999A. V. supra, note #128 (Chapter 2), p. 104, concerning this genitive form.

[94] E.g., *puer Maurus annorum quinquae mensorum tres* (1527); *puella annoro.... et.... misoro* (4020); *Leo defuntus annoru II mesoru X* (2797B), and *passim*.

being 14 to 4. It may be of interest to observe that this form was not found in any of the other areas, although it would seem reasonable to assume that wherever the genitive in *-um (-ium)* was likely to be replaced by *-orum,* the form *mensorum* (and its variants) was not unknown.

In discussing the genitive form "du type *fratrorum*" in Late Latin texts Uddholm comments,

> Dans l'histoire du latin on peut relever une certaine concurrence entre cette terminaison et la terminaison en *-um* (58)

and further remarks that the *-orum* ending is by far the preferred form in the spoken language (cf. also Pirson, 125). Reflexes of forms like *parentorum* and *martyrorum* in the Romance languages would tend to confirm this view, e.g., Prov. *parentor* 'famille' and *martror* 'La Toussaint' (< *dies martyrorum*) (*ibid.,* 60). In any event, our material gives clear evidence of this innovation, pointing once again to the area of *Rome* as its focal point.

For the periphrastic genitive construction *membra ad duus fratres* (for *duorum fratrum*), v. *supra,* 2.22, p. 106.

3.23 *Dative*

This case does not occur frequently either. When it does, it is generally limited to the forms *fratribus, parentibus,* and *martyribus,* in accordance with the phraseology commonly encountered on tombstone inscriptions, e.g., *fecit (titulum) parentibus.*

Sittl has stated:

> Die Endung des Dativs der dritten Deklination war wegen ihrer Länge und des proparoxytonen Accentes unbequem. Daher wurde sie vom Mittellatein nicht mehr als eine lebende Form übernommen (*Mittellatein,* 563-564).

The dative (and ablative) *-ibus* form left no trace in the Romance languages.[95] It is said to have been replaced by an analytic form with *ad* which finally eliminated the classical Latin ending (Meyer-

---

[95] Contrary to the dative/ablative in *-īs* which may be reflected in the plural *-i* ending of second declension Italian nouns. V. *supra,* Note #158 (Chapter 2), p. 113.

Lübke, *Grammatik*, II, 26). As to the final victory of this periphrasis, Muller (*Préposition "à"*, 179) places it not before the eighth century.

As far as the Merovingian documents go, the replacement of the dative case in *-ibus* by the endings *-es* or *-is* frequently preceded by the preposition *ad*, is reported by both Pei (*Texts*, 223) and Sas (265). If we interpret the phrase *menbra ad duus fratres* from the oftquoted inscription from *Briord* (*Lugdunensis*)[96] as a so-called possessive dative[97] rather than a genitive,[98] then, it would seem, we have here an instance of the replacement of *duobus fratribus* by a periphrasis with *ad*. The handful of occurrences of the dative in *-ibus* are, otherwise, unchanged.[99]

Politzer notes that in eighth-century Lombardic documents "the ending *-ibus* in the dative is generally preserved" (*Lomb. Docs.*, 84), with an occasional substitution of the second declension *-is* ending which seems to increase in frequency as one moves toward the south (*Rom. Trends*, 28). The only examples of this kind of substitution that we found in our material come from the area of *Rome*, where we read on two epitaphs

Aurelius Felicissimus fratris.... f(ecit) (766)
benemerentis filiis dulcissimis (4643 a. 390)

The apparent hesitation between the dative in *-ibus* and that in *-is* (second declension) is also apparent in *Fl. Crescentianus alumnibus fecit* (759), (while on another epitaph from the same place in Rome we read *alumnis dulcissimis* (759 ad.) and *fecit filibus duobus* (4487) where, however, the influence of the attested dative form *filiabus* (v. supra, 1.23, p. 52) may also be envisaged.[100]

The paucity of our data does not, of course, warrant any firm conclusions; yet, even the few examples of this shift between datives in

---

[96] *Hic requiscunt menbra ad duus fratres Gallo et Fidencio qui foerunt fili Magno cl....* (150).

[97] Cf. Stolz-Hofmann, 86.

[98] Cf. Bourciez, *De praepositione 'ad,'* 45 (cf. also our note #132 (Chapter 2), p. 106). For the interpretation of *ad duus fratres* = *duorum fratrum*, cf. also Schuchardt, III, 196.

[99] Note that Sas (265) still finds 80 % use of the dative in *-ibus* in the mid-seventh century Marculf Formulary.

[100] For this analogical masculine formation, cf. also Uddholm, 60.

-*ibus* and -*is* seem to point to the desire on the part of the speaker to eliminate an ending that must have seemed cumbersome to him.

3.24 Accusative

Grandgent notes that "in the accusative plural there was ... confusion of -*īs* and -*ēs* (*nubēs, nubīs,* etc.) both in Classic and in Vulgar Latin" (*V.L.*, 152). This "confusion" is well attested in our material, except for some seemingly conservative regions where the -*es* ending is quite stable.

1. Consonant stems in -*es*

The orthographic change of -*es* to -*is* is particularly frequent in connection with the accusative form *menses* alternating with *mensis*. Examples of this deviation will, therefore, generally be limited to words other than this one.

A. *Iberian Peninsula*

No occurrences of forms in -*is* for -*es* were found in either *Baetica* or *Lusitania*.

In the *Tarraconensis* region, on the other hand, we found two examples of *mensis* on the same epitaph (V253, ca. late 4th-early 5th cent.). As with all instances of a single deviation it is difficult to say just how widespread the use of -*is* for -*es* in this case ending may have been.

B. *Gaul*

(a) *Narbonensis*: The spelling -*is* for -*es* is confined to the form *mensis* for *menses*, in both dated and non-dated inscriptions, e.g., *vixit annos XVI et minsis VI* (2779 a. 516).

(b) *Lugdunensis*: In addition to several accusative forms *mensis*, also in non-dated inscriptions, e.g., *vicxit in deo anos IIL mesis hocto* (3246, 7th cent.), this deviation was also found in

>*passiins* (= *patiens*) *compascere litis* (1075 ca. a. 630)[101]
>*magnas dum feneraris opis* (1076 a. 632)

---

[101] The author of the epitaph must have meant *compescere* 'to hold in check.'

> dignit (= dignet) orare pro parentis suus (= suos) (2340 ca. 7th cent.)
> militavit inter ... senioris (552)

C. Italy

While in the *Central* and *Southern* regions forms in *-is* for the expected *-es* are restricted to *mensis* (also *mesis*), e.g., *vixit cum marito suo annos V mesis V et dies XXVII* (2817 a. 344), and *passim* in non-dated epitaphs also, examples of consonant-stems with an accusative ending in *-is*, in addition to *mensis*, occur in the *Northern* area, namely

> centenarius de equitum comitis (506, 4th-5th cent.) [102]
> nominis sui conscribi iussit (849, 4th-5th cent.) [103]
> has sedis spectaculi fieri precepet (39 a. 528)

D. Rome

The great majority of deviations again involve the form *mensis* (also spelled *mesis, minsis, misis*). The *-is* spelling, however, also occurs in the following non-dated examples:

> de tres fratris cursoris (381[b])
> cum tecusa sua et sororis suas (808A ad.)
> inter innocentis (2500B)

as well as in the accusative absolute construction *locum emerunt presentis omnis fossores* (3761), in which the deviant *-is* and correct *-es* endings occur side by side.

These examples of the alternation of accusatives in *-is* and *-es* support our belief that we are faced with a morphological rather than

---

[102] *De comitis* (cl. Lat. *comites*) for the expected *de comitibus*. (For similar uses of *de* to show provenience or origin, cf. *ducenarius de Batavis* (498), or *de numero Batavorum* (499), and *passim*, frequently attested in epitaphs from the Concordia military cemetery.) The *comites equitum* seem to refer to the cavalry units mentioned by Pauly-Wissowa: "Als das Gefolgewesen im 5. Jhdt. auch in das römische Heer eingedrungen war [the system of attendants to chiefs and kings, referred to as *comites* by Roman writers, being a Germanic custom], erscheinen mehrere Reitercorps, die Comites heissen...." (IV, 1, 623).

[103] Also noted under 3.21, neuter to masculine gender shift, v. *supra*, p. 158.

phonological phenomenon (*v. supra,* note #88)[104] and that the indiscriminate use of these endings in this grammatical function is but a continuation and extension of the alternation between consonant and *i*-stems in Classical Latin.[105]

In order, however, not to base such a conclusion on this one-way development alone, that is, on the orthographic change from the classical accusative in *-ēs* to *-is,* let us see if our findings may be verified by establishing a correlation between the *-es* > *-is* orthographic change and the reverse substitution of *-es* for the Cl. Latin *-īs* accusative ending of *i*-stems. Should the evidence indeed show that this kind of substitution is just as frequent as the *-is* spelling for the Cl. Latin *-ēs,* there would be little doubt as to the allomorphic nature of these two accusative plural endings.

2. *i*-stems in *-is*

Latin grammarians tell us that *i*-stems should show *-īs* in the accusative plural in conformity with the *-ium* ending in the genitive plural.[106] Accordingly, substantivized adjectives of the *Aprilis* type should have an *-īs* ending in the accusative plural, seeing that they end in *-ium* in the genitive.[107] There seems to be, nevertheless, considerable hesitation in the use of orthographic *-īs* and *-ēs* already in classical authors (e.g., *Apriles* for *Aprilīs, Decembres* for *Decembrīs*) with, perhaps, a preference for the *-ēs* ending.[108] It may be a moot question, therefore, whether to consider the accusative form *Aprilis* or *Apriles* to be a deviation from the classical norm, although

---

[104] Cf. in this connection also Uddholm's statement quoted in our note #154 (Chapter 2), p. 112.

[105] Concerning the alleged parallelism between the frequent alternation of *-os* and *-us* in the accusative of second declension nouns and that of *-es* and *-is* in the third declension, *v. supra,* note #153 (Chapter 2), p. 112.

[106] Cf. Neue, *Formenlehre,* I, 246, with copious quotations from Priscian on this question. For analogical *mensium, v. supra,* note 90, p. 159. The *-i* ending of the ablative singular, also a characteristic feature of *-i* stems, is mainly restricted to third declension adjectives and substantivized adjectives of the *Aprilis* type, e.g., *mense Aprili* (Cicero, *Phil.* 2, 39, 100) and neuter nouns in *-e, -al,* and *-ar,* cf. Kieckers, II, 56-57.

[107] E.g., *sub id. Aprillium* (4430 a. 551), *pridie Septemb(r)ium idus* (274 a. 642), *id. Nobenbrium* (304 a. 490), *XIII kal. Decembrium* (V219), and *passim,* attested in our material. Cf. also Sommer, 386.

[108] Cf. examples given by Lewis-Short under the respective entries: *Aprilis* (145), *September* (1674), *October* (1254), and *December* (517).

THIRD DECLENSION

it seems to us that these original adjectives do conform to the pattern of *i*-stems and that there is justification to regard forms like *Apriles, Septembres, Decembres,* etc. as not being in accord with the rules of grammar.

I-stems in our material are just about restricted to these names of the months. They occur with some frequency in both dated and non-dated inscriptions.

A. *Iberian Peninsula*

In speaking of the *i*-stem accusative plurals, Carnoy has stated that

> l'accusatif en -*is* n'apparaît en Espagne que dans les inscriptions officielles d'un latin rigoureusement classique. Ce fait est en conformité avec la nature de cette terminaison *is* qui... n'a jamais eu de racines bien profondes dans la langue populaire (219).

The trend toward a general -*es* ending in the regions of *Baetica* and *Lusitania* is quite evident from our data and confirms this scholar's statement. Forms like *Apriles* and *Decembres* also appear on non-dated epitaphs and even on verse inscriptions.[109]

As to the *Tarraconensis* region, the situation is less clear. Comparing the orthographic changes of -*es* > -*is* and -*is* > -*es*, it would seem that there also existed the kind of alternation observed in *Gaul* and *Italy* and that the accusative in -*is* may have been more widespread in the spoken language than Carnoy would have us believe. However, in the absence of more abundant data, this conclusion must remain very tentative.

B. *Gaul*

The orthographic change of -*is* to -*es* (generally also limited to the names of the months) is evident. However, it may be of interest to note that while the shift from -*is* to -*es* increases in *Narbonensis* by the 6th cent., the -*is* ending in *Lugdunensis* becomes more stable. In fact, when we compare the tables of orthographic -*es* > -*is* and -*is* > -*es* we find that in the *Narbonensis* region this interchange

---

[109] E.g., Nos. V272 and V273 (a. 641), both from *Baetica*.

occurs in an approximately 50:50 ratio, whereas in the *Lugdunensis* region the *-is* ending clearly takes the upper hand.

Except insofar as the *-es* > *-is* trend in the latter region finds confirmation in the extension of the nominative/accusative *-is* ending in later northern French documents (*v. supra*, our note #77, p. 155), this morphological phenomenon [110] is of no consequence for the subsequent development of French, since the vowel of the ending was lost in this language anyway. [111]

C. *Italy* (including *Rome*) [112]

Again, the available data show the alternation between expected forms in *-is* and those in *-es*, both in dated and non-dated epitaphs. A close look at our figures (table #6) reveals a progressive decrease of the orthographic *-is* to *-es* change, so that by the 6th-7th centuries we find only a few or no changes at all. If we now compare the *-is* > *-es* column of our table with that of the reverse phenomenon (*-es* > *-is*), we are struck by the fact that during this same period the ratio of *-is* spelling for *-es* is also on the increase (though in some regions it is high even before the 6th century). Such a trend is more than a coincidence and clearly points to the extension of the *-is* plural ending which, as was seen in connection with our discussion of the nominative (*v. supra*, p. 152 ff.), was also extended to this function. Indeed, a summary of the ratio between *-es* and *-is* in both nominative and accusative shows the following:

	Area	Century	-es	-is
(a)	No. Italy	4th-5th	11	11
		6th	6	7
(b)	Ce. Italy	3rd-4th	35	2
		5th	6	3
		6th-7th	3	6

---

[110] A proposition which we believe to have demonstrated, despite such claims that the alternation of these formal devices merely reflect "a weakening of the unaccented final syllable" (Sas, 276).

[111] Cf. Pei, *Texts*, 45.

[112] Because of the implication that, we believe, this alternation of *-es* and *-is* endings have in connection with the problem of the origin of the *-i* plural ending of third declension nouns in Italian, we have included the area of *Rome* under this heading.

(c)	*So. Italy*	3rd-4th	7	4
		5th	7	4
		6th-7th	13	18
(d)	*Rome*	3rd-4th	67	44
		5th	29	15
		6th-7th	3	11

This kind of evidence is difficult to reconcile with Grandgent's statement to the effect that "Apparently -ēs crowded out the rarer -īs, which left no sure traces" (*V. L.*, 152). The evidence presented here seems to suggest, on the contrary, that not only did the alternation between -ēs and -īs plurals (i.e., between consonant and *i*-stems in Cl. Latin) survive but that, as Bourciez had already suspected,[113] the -īs ending gained considerable ground in Vulgar Latin. Thus, our inscriptional evidence lends strong support to the theory that the final -*i* outcome of Italian nouns of the (*i*) *cani* type is, ultimately, a survival of the -īs ending of old Latin *i*-stems.

3.25 *Ablative*

The ablative in *-ibus* does not occur frequently in our material. Except for an occasional phrase like *ora pro parentibus tuis* (2338), and *cum fratribus* (2267A) it is principally limited to ablative absolute constructions of the *Optato et Paulino consulibus* type (quite infrequent in the *Iberian* area and restricted to the *Tarragona* region) and indications of extent of time, as *in vixit annis* (*tot*) *mensibus* (*tot*) *dies* (*tot*).[114]

In the fourth edition of their monumental *Lateinische Grammatik*, Stolz-Schmalz state:

> Die plebejische Sprache hat schon frühe *cum sodales* gesagt, wie die pompejanischen Wandinschriften zeigen ... es scheint

---

[113] *V. supra*, under 3.21, p. 155.

[114] Concerning the use of the classical accusative and ablative to show extent of time, *v. supra*, note #66 (Chapter 2), p. 80. The form *mensibus* was omitted from our count because of its interchangeability with *menses* in these time expressions (although much less frequent than the alternation of *annos* and *annis* in time expressions also). We also omitted *consulibus* which occurs only in fixed ablative absolute constructions indicating the consular year in which a particular inscription was written.

demnach der spätere Universalkasus in der gewöhnlichen Sprache schon frühe vorhanden gewesen sein (393). [115]

The replacement of the ablative in *-ibus*, particularly when preceded by a preposition, is attested in all areas except the *Iberian*. However, let us recall that in this area we did find a few instances of the replacement of second declension ablatives in *-is* by the classical accusative form in *-os* (e.g., *cum beatos*, attested in the 4th century, *v. supra*, 2.25, p. 144), so that it would seem reasonable to assume that the substitution of the classical accusative in *-es* for the ablative in *-ibus*, e.g., *cum fratres*, was not unknown here either. [116]

The hypercorrect *annibus* in *Savinus in annibus viginti duos* (V187, ca. 7th cent. or later), found on an epitaph from *Gallaecia* (included in our material from *Lusitania*), is most likely analogical on the pattern of *in diebus* and *in mensibus* [117] and seems to reflect the residual nature of the *-ibus* ablative form relegated to the written language and formulaic expressions. [118]

---

[115] Let us also add the occurrence of *cum discentes suos* reported by Väänänen, *Inscr. pomp.*, 121. Sas (277) erroneously attributes to Muller the statement that *cum discentes* must be interpreted as *cum discentis* (for *discentibus*), there being only one form in *-is* for the plural of the second and third declension in Vulgar Latin. Actually, this statement originates with Mohl (216 ff.). Sas has apparently misread Muller who, on the contrary, expresses disbelief at such a claim: "Who can believe — he says — for instance.... that the famous cum discentes of the Pompeian inscriptions must be interpreted as cum discentis for *-ibus*, one form: *-is* for the plural of the second and third declensions" (*Chronology*, 1).

[116] Cooper (54) reports the interchange of forms in *-ibus* and *-is*, and *-es* (*-is* being the second declension ablative plural morpheme rather than the third declension accusative plural variant) in the eighth century *Forum Judicum*. Jennings, on the other hand, observes that by the time of the *Cartulario* the *-ibus* form is rare and appears for the most part in formulaic expressions and that "the most common substitute for *-ibus* is naturally *-es*" (100).

[117] For the ablative of time *within which*, cf. Allen-Greenough, 266. Carnoy's comment concerning *in annibus* is worth quoting: "Le graveur a voulu latiniser une locution de la langue vulgaire se rapprochant de *en años veinte dos*. Il a transcrit *veinte dos* en *viginti duos*, opération à laquelle il était probablement habitué, mais il s'est rappelé qu'en latin correct on introduisait les nombres par des expressions telles que *in diebus, in mensibus*, ce qui l'a porté à commettre le barbarisme *in annibus* qu'il a accolé tel quel à *viginti duos* (268).

[118] This example should properly have been included with "deviations" from the second declension ablative plural in *-is*. We have included it here precisely to suggest the residual nature of the *-ibus* form.

The following replacement of the ablative in *-ibus* was found on an epitaph from *Lugdunensis (Gaul):* ... *orare pro parentis suus Agecio et Mellito* (2340, ca. 7th cent.).

What is of particular interest is that *parentis* and *suus* reflect the classical accusative plural (i.e., *parentes* and *suos*), while the proper names *Agecio* (for *Agrecio* or, possibly, *Agrecia*) and *Mellito* (or *Mellita?*) reflect the classical ablative singular.[119] This concurrent use of accusative plural and ablative singular is a rather clear indication, we believe, that in the *plural* it is the classical accusative that tends to supplant the ablative and, eventually, all *casus obliqui* as the "Universalkasus" but that in the *singular* it is neither one nor the other, but a merger of the two that gives rise to a generalized oblique case whose form in the three major declensions happens to coincide with the classical ablative.[120]

To further illustrate the trend to replace the ablative by the classical accusative in the plural, we may adduce two instances of *pro nus* (= *nos*) (2352, 2353A, ca. 7th cent.) from this area also.

For the replacement of the ablative in *-ibus* by the classical accusative in *-es* (and its variant *-is*) in 7th and 8th cent. northern French documents, particularly after prepositions, cf. Pei, *Texts*, 148, and Sas, 277-284.

In the *Italian* area, outside of *Rome,* the use of the classical accusative for the expected ablative in *-ibus* is attested in three examples,

> Northern: *centenarius de equitum comitis* (506, 4th-5th cent.)[121]

---

[119] Both the names *Agroecius* (*Agrecius*) and *Agroecia* (*Agrecia*) are attested, as well as *Mellita* side by side with *Mellitus*. It is difficult, therefore, to decide which is the father's and which is the mother's name.

[120] Our skepticism regarding the *universal* extension of the Latin accusative case in *both* singular and plural is also implicit in Maurer: "De fato, a documentação epigráfica.... nos dá o acusativo no plural, quase sem exceção. No singular é que se encontra ora o acusativo, ora o ablativo, mas aqui o ablativo.... confundia-se, mesmo formalmente, con o acusativo.... Mas a notável preferência dada ao acusativo nos textos incorretos e nas inscrições (*naturalmente referimo-nos apenas ao plural*) [italics are ours] denota claramente qual a tendência popular" (89). Cf. also Pei's observation concerning the predominant use of the apparent ablative in the singular and the apparent accusative in the plural after prepositions, "both being thinly disguised forms of the single oblique case" (*Texts*, 235). For the oblique case theory cf. also Taylor, 64 ff.

[121] For the meaning of *comites equitum, v. supra,* note #102, p. 163.

> Central: orate pro nobis peccatores (2355, ca. 6th-7th cent.) [122]
> Southern: qui eum locum sine parentis aperuerit (2360 a. 612) [123]

Although our evidence is quite scanty, the replacement of the ablative form in *-ibus* is amply borne out by subsequent documentary attestations, cf. Politzer, *Rom. Trends*, 29.

Our examples from the area of *Rome* illustrating this phenomenon are, naturally, more abundant. Most of them occur in non-dated epitaphs, so that the general trend to replace the ablative by the classical accusative when preceded by a preposition is poorly reflected in our table. However, a comparison taking into account the *total* number of occurrences of the *-ibus* ablative form and its replacement by the accusative in *-es (-is)* and *-a* (7 + 18 *-ibus* versus 2 + 7 *-es (-is)* and *-a*) reveals a slightly better than 26 % substitution of the accusative for the ablative.

Here are some examples of the use of the classical accusative with prepositions that traditionally govern the ablative:

> *semper cum omnes* (1139 ad. a. 565/578)
> *cum sororis suas* (808A ad.); *con parentes* (3829)
> *de tres fratres cursoris* (381ᵇ); *a parentes* (4475)
> *roga pro fratres et sodales tuos* (2343)
> *in mente habeas in hortationes Aureliu* (2324ᵈ), etc.

This replacement is also attested with neuters, as in *de sua omnia possedit domum ista* (1464 a. 380).

In the phrase *vixit cum parentibus suo* (2267A), it would seem that the stonecutter omitted final *-s* (which is also missing on the subsequent *mense X* for the expected *menses*), in which case we would have an ablative and an accusative used concurrently. Indeed, if we assume that the writer meant *suos*, we could almost consider

---

[122] Note, however, the use of *nobis*, probably under the influence of the stereotyped formula: *ora pro nobis!*

[123] Diehl, *De m finali*, 52, interprets the form *parentis* (and all similar forms in *-is*) as an analogical second declension ablative plural form. This is hard to believe, particularly in the broader context of similar replacements where accusative forms in both *-es* and *-is* occur on the same inscription. Cf. the previously encountered *pro parentis suus*.

parentibus a hypercorrect form for *parentes*, the more likely form in the spoken language.

In two instances an ablative absolute construction is replaced by what appears to be an accusative absolute:

> *locum sibi emerunt presentis omnes fossores* (3761)
> *Concordia et Tigrinus se vivo fecerunt filius iscientes* (4154A)

for the expected *filiis scientibus*.

These examples seem to point clearly to the use of the classical accusative with prepositions that traditionally (i.e., according to Latin grammar) would call for an ablative in *-ibus*. Thus, our inscriptional evidence from this area is in accord with the statement of Stolz-Schmalz quoted earlier, also bearing out Väänänen's findings in Pompeian *graffiti*, at least as far as the replacement of *plural* ablatives is concerned. [124] And while we cannot draw the same conclusion with respect to other areas (with only an educated guess as far as the *Iberian* area goes), we believe that the few examples found there may be taken as an indication as to a similar trend.

In the absence of more dated examples, furthermore, it is also difficult to establish a chronology of the replacement of the ablative form in *-ibus* by what appears to be the classical accusative. However, the evidence furnished by Pompeian inscriptions would seem to suggest that by the time of the appearance of the bulk of Christian inscriptions (4th cent. in *Italy*, particularly *Rome*, 5th-6th cent. elsewhere), the ablative in *-ibus* may no longer have been a popular form, having become relegated to the status of a residual written form used mainly in stereotyped and formulaic expressions. [125]

---

[124] On the basis of the examples of the use of prepositions with the apparent accusative, both singular and plural, for the expected ablative, the Finnish scholar states that it was the accusative which was to become "le cas prépositionnel par excellence" (*Inscr. pomp.*, 121). In view of what we said in the foregoing paragraphs (cf. also our note · #120, p. 169), we can subscribe to this statement only as far as the *plural* is concerned.

[125] Cf. Mihăescu who states: "Construcţia cum + acuzativul este un indiciu că desinenţia de ablativ în *-ibus* nu era populară" (172). In the same vein, Norberg comments: "Wenn der Ablativ nicht nur durch eine Präposition + Akk. sondern auch durch einen einfachen Akk. ersetzt werden konnte, wurde er als selbständiger Kasus ziemlich überflüssig" (*Synt. Forsch.*, 41).

3.3 Summary

Here is a brief summary of our findings concerning the third declension.

3.31 Singular

3.311 *Nominative*

The deviation which seems to have morphological significance is the *-es* spelling of parisyllabics in *-is* (e.g., *cives* for *civis;* *dulces* for *dulcis*), attested in virtually all areas under investigation.

Since the reverse phenomenon (e.g., *milis* for *miles*) is quite rare, it would appear reasonable to interpret this orthographic change as a trend toward the extension of the thematic /e/ of accusative/ablative, which has become the characteristic ending of third declension singular nouns in Italian and Spanish.

3.312 *Genitive*

(a) The *-es* spelling for the expected *-is* closely parallels the situation found in connection with the nominative.

(b) A few instances of what appears to be the extension of the oblique in *-e* were also noted in the areas of *Gaul* and *Rome*. (Let us recall that examples of the use of the apparent oblique form in *-o* in the genitive function were also found in these areas, *v. supra*, 2.12, p. 66 ff.).

(c) There are sporadic occurrences of genitive forms in *-i* for *-is*, particularly in proper names. However, in most cases this deviation may be accounted for by analogical influence of a preceding or following second declension genitive form. [126]

(d) The prepositional replacement of the classical genitive form, that is, a construction with *de* followed by a form in *-e*, is attested in an inscription each from *Tarraconensis* (7th cent.) and *Narbonensis* (5th cent.). Noteworthy is the circumlocution *de sorore nepus* found in the latter area, which is a good illustration of a periphrastic genitive

---

[126] Cf. Paul A. Gaeng, *art. cit.* in footnote #9 (Chapter 2), p. 60.

construction that expresses the idea of possession. It is of interest to note that proper names regularly appear in their classical genitive form.

3.313 *Dative*

(a) The *-e* spelling for *-i* is sporadically attested in our material; nevertheless, it may be said that on the whole this case ending is quite stable, as evidenced by the correct *-i* spelling in those areas in which this case occurs with some frequency. The few examples that show up with *-e* should not be dismissed, however, since they would also seem to point in the direction of a trend toward the emergence of a single *-e* ending in the oblique.

(b) Three non-dated examples of a periphrastic construction with *ad* followed by forms in *-e* or *-em* were also found (one in *Lugdunensis*, two in the *Italian* area), as an alternative to the synthetic dative.

3.314 *Accusative*

The omission of *-m* is quite frequent in all areas under study, both in direct object function and after prepositions. Instances where this case is represented by forms in both *-e* and *-em* occurring side by side, in particular, suggest the residual nature of *-m* as a morphological marker, limited to written representation, with *-e* as the normal ending on the level of speech.

3.315 *Ablative*

(1) Consonant-stem ablatives in *-e* clearly predominate in all areas.

(a) An occasional *-i* spelling for the expected *-e* is attested sporadically, except in the *Iberian* area. Although one might be tempted to interpret this phenomenon as a reflection of the phonetic coalescence of unstressed /ē/ and /ĭ/, the morphological nature of this orthographic change looms large, particularly when we compare it with the reverse phenomenon, the *-e* spelling of *i*-stem ablatives traditionally ending in *-i*.

(b) A sporadic hypercorrect form in *-em*, particularly after prepositions, was also found in all areas under study. While the *-e* ending overwhelmingly predominates, the occasional use of forms in *-em* in classical ablative function does indicate, it seems, that the case consciousness between classical accusative and ablative is lost for all practical purposes.

(2) The *-e* spelling for the expected *-i* of *i*-stem ablatives (particularly adjectives) is also attested here and there, even though the occurrence of these ablatives is quite rare. This morphological confusion seems to stem from the shift of *i*-stem ablatives to what speakers must have regarded as the regular pattern in *-e,* while, at the same time, also being in accord with the trend to generalize the vowel /e/ in all morphological endings in the singular.

Thus, the drift seems to be in the direction of two endings in the singular: *-es* for nominative and genitive and *-e* for dative, accusative, and ablative. Although it is most noticeable in the *Italian* area, with *Rome* as the probable focal point, our material seems to indicate that all areas are affected to a greater or lesser extent. Some conservative regions, particularly *Baetica* and *Lusitania,* seem to hang on to the Classical Latin system quite tenaciously; the latter seems to participate least in these innovations.

3.32 Plural

3.321 *Nominative*

Noteworthy is the occurrence of the *-is* ending for the expected *-es* in the areas of *Gaul,* specifically *Lugdunensis,* and *Italy,* which we have interpreted as a morphological variation between the Cl. Lat. *-es* nominative ending and the *-is* accusative ending of old *i*-stems that seems to have survived in Late Latin. This variation is, we believe, of considerable interest in connection with the problem of the plural of the third declension nouns in *Italian* of the (*i*) *cani* type. Our material seems to suggest (particularly in light of available documents of a later period in which the apparently allomorphic relationship between *-is* and *-es* finds ample confirmation) that the origin of these plurals may, indeed, be traced back to the old Latin *-īs* accusative of *i*-stems, which was then extended to non-*i*-stems in both the accusative and the nominative. The two endings having thus become variants, they existed side by side for a considerable period of time, until the eventual choice of *-i* as the characteristic plural morpheme after the fall of final *-s,* a choice that was no doubt favored by the analogical pull of second declension *-i* plurals.

3.322 *Genitive*

Except for the *Iberian* area, the expected *-um* or *-ium* endings of this case are occasionally replaced by the second declension *-orum* form. This substitution also confirms the findings of other scholars concerning the apparent competition between analogical genitives like *parentorum* and the classical *parentum*. In the area of *Rome*, the form *mensorum* (also *mensoro* and even *misoro*) is particularly frequent in both dated and non-dated epitaphs.

For the periphrastic construction *ad duus fratres, v. supra,* 2.322, p. 125.

3.323 *Dative*

The infrequent occurrence of this case does not permit drawing any specific conclusions. In fact, whenever this case is attested it is correctly spelled, except for two instances in *Rome* where the second declension *-is* ending is substituted for the expected *-ibus*.

3.324 *Accusative*

The alternation of *-is* and *-es* in the accusative, attested in all areas except *Baetica* and *Lusitania* (where the expected *-is* of *i*-stems almost invariably shows up as *-es*) seems to confirm the fact that this is a *morphological* rather than a *phonological* phenomenon. The allomorphic nature of these two endings becomes quite evident when the *-es* > *-is* orthographic change is brought into correlation with the reverse phenomenon, the *-es* spelling for the expected *-is* ending of *i*-stems.

While it would seem that in *Baetica* and *Lusitania* the *-es* ending is by far the preferred morpheme, the situation in *Tarraconensis* is more difficult to assess in the absence of sufficient data. Nevertheless, a few instances of *-es/-is* alternation would suggest that in this region the *-is* ending may have been an acceptable variant also.

While the *-es/-is* alternation seems to occur in about equal ratio in *Narbonensis*, the *-is* ending clearly takes the upper hand in the

Lugdunensis by the 6th century. This trend is confirmed by the extension of *-is* at the expense of *-es* in later Merovingian documents.

A summary of the ratio between *-es* and *-is* in the whole *Italian* area gives a rather clear indication of the extension of *-is* which seems to become the predominant ending by the 6th century. This evidence tends to lend further support to our claim made in connection with the plural nominative, namely that there is a chronological continuity between the *-is* ending of Latin *i*-stems and the third declension Italian plurals in *-i*.

3.325 *Ablative*

The replacement of the ablative in *-ibus* by the classical accusative form in *-es* (and its variant in *-is*), particularly after a preposition, is attested in epitaphs from *Gaul* and *Italy*, e.g., *pro parentes* for *parentibus*. Except for *Roman* inscriptions where a significant encroachment of accusative upon ablative was observed, amounting to better than 26 % of the total material (both dated and non-dated), this case occurs quite infrequently for specific conclusions to be drawn. However, substitutions of oblique forms in *-es* or *-is* found in other areas would suggest that this trend was not confined to a single region.

Once again, *Baetica* and *Lusitania* seem to be most conservative in holding on to the classical Latin paradigm, with *Tarraconensis* forming the bridge between this conservatism and the more innovative area of *Gaul*. The trend toward simplification of the declensional pattern is most evident in *Rome* where the plural endings tend to be reduced to *-es* (*-is*), with an analogical *-orum* (*-oro*) genitive. There are definite signs of a similar trend in the rest of *Italy* and in *Gaul*; unfortunately, our material from these areas is not sufficient enough to be more specific.

Chapter 4

FOURTH AND FIFTH DECLENSIONS

No tables are given for either the fourth or fifth declension because of the infrequent occurrence of nouns belonging to these declensional classes and the fact that when they do occur, they are generally found in the same case functions (such as the forms *idus* and *dies* used, for the most part, in the accusative plural). Besides, it is generally recognized that *u*-stems were absorbed by *o*-stem nouns [1] *ē*-stems joined the first declension *a*-stem nouns, [2] so that a separate discussion of the case reduction in these inflectional classes (even if there were enough linguistic material available) would be merely a repetition of what has already been said in connection with the first and second declensions. Hence, we shall limit our discussion to ascertaining the extent to which these declensional shifts are attested in our inscriptional material.

4.1 Fourth Declension

Carnoy states that "une tendance générale du latin tardif c'est de faire passer la 4ᵉ déclinaison à la seconde" (224) and he offers the occurrence of *arcos* to support his claim. [3]

---

[1] Except for *nurus* and *socrus* which were absorbed by the first declension, cf. *nurus non nura* and *socrus non socra* in the *Appendix Probi*.

[2] Cf. Väänänen, *Lat. Vulg.*, 113.

[3] Taken from two inscriptions found on public buildings: *binos porticos arcos* (V362 a. 589) at *Cartagena* (*Tarraconensis*) and *construxit arcos* (V363 a. 483) at *Mérida* (*Lusitania*), the latter commemorating the restoration of the Roman bridge in that city.

Pirson (122) devotes less than half a page to the fourth declension and mentions the form *nuru*, which he considers to be a contraction of the classical form *nurui*.

Grandgent states that "the transfer from the fourth to the second began in Classic Latin and continued in vulgar and late speech" (*V.L.*, 148), while Bourciez claims that both the fourth and fifth declensions "ont eu de bonne heure tendance à se fondre dans les autres" (*Éléments*, 86-87) and mentions the genitive forms *fructi*, *gemiti*, and *tumulti* attested in Plautus, Terence, and Cato.

Instances that would point to the absorption of the fourth declension by the second are found in our material from all areas under study.

A. *Iberian Peninsula*

The only clear-cut example is the above-cited form *arcos* (cf. our note #3). The hypercorrect *consulatum primu* (V189 a. 393, Tarraconensis) (for the expected ablative absolute construction *consulatu primo*), where final *-m* is incorrectly added, as in many ablatives of second declension nouns (*v. supra*, 2.15, p. 94 ff.), may also suggest the treatment of *consulatus* as an *o*-stem noun, in view of what has been said earlier concerning the orthographic confusion of *-um* for *-o* and *-u* for either *-um* or *-o*, which we have interpreted as the reflex of an [o] pronunciation (*v. supra*, p. 99 ff.).

B. *Gaul*

Nouns belonging to the classical fourth declension are generally limited to *idus* and *consulatus*. The treatment of the latter as an *o*-stem noun may be seen in the formula *post consulato* attested three times in *Narbonensis* (1587 a. 491; 1672 a. 540; 3284 a. 563) — as against one occurrence of *pos(t) consulatum* (2256 a. 509) — and once in *Lugdunensis* (4823 a. 510) (the only occurrence of this formula).

In a non-dated epitaph from the latter region we read *innocenti spirito* (735) for the expected *spiritui*.

C. *Italy*

(a) *Northern*: The expected ablative *consulatu* appears once as *consulato* (343 a. 432), being correctly spelled three times. A declensional shift may also be observed in the dative form *spirito* (2369; 3345), as well as in the plural *ad spirita sancta* (3361). The latter is of particular interest since it suggests that speakers treated the plural of *spiritus* as a collective neuter, maybe on the analogy of *astra*, cf. *fecit ad astra viam* (316 a. 382).

The plural nominative form *mani* is attested in *ut mani eius precidantur* (545 a. 394/402).[4]

(b) *Central*: Evidence of declensional shift is found in *post consulato* (323 a. 386) (the only occurrence of *consulatus* in any function) and the dative form *spirito* (3397 ad.).

(c) *Southern*: The dative forms *spirito* (3400) and *ispirito* (3396; 3399), as well as the ablative in *spirito sancto* (1010; 2443 ad.) illustrate the absorption of *spiritus* to the second declensional class. The noun *consulatus* occurs once in *pos consulatum* (582 a. 392).

D. *Rome*

While the form *consulato* is not attested in this area, there are quite a few instances of *consulatu* alternating with *consulatum* in the ablative function, even in the same inscription, as in *consulatu Maximo Augusto consulatum* (3287 a. 384/388), with the obvious meaning of 'in the consulship of ...'[5] The construction *post consulatum* is also quite frequent, although more often than not appearing as *post consulatu*.[6] Despite the absence of an attested *consulato*, however, and in view of the orthographic confusion of -*um* and -*u* in the same grammatical function, which we have interpreted as reflecting an [o] pronunciation, it seems reasonable to assume that this word was treated as a second declension noun already by this time (end of 4th cent.). This assumption is strengthened by the fact that *consulato* is attested in less innovative areas than Rome, *v. supra*, Central Italy.

The other frequently used word originally belonging to the Latin fourth declension is *spiritus*. The first evidence of its shift to the *o*-stem class occurs on an epitaph written with Greek characters,

---

[4] Cf. It. *le mani*, the only *u*-stem noun become *o*-stem that has retained its original feminine gender. Cf. Meyer-Lübke, *Ital. Grammatik*, 190.

[5] We counted a total of 11 occurrences of *consulatu* against 6 *consulatum* in this function.

[6] A ratio of 8 cases of *post consulatu* to 3 of *post consulatum*.

which, in transliteration, reads as follows: *eispeireito sankto touo* (3391 a. 269). The form *spirito* (also spelled *ispirito* and once even *sbirito* (3392)) occurs a total of 16 times and is always spelled with -*o*. Twice it occurs in the ablative: *in spirito* (2230) and *pro spirito* (2333 ad.). We also found one hypercorrect *cum spiritum tuum* (3389).

Of interest is, furthermore, the occurrence of *ispirito* in the apparent nominative function: *Indelecia, ispirito tuo in irene* (2718) (but cf. *ispiritus tuus in pace* (3404)), as well as the use of *spiritum* in this same function as in

> *spiritum Parhesiastae in pace* (3403 ca. 3rd cent.) [7]
> *Agatemeris, spiritum tuum inter sanctos* (3356)
> (but cf. *Vernacla, ispiritus tuus cum sanctis* (3356A))
> *Ilara ispiritum tuum santum* (3391A)

In all these cases it is, of course, possible that something like *Deus accipiat* or *refrigeret* is to be understood which, for lack of space, the writer was unable to fit in. Let us recall, however, that forms in -*o* in the nominative function have also been found in connection with second declension nouns (v. supra, 2.11, p. 62 ff.), so that here, too, it would appear reasonable to postulate the extension of the oblique form (written -*o* or -*um*, as well as -*u*) [8] to the nominative.

The expected plural form *spiritus* is invariably replaced by *spirita*, as in *spirita sancta in mente habete Bassu cum suis omnibus* (2325 ca. 4th cent.). In addition to the use of this form in -*a* in both subject and direct object functions, it also appears regularly with prepositions that would require the classical ablative form *spiritibus*, e.g., *refrigera cum spirita sancta* (2305 a. 291). (For the replacement of ablatives in -*ibus* by accusative forms, v. supra, 3.25, p. 168 ff.).

While the dative/ablative form *spirito* has repeatedly been pointed out as being illustrative of the shift from fourth to second declension, [9]

---

[7] A similar use also appears in *spiritum Caprioles in pace* (3403A). For the -*es* genitive ending for -*ae* in feminine proper names, v. supra, 1.12, p. 29 ff.

[8] Occurring, as a matter of fact, in *Augende spiritu cum iren* (2731A) (nom. *Augenda*) and *cuius spiritu in bono que(s)quat* (2285A adn.).

[9] Thus Schuchardt, II, 188; Rónsch, 261; Grandgent, *V.L.*, 148. That the final -*o* is not due to a "purely phonetic phenomenon due to the interchange of *o* and *u* in the final syllable," as suggested by Pei (*Texts*, 151), has been clearly shown by Schuchardt, *ibid.*, 189.

the plural *spirita* has received, as far as we are able to determine, no special comment.[10] As suggested already in connection with the occurrence of this form on an epitaph from *northern Italy*, we believe that this shift to the second declension neuter plural must be sought in the treatment of this word as a collective noun, possibly in the meaning of *sancti*, seeing that it usually occurs in the combination *spirita sancta*.

In summary, it would be fair to state that the absorption of *u*-stem nouns by the *o*-stem class is quite well attested in the few fourth declension nouns that appear in our material. Notable exceptions are the plural genitive *iduum*, the accusative *idus*,[11] and the ablative *idibus*,[12] which appear in stereotyped expressions of date. However, the small number of fourth declension nouns that we have found does not allow us to draw general conclusions concerning the disappearance of this declensional class during the period under study.

4.2 Fifth Declension

Gerhardt Rohlfs states that

> die einstige fünfte lateinische Deklination wurde in der vulgären Sprache als ein entbehrlicher Luxus betrachtet. Wörter, die ihr einst angehörten, haben sich der ersten Deklination angeschlossen; so wurde d i e s zu *d i a, f a c i e s zu f a c i a.[13]

Rönsch (259) cites *effigia* for *effigies* in Plautus, while Sommer (402) mentions the form *materiam* attested in an inscription dating back to 117B.C. (CIL I, 584). The alternation of nouns in *-ies* and *-ia* (e.g., *materies/materia*) is also found in classical authors and is

---

[10] Betty I. Knott, who has devoted a special study to the vocabulary in Christian inscriptions, does not mention this form at all. *Art. cit.* in our note #14 (Chapter 1), p. 29.

[11] But even *idus* seems to have been subject to a declensional shift, cf. *idos Octobri* (2816 adn.). For a list of fourth declension accusatives in *-os*, cf. Schuchardt, II, 189.

[12] In two inscriptions from the *southern Italian* area we read: *idis Septembris* (4677 a. 529) and *iris Iuliis* (1419), respectively, also suggesting a shift to the second declensional pattern. For the substitution of /r/ for intervocalic /d/ in southern Italian dialects, cf. Rohlfs, *Grammatik*, I, 352.

[13] *Vulgärlatein*, 68.

generally considered to be the point of departure for the absorption of ē-stem nouns by a-stems.[14] For the survival of nouns in -ies in some regions of Romania, cf. Grandgent, *V.L.*, 148.

The fifth declensional class is poorly represented in our inscriptional material. At any rate, no examples were found[15] that would show a shift from the fifth to the first declension, since nouns belonging to the ē-stem class are just about confined to *res, spes, fides,* and *dies*,[16] which were assimilated to the third declension.[17] In fact, we find some of the same phenomena that were observed in connection with third declension nouns: the absence of final -*m* in the accusative singular, the hypercorrect addition of -*m* in the ablative, and -*is* for -*es* in the nominative and accusative plural. A few random examples taken from those areas in which such deviations occur will suffice:

Lugdunensis: ubi ficet de Abrilio diis XV (2456, ca. 7th cent.)
vixit annos V et diis XLV (2910 a. 466)
No. Italy: de rem sua conparaverunt (521, ca. 4th-5th cent.)[18]
deposita diem Veneris (4214)[19]

---

[14] Väänänen, *Lat. vulg.*, 113. Tekavčić, II, 50, places the shift of nouns from the fifth declensional class to the first one in the period of what he calls "tardo latino parlato," which he seems to place between the sixth and eighth centuries.

[15] The fact that forms in -*ies* were still in use at this time is suggested by the word *blandities* found on a Roman epitaph (3887). The alternate form *blanditia* (surviving in Rum. *blindeţe*, cf. REW #115) seems to have been the more usual one already in classical authors, cf. Lewis-Short's entry under *blanditia*, 241.

[16] This word is found mainly in time expressions like *vixit annos.... menses.... dies* (sometimes also in the ablative, as in *annis.... mensibus.... diebus*) and in the frequent formula *depositus die* (or *sub die*) followed by a numeral and an indication of the month.

[17] Cf. Grandgent: "Fifth declension nouns not in -*ies* went to the third" (*V. L.*, 148). *Dies* was also assimilated to the third declension but was rivalled by a form *dia* (cf. OIt., Prov., Sp., Port., Cat. *dia*, REW #2632) which, however, is not attested in our material.

[18] Lucien Beszard, *La langue des formules de Sens* (Paris, 1910), is reported to have claimed that the form *rem* had become invariable in Late Latin, cf. Pei, *Texts*, 153, whose documents seem to substantiate this claim, since -*m* in this word is never dropped in the accusative and is incorrectly added in the ablative. The same substitution of *rem* for the expected *re* in the ablative is also reported by Politzer, *Lomb. Docs.*, 88.

[19] In the preceding line we read *deposita die VII kal. Decemb.* evidencing the use of forms in -*em* and -*e* in the same function.

So. Italy:	*recessit diem Mercuris* (1358 a. 415)[20]
	defuncta ... hora die prima (1549)[21]
Rome:	*dipositos diem III kal. Iun.* (2917 a. 397)[22] and *passim,*
	usque at die mortis (2805)
	qui vixit.... diis (265ª a. 355) and *passim,*
	fide percepit (1529A ad.); *integre fide* (1339),[23] etc.

In an epitaph from this area we also found the form *diero* (4575) for the expected *dierum,* modelled, no doubt, on the frequently attested *annoro* and *mesoro* forms, *v. supra,* 2.22, p. 104, and 3.22, p. 159.

Clearly, then, the virtually total absence of fifth declension nouns that were eventually absorbed by the first declension makes it impossible to ascertain to what extent this shift had already taken place during the period covered by our inscriptional material.

---

[20] In re *Mercuris, v. supra,* 1.12, p. 31 ff.

[21] Concerning the occurrence of the gen. sing. form *die* in other texts, cf. *Thesaurus,* V, 1022, 19 ff., where the following statement is made: "C. Caesar in libro de analogia secundo 'huius -e'.... dicendum putat." Could the use of *die* in the genitive function not reflect the extension of a single oblique form? *V. supra,* 3.12, p. 132.

[22] For an attempt to account for the *-os* ending in the nominative singular of second declension nouns that makes no appeal to the phonological merger of Lat. /ŭ/ and /ŏ/ in unstressed syllable, *v. supra,* 2.11, p. 59.

[23] A genitive of quality along the lines of *bonae memoriae.* A few other occurrences of this genitive show the correct form *fidei,* e.g., *fidei catholicae* (115), *fidei sanctae* (4708), etc. Cf. also *sanctae fide* from a late second cent. inscription from *Rome* (Diehl, *V. I.,* #642). Concerning this gen. form *fide,* cf. our comments in connection with gen. *die, supra,* note #2.

CHAPTER 5

GENERAL SUMMARY AND CONCLUSIONS

We may now conveniently summarize inflectional phenomena found in Christian inscriptions from Western Romania. For the purposes of this *vue d'ensemble*, we thought it might be again useful to offer tables showing a case by case comparison of the various areas under study [Tables nos. 7-16 in the Appendix].

5.1 NOMINATIVE SINGULAR

5.11 First Declension

In both dated and non-dated inscriptions from all areas, the nominative shows the classical Latin ending in 100 % of all instances. It invariably ends in *-a*.

5.12 Second Declension

The evidence shows that the classical Latin *-us* ending is used rather consistently. Nevertheless, sporadic nominative forms in *-os*, *-u*, and *-o* were found in both dated and non-dated inscriptions.

(a) Forms in *-os* for *-us* occur mainly in proper names in *Gaul* and *Italy*. These may be due to Greek influence (e.g., *Marcellinos* by analogy of *Antiochos*), although they could also reflect the phonetic merger of Latin /ŏ/ and /ŭ/ in the unstressed syllable, particularly in those regions (*Gaul* and *No. Italy*) where the *-us* > *-os* orthographic change also occurs in non-morphological endings. On the other hand, whenever the *-os* ending is found only in morphological

GENERAL SUMMARY AND CONCLUSIONS   185

endings (e.g., *iustos* for *iustus*), as in the *Iberian* area and the rest of *Italy*, we may also envisage the possibility of the use of an oblique form in *-o* (*iusto*) to which a subsequent *-s* was added as a reminiscence of the classical nominative case.

(b) Nominatives in *-u* invariably raise the question as to whether the final *-s* was simply omitted on the epitaph for lack of space, or whether the form in *-u* indeed reflects a feature of the spoken language, namely a "compromise between the popular oblique in *-o* and the learned form in *-us*" as has been suggested (*v. supra*, 2.11, p. 60). While this phenomenon is quite sporadic in other areas, forms in *-u* occur with some frequency in non-dated epitaphs from *Rome*, particularly in proper names.

(c) The morphological substitution of a form in *-o* for the expected *-us* is sporadically attested throughout our material, although most of our examples come from *So. Italy* and *Rome*.

On the basis of the available evidence, it would seem that the masculine *-us* ending is still quite firmly entrenched in the writer's mind, though no longer 100 % in some areas. The occasional extension of a form in *-o* to the subject case would indicate that, on the level of *parole*, the nominative is being encroached upon by an oblique form to a greater extent than is reflected in written material.

The occurrence of the nominative of neuter nouns is practically limited to the area of *Rome*. Here, too, forms in *-u* (omission of final *-m?*) and the substitution of forms in *-o* for the expected *-um* were recorded.

5.13 Third Declension

The orthographic change that seems to have morphological significance is the *-es* spelling of parisyllabics in *-is*, attested in just about every area under study. Since the reverse phenomenon (*-is* for *-es*) is quite rare, we suggest that this deviation points toward the extension of a universal /e/ in the final syllable, which has become the characteristic vowel ending of the third declension nouns in Italian and Spanish.

5.2 Genitive Singular

5.21 First Declension

The classical genitive written *-ae* or *-e* is still the predominant form.

(a) Of particular interest is the occurrence of a periphrastic construction with *de*, generally followed by a form in *-a*, as a substitute for the synthetic genitive. This periphrasis, which clearly points to the existence of a spoken language trend to express genitive function "analytically," is sporadically attested in the area of *Rome* and once in the *southern Italian* region.

(b) In the *central* and *southern Italian* areas, in *Rome* and, sporadically, in *Baetica* and the southern region of *Gaul*, the genitive ending is sometimes replaced by *-aes* or *-es*, particularly in feminine proper names, probably under the influence of Greek genitives in *-ης*.

(c) Noteworthy is also the occurrence of *Lunis* throughout the *Italian* area, suggesting that the analogical sigmatic form may have been in greater general use in the spoken language than the classical form *Lunae*, and that the Italian *lunedì* may ultimately derive from this sigmatic genitive form rather than the generally postulated *Lunae die*, just as It. *giovedì* < *Jovis die*.

5.22 Second Declension

The classical *-i* ending appears to be quite stable throughout our material. Noteworthy, however, are the following substitutions.

(a) What appears to be the oblique form in *-o* is occasionally attested as a substitute for the genitive in *-i*, notably in *Gaul* and the *Italian* area. In the latter, it frequently occurs in expressions indicating a consular year, so that forms in *-o* could be due to a confusion in formulae, like *consulatu Eusebi* and *consule Titiano*. In the *Lugdunensis*, on the other hand, this substitution is quite extensive and is used in better than 30 % of all instances by the sixth century.

(b) An example each of the periphrastic genitive construction with *de* followed by a form in *-o* (also *-u*) was found in *Tarraconensis*

(7th cent.) and *Narbonensis* (5th cent.), while three examples were found in *Rome*, the earliest one dating back to the 4th century.

(c) The analogical sigmatic genitive forms *Mercuris* and *Saturnis* (paralleling *Lunis* in the first declension) is also worth noting.

5.23   *Third Declension*

(a) As in the nominative, the *-is* ending is occasionally replaced by *-es*, except in *Baetica* and *Lusitania*, where the genitive always appears in its classical form. (But note that *-es* for *-is* in the nominative is attested in the former.)

(b) A few instances of the apparent extension of the oblique in *-e* were also noted in *Gaul* and *Rome*, precisely those regions where oblique forms in *-o* are also attested in the genitive function.

(c) Sporadic occurrences of genitive forms in *-i* for *-is* are attested with proper names, in particular. It seems, however, that most of these deviations may be ascribed to analogical influence of preceding or following second declension genitive forms.

(d) The periphrasis with *de* followed by a form in *-e* is attested only in an inscription from *Tarraconensis* (7th cent.) and *Narbonensis* (5th cent.). The circumlocution *de sorore nepus* found in the latter area is of particular interest, because it is a good example of a periphrasis with *de* which expresses the idea of *possession*. It is worth pointing out, however, that proper names regularly appear in their classical genitive form.

5.3   DATIVE SINGULAR

5.31   *First Declension*

It was found that in the few instances in which this case occurs, the classical dative ending *-ae* alternates with the *-e* ending, reflecting what seems to be a conflict between the monophthongization of the /aj/ diphthong in speech and orthographic tradition.

5.32 Second Declension

The dative generally appears spelled with -*o*. However, a few examples of the use of what appears to be the genitive in -*i*, observed in *northern Italian* inscriptions, in particular, may illustrate what Norberg has called "die dativische Funktion des Genitivs," attested in other Late Latin texts.

5.33 Third Declension

(a) On the whole, the classical -*i* spelling is quite well preserved. Sporadic examples of the orthographic substitution of -*e* (mostly limited to the *Italian* area) seem to point to a trend toward the emergence of a single -*e* morpheme in the oblique.

(b) The periphrasis with *ad* followed by forms in -*e* or -*em*, as a substitute for the classical dative, is attested in three non-dated inscriptions from *Gaul (Lugdunensis)* and the *Italian* area (*No. Italy* and *Rome*).

5.4 ACCUSATIVE SINGULAR

5.41 First Declension

The -*am* inflection that characterizes the classical accusative is frequently replaced by a form in -*a*, in all areas under study, both after verbs and prepositions. This would seem to suggest that, at least on the level of speech, final -*m* is no longer to be a morphological marker (residual forms in -*am* being relegated to written expression), and that there is emerging a general oblique case ending in -*a*.

Our material does not permit us to establish a possible chronology of the disappearance of final -*m* as an inflectional morpheme.

5.42 Second Declension

The classical accusative form in -*um* is frequently replaced by forms in -*u* and -*o*, except in *Baetica* and *Lusitania* where this case is consistently marked by -*um* in both dated and non-dated inscriptions.

(a) The orthographic change from -*um* to -*u* is mostly attested in the *Italian* area (a few examples were also found in *Lugdunensis*), although orthographic retention of final -m is somewhat greater in the *northern* and *central* regions than in *Rome* and the *southern Italian* regions. Nevertheless, there seems to be enough of a hesitation in the use of forms in -um and -u (including the many instances of *annu* for the expected *annum*), so that it may be fair to state that -m as a direct object marker is more a matter of traditional orthography than one of speech; and while some speakers may use the residual form in -um in orthography, as a reminiscence of classical Latin grammar, on the level of *parole*, at least, final -m is no longer regarded as an indispensable inflectional morpheme to mark grammatical opposition, much like final -m in *who did you see* or *the man who you talked to yesterday* for the "grammatically correct" *whom*.

(b) The morphological replacement of the classical accusative form in -um by an apparent ablative form in -o is attested in most areas, *Baetica* and *Lusitania* being the exceptions. Of interest and some significance is the fact that forms in -o for -um also occur in highly formulaic expressions (where we might expect greater adherence to traditional orthography), and that occasionally both the residual -um and the innovative -o forms appear side by side on the same epitaph, in the same function. Such examples would, indeed, suggest that the opposition between the classical accusative in -um and the ablative in -o is no longer a *grammatical* but a purely *formal* one and that there has emerged a general oblique form marked by -o (but *v. infra*, ablative of second declension nouns for possible "intermediate stage"), which fulfils several syntactic functions.

5.43 *Third Declension*

The omission of final -m is frequently attested in all areas under study, both in direct object function and after prepositions. The situation that obtains in this declensional class closely parallels the one found in the first declension. Here, too, it would seem that forms in -em should rather be interpreted as residual forms, essentially limited to the written language, while on the level of speech forms in -e have become the norm. This conclusion is further strengthened by instances in which the classical accusative is represented in forms in -em and -e occurring side by side on the same inscription.

It will be seen from the foregoing, then, that the classical Latin verb and prepositional objects in -am, -um, and -em are no longer the rule in our inscriptional material. Stonecutters freely use forms in *-a, -u* or *-o,* and *-e* as alternative endings to mark this case in the three major declensions. It is of interest to note, however, that while neither forms with *-m* nor those without *-m* are used exclusively in most areas under study, the classical accusative of *second* declension nouns and adjectives is invariably marked by *-um* in *Baetica* and *Lusitania.* But even in those areas in which *-m*-less forms do occur in this declension, the percentage of forms with *-m* is higher than in the first and third declensions. This may be more than just a coincidence; in fact, Veikko Väänänen has said that the greater frequency of forms in *-um* found in later Latin texts, with respect to those in *-am* and *-em,* is due to the greater resistance of final *-m* after the [u] in the spoken language.[1] This would certainly account for the longer survival of *-um* as a residual accusative form and the earlier fall of *-m* in the first and third declensions. Our inscriptional material, which also reflects this situation, seems to lend support to these views expressed by the Finnish scholar.

5.5 Ablative Singular

5.51 *First Declension*

An occasional hypercorrect form in *-am* for the ablative in *-a* is attested in all areas, although the proportion of cases of this orthographic change is far smaller than the spelling of *-a* for *-am* in the accusative.

While a reminiscence of the classical case system may still be reflected on the level of form, the concurrent use of forms in *-a* and *-am* clearly suggests an obliteration of case consciousness on the level of content.

5.52 *Second Declension*

The ablative ending in *-o* is the rule. Substitute forms in *-u* and *-um* (hypercorrections?) are also attested here and there, the forms

---

[1] Speaking of Pompeian *graffiti,* Väänänen, in fact, states that "L'omission de *-m* y est fréquente en toute position, et confirmée de surcroît par des contrépels.... Cependant, il apparaît que *-m* a mieux résisté après *u* qu'après *a, e,* et *i*" (*Lat. vulg.,* 69).

with *-um* occurring mainly with prepositions that traditionally govern forms in *-o*.

(a) Forms in *-u* for the expected *-o* ablative ending do not occur in either *Baetica* or *Lusitania*. (Let us recall that in these areas the classical accusative is invariably spelled with *-um*, indicating, perhaps, a greater orthographic tradition of keeping forms in *-o* and *-um* apart than is the case in other regions.) The orthographic change of *-o* > *-u* occurs with greatest frequency in *southern Italy* and *Rome*. Whether the *-u* spelling represents a classical accusative without final *-m* or an ablative in *-u* for the expected *-o* is difficult, if not impossible, to decide and any interpretation of the phenomenon must remain tentative and subjective, at best. For reasons that we have advanced on the basis of a comparison of accusative and ablative cases (assuming that at this point in time, say, beginning with the fourth century A.D., it is still legitimate to speak of "accusative" and "ablative" cases), we believe that these forms in *-u* reflect an attempt to represent what Schuchardt has called "ein Mittellaut" — that is, an [u] -colored [o] or an [o] -colored [u] — as a first stage in the morphological collapse of the opposition between classical accusative and ablative, resulting in the emergence of a single oblique case form, generally signalled by *-o*.

(b) The substitution of forms in *-o* by those in *-um*, particularly after prepositions, is also attested in virtually all areas. (We even found a few examples of this replacement in otherwise seemingly conservative *Baetica*.) Of special interest are those instances (not limited to a specific area) in which forms in *-o* and *-um*, used concurrently in the same epitaph, are governed by the same preposition. Would this not also indicate, in addition to the collapse of the accusative/ablative opposition on the expression level, that the speaker's attention is focused on the preposition rather than on the ending of its complement, it being irrelevant for all practical purposes whether this ending shows a form in *-o* or *-um*?

5.53 *Third Declension*

(1) The overwhelming majority of nouns are of the consonant stem variety, and, hence, take the *-e* ending in the ablative singular:

(a) An occasional -*i* spelling for the expected -*e* is attested sporadically in every area save the *Iberian* (where only the reverse phenomenon was found, i.e., the -*e* spelling for an -*i* of *i*-stem nouns and adjectives). For reasons that we have advanced earlier (*v. supra*, 3.15, p. 152) we interpret this orthographic change as the reflection of a morphological rather than phonological phenomenon.

(b) Hypercorrect forms in -*em*, occurring particularly after prepositions, are also attested in every region under study in dated and non-dated epitaphs. These instances, when brought into relationship with forms in -*e* for those in -*em* in the accusative, clearly reflect the kind of confusion between classical accusative and ablative that was observed also in the other declensions.

(2) The expected -*i* ending of *i*-stem nouns and adjectives occurs very infrequently; but where it does occur, it is sometimes replaced by a form in -*e*.

Although the scarcity of material at our disposal imposes some caution in drawing general conclusions, it would seem reasonable to see in the -*i* spelling for -*e*, as well as in the reverse phenomenon, a morphological confusion resulting from the shift of all *i*-stems to a generalized form in -*e*, which also ultimately emerges as the single oblique form (*v. supra*, 5.43).

5.6 Nominative Plural

5.61 First Declension

(a) In inscriptions from the *Iberian Peninsula* and *Gaul* the classical nominative prevails, although generally spelled with -*e* rather than -*ae*, reflecting the monophthongal pronunciation of the inflectional ending.

(b) Sporadic occurrences of the nominative in -*ae* or -*e* in the *Italian* area are outnumbered by a more frequent sigmatic form in -*as* (regarded by some as a reflex of the Indo-European nominative in *-*as* preserved in some Italic dialects, rather than an extension of the classical accusative case). The extensive use of this new nominative inflection has raised the question as to whether the feminine -*e* plurals of standard *Italian* might not be the historical continuation of this

GENERAL SUMMARY AND CONCLUSIONS 193

-*as* form rather than the classical -*ae* (Vulgar Latin -*e*) ending, as suggested by traditional theory. It is worth noting, furthermore, that there is no trace of this sigmatic nominative in either the *Iberian* area or *Gaul*, suggesting that the new -*as* inflection may not have reached these areas before the late sixth or early seventh centuries.

5.62 *Second Declension*

Masculine nominatives invariably end in -*i*. Some of the few occurrences of neuters in -*a* appear to be used as feminine singulars. Except for a single fourth century example from *Rome* (*opera*), instances of this shift, observed in the *Iberian* area and *Gaul*, are not attested before the seventh century.

5.63 *Third Declension*

No occurrences of this case were found in the *Iberian* area.

In both *Gaul* (specifically *Lugdunensis*) and the *Italian* area a number of instances of nominative forms in -*is* were observed, alternating with those in -*es*. These "deviant" forms in -*is*, which may well reflect an extension of the -*is* accusative inflection in Old Latin -*i*-stems, are of some interest in connection with the problem concerning the genesis of Italian third declension plurals of the (*i*) *cani* type. Indeed, there seem to be strong reasons to suspect that the origin of these plurals ultimately goes back precisely to this old accusative inflection.

5.7 GENITIVE PLURAL

5.71 *First Declension*

The classical -*arum* ending is used in the few occurrences of this case, except for one instance of an "analytic" construction with *de* followed by an apparent accusative form in -*as*, found on a non-dated *Roman* epitaph.

5.72 *Second Declension*

(a) In the *Iberian* area and *Gaul* the -*orum* ending is intact. In the *Italian* area it is also used in the majority of cases; but here it is sometimes written *-oru* and *-oro*. Whether the form *-oru* is due to the omission of final *-m* on the part of the stonecutter, or, as we believe, to a "compromise spelling" between traditional *-orum* and innovative *-oro* forms — possibly reflecting an [u] -colored final [o] sound — is, of course, difficult to decide. Nevertheless, instances of the morphological replacement of *-oro* for *-orum*, as well as the concurrent use of both forms in the same epitaph, would seem to suggest that on the level of speech the inflectional ending is realized as /-oro/ and that the *-orum* (and *-oru*) ending is a residual form which was continued to be written in accordance with orthographic tradition (much like the classical *-um* ending in the accusative singular, *v. supra*, 5.42 (b)).

(b) The genitive is replaced by a periphrastic construction introduced by *ad* and followed by the classical accusative in the oft-quoted phrase *membra ad duus fratres* found on an epitaph from *Lugdunensis*.

5.73 Third Declension

Occurrences of this genitive plural inflection in *-um* or *-ium* are infrequent. Notable is the morphological replacement of these classical forms by the second declension *-orum* form in several instances on epitaphs from *Lugdunensis* and the *Italian* area.

For the periphrastic *ad fratres* for *fratrum*, *v. supra*, 5.72.

5.8 DATIVE PLURAL

5.81 First Declension

Occurrences of this case are very rare; none in dated material and only sporadic attestation in non-dated epitaphs. Noteworthy is the extension of feminine formations in *-abus* even in cases where there is no need for gender distinction (as in *filiis* versus *filiabus*), e.g., *reliquiabus*. Although instances of new *-abus* formations were observed only in the areas of *Gaul* and *Italy*, studies by Hehl, Carnoy and Pirson suggest that they must have been used more extensively than our material would suggest.

5.82 Second Declension

The classical *-is* ending is generally preserved in the few occurrences of this case. On an epitaph from *So. Italy* the expected dative in *-is* is replaced by an apparent accusative form in *-os* after a verb that traditionally governs the dative case.

5.83 Third Declension

Limited to formulaic phraseology of the *fecit parentibus* type, this case is attested much too infrequently to permit drawing specific conclusions as to its viability. On two *Roman* epitaphs the *-ibus* inflection is replaced by the second declension *-is* dative ending, seemingly pointing to a conflict between these two inflections, particularly in view of such hypercorrect forms as *alumnibus* also found in this area.

5.9 ACCUSATIVE PLURAL

5.91 First Declension

Occurring mostly in expressions of date (as in *Kalendas Augustas*) this case regularly appears spelled with *-as*.

5.92 Second Declension

(a) The orthographic change of the classical *-os* inflection to *-us* is attested in inscriptions from *Gaul* and *Italy*. The concurrent use of both forms on the same epitaph was also noted.

Seeing that this *-os/-us* alternation occurs in morphological endings only, we have interpreted this phenomenon as being of a morphological rather than a phonological nature. On the phonological level, this alternation probably reflects a very close final [o] sound (an [u] -colored [o], perhaps), much like the situation in the singular where the frequent alternation of *-o* and *-u(m)* endings may also be a reflex of a close pronunciation of final [o], represented by either spelling.

(b) Sporadic examples of forms in *-is* were found in *Italy* and *Gaul* instead of the expected accusative in *-os (-us)*, after prepositions that traditionally govern the latter case. These hypercorrections would seem to support the view that at this point in time (about 4th century) it is the preposition itself that marks the function of the noun in the sentence, rather than the flectional ending it governs.

5.93 Third Declension

Except for the *Baetica* and *Lusitania* regions (where *-es* appears to be the rule) there is a regular morphological alternation of *-es* and *-is* inflections (i.e., orthographic *-is* for *-es* and vice versa), regardless of the traditional classification of nouns and adjectives as to consonant and *i*-stems. It is more than worth remarking, however, that by the sixth century, in both *Lugdunensis* and the *Italian* area, the *-is* inflection definitely takes the upper hand with respect to *-es*. While of no particular consequence for later developments in *Gallo-Romance*, this extension is quite significant for what we believe to be a chronological continuity between the *-is* accusative ending of Latin *i*-stems and third declension *Italian* plurals in *-i* (v. supra, 5.63).

5.10 Ablative Plural

5.101 First Declension

Worthy of note is the replacement of the ablative form *-is* and *-abus* (v. supra, 5.81) by the classical accusative in *-as* (e.g., *cum filias*). This substitution also occurs in the absolute construction *se vivas* for the expected *se vivis* (corresponding to the singular *se viva*). However, since occurrences of this case have been found only in the *Italian* area, more particularly in *Rome*, any reading of the evidence can only refer to this region. This limited evidence suggests that in this area, at least, there is a definite trend to substitute the *-as* form for the ablative in *-is* and *-abus*.

It would seem that conditions for the development of a plural oblique in *-as* were readily set by the emergence of an oblique singular in *-a* (the only factor differentiating singular from plural being the *-s* marker), further favored by the morphological identity of the popular nominative in *-as* and the accusative.

5.102 *Second Declension*

Although generally speaking poorly represented in our epigraphic material, particularly in *Gaul* and the *Iberian Peninsula*, substitutions of forms in *-os* (masculine) and *-a* (neuter) are attested in all areas under investigation (except that this case does not occur in *Lusitania*). While conclusions are difficult to draw as regards those areas where the occurrence of the ablative is infrequent, the sporadic replacement of this case by the classical accusative nevertheless suggests a trend toward a universal oblique in the plural, represented by either *-os* or *-a*, depending on the noun gender.

This trend toward substituting the classical accusative for the ablative is quite pronounced in the *Italian* area. It is of interest to note, however, that in both the *northern* and *southern* regions, this substitution involves neuter forms in *-a* (whereas masculine ablatives are not likely to be replaced by forms in *-os*), while the masculine ending in *-os* as a substitute for ablatives in *-is* are only attested in the *central* region and in *Rome*. Despite the general trend to replace the prepositional ablative by the classical accusative forms, it must be said that these two cases are still fairly well kept apart, better at any rate than in the singular.

The substitution of accusative for ablative is particularly evident in the *se vivos* construction, for the expected *se vivis*. Since this expression appears as *se vivo* in the singular, it is likely that the plural form *vivos* (as well as other substitute forms in *-os* for those in *-is*) reflects a popular trend to tack *-s* on to the singular form by analogy of first and third declension nouns, thus bringing about a kind of symmetry in the plural oblique system.

5.103 *Third Declension*

The replacement of the *-ibus* ablative ending by the classical accusative in *-es* (and its *-is* variant) in both absolute constructions and following a preposition is attested in epitaphs from *Gaul* and *Italy*. Except for the area of *Rome*, however, where forms in *-es* (*-is*) replace those in *-ibus* in better than 26 % of all instances, the occurrence of the ablative is too infrequent to draw specific conclusions as to the trend to universally replace the ablative by the classical accusative. Nevertheless, a few examples of this morphological substitution that were found in other *Italian* areas and in *Gaul* suggest that the ablative in *-ibus* may have been little more than a residual written form, used mainly in stereotyped formulae.

★ ★ ★

The conclusion that seems to emerge from the evidence presented in these pages might, perhaps, be summed up in the following manner: while not yet essentially different from the classical Latin declension system, it is undeniable that this system is undergoing an unconscious reorganization, with old and new endings existing side by side. Indeed, it would appear that, on the whole, the average stonemason (and, hence, the average speaker with some schooling) was fairly conversant with classical Latin morphology and syntax (even though he may no longer have had full awareness of specific case-endings required by prepositions), and that the greater or lesser amount of deviation in the various areas under study may well reflect his training in Latin grammar.

Our analysis suggests that throughout our material some case-endings continue unchanged with respect to the classical Latin system, while others are subject to replacements by either existing endings or new formations. Deviations from the classical norm occur chiefly in the oblique cases,[2] rarely in the nominative (the *-as* nominative plural

---

[2] Particularly in the accusative and ablative cases, specifically in the singular, where the greatest amount of confusion occurs. Let us recall that it is precisely this constant use of one case for another (in terms of classical Latin case distinction) that has led us to postulate the emergence of a single oblique form (which is then also used in periphrastic genitive and dative constructions) and to call into question the generally accepted theory that Romance nouns and adjectives are directly derived from the Latin accusative case in *both* singular and plural. While we have no quarrel with this "accusative theory" as regards the *plural* (where indications that it is indeed the Latin accusative form that tends to supplant the other oblique cases are quite clear), we suggest that as far as the *singular* goes, the "Universalkasus" in the modern Romance languages represents an early merger of Latin accusative and ablative into a single form that, generally speaking, happens to coincide with the classical ablative form in the three major declensions. This view in no way precludes individual survivals of the classical accusative case (e.g., *rem* and other monosyllables; survival of the imparisyllabics of the *corpus* type; *Logudorese* that distinguishes final *o*'s and *u*'s in *otto* vs. *kentu*), just as there are sporadic survivals of classical nominatives, genitives, and ablative/locatives, e.g., *Florentiae*. See our discussion of this point under 3.25, p. 167 ff. and our note #120, p. 169. For the most eloquent defense of the

GENERAL SUMMARY AND CONCLUSIONS

in the *Italian*, specifically *Roman* area being a notable exception), but even in those more "progressive" areas where such deviations occur with greater frequency, there seems to be no clear-cut chronological evolution, no even progression from the classical declensional system into a system which could be called proto-Spanish, [3] proto-French, [4] or proto-Italian. [5] Some "conservative" areas like the *Iberian Peninsula* (although, as was seen, occasionally *Tarraconensis* seems to deviate from both *Baetica* and *Lusitania* in a number of respects) are still surprisingly classical in their declensional make-up. [6]

It is clear, then, that the evolution of non-classical formations (shall we call them pre-Romance?) is not regular and cannot really be said to dominate any one region in our corpus. Nevertheless, we believe that we were able to show some significant regional differences in the preferential use of certain morphological forms, e.g., (a) the *-as* nominative plural ending in *Italy* versus its total absence in *Gaul* and the *Iberian* area; (b) the *-o* ending in the second declension

---

"oblique theory" consult M. Pei, *Accusative* (cf. Bibliography for details). (It is unfortunate that this article has not attracted the attention of Romanists that it deserves.) For a view that attempts to conciliate both theories and is very much in line with our own views arrived at as a result of the analysis of inscriptional material, cf. Väänänen, *Lat. vulg.*, 124.

[3] A perusal of Carnoy's study of inscriptions from Spain reveals next to nothing that would appear as essentially Spanish-Romance. Possibly the most striking feature we found that sets at any rate *Baetica* and *Lusitania* apart from *Gaul* and *Italy* is the consistent use of *-es* as the third declension plural nominative/accusative ending.

[4] In his study of the Merovingian noun-declension system, Sas also states that deviations from the Classical Latin pattern do not necessarily represent "the embryonic forms of a future Old French system" (481) and that "clues offered by the Merovingian declension system do not indicate that Old French was already in existence" (484). The primitive form of the Old French system — Sas goes on to say — does not become evident until the latter part of the eighth or the early part of the ninth century (485).

[5] The comments by P. Tekavčić are very appropriate in this connection: "Su quello che poteva essere, nel tardo latino parlato, il sistema morfo-sintattico nominale.... è quanto mai arduo, anzi addirittura impossibilie stabilire le singole tappe dell'evoluzione e darne delle sezioni sincroniche. Nel tardo latino coesistono certamente l'antica flessione sintetica, moribonda, e il nuovo modo di esprimere le funzioni mediante le perifrasi; tuttavia la proporzione dell'una e dell'altra oggi naturalmente ci sfugge" (II, 49).

[6] Carnoy sums up the morphological system reflected in his inscriptional material from Spain as follows: "Le latin d'Espagne se distingue par la conservation, jusqu'à des époques relativement récentes, de quelques formes casuelles qui généralement ont disparu ailleurs à l'époque impériale et même de réels archaïsmes" (222).

genitive singular which is on the increase in sixth century epitaphs from *Lugdunensis,* while other areas substantially hold on to the classical Latin *-i* ending; (c) the alternation of *-os* and *-us* in the plural accusative in *Gaul* and *Italy,* while completely absent in *Baetica* and *Lusitania,* with only an occasional attestation in *Tarraconensis*; and (d) *-is* third declension plural nominative and accusative forms in *Gaul* and *Italy* — and their extension in the latter region beginning with the sixth century at the expense of *-es,* — while in the *Iberian* area even the old *i-*stems are spelled with *-es.*

As stated earlier, our inscriptional material gives no clear indication of what the nominal system may have been at a given point of time as a result of morpho-syntactic transformations with respect to the Classical Latin system. Romanists are generally agreed upon a two-case declensional system "como último resto do sistema latino" [7] before the individual Romance areas went their separate ways, but it is the progression from the classical system to the proto-Romance one that seems to elude us. This does not mean, however, that with the clues at our disposal we may not attempt to give a *general* pattern of the system which is revealed to us through the study of written monuments. Bearing in mind the very tentative nature of any reconstruction and our inability to set up clear-cut chronological stages of development, this is how we might visualize this pattern as it emerges from our later (6th-7th century) inscriptional material: [8]

First Declension

	Singular		Plural
Nom.	*-a*	Nom.	*-e (Gaul, Spain); -as (Italy)*
Gen.	→ *de* + *-a* / *-e*	Gen.	*-arum; de* + *-as*
Dat.	→ *ad* + *-a(?)*	Dat.	*-abus; ad* + *-as(?)*
Acc.	*-a*	Abl.	*-as*
Abl.		Acc.	→ *-abus*

---

[7] Maurer, 93.

[8] The declensional endings refer to all areas, unless otherwise specified. Since we are attempting to give a *general* pattern of the declensional system in the Latin of the sixth/seventh centuries, it may be more convenient to give an overall synoptic representation of it rather than one for each area.

Taking the first declension as a whole, we may note that the *-a* ending dominates the *singular*. The *-e* ending of the synthetic genitive/dative is still well represented, however. As to the periphrastic constructions to express these case relationships, the following comments may be in order.

Although the periphrasis with *de* to express *genitive* relationship is found only in the *Italian* area in connection with first declension nouns, similar constructions attested in the second and third declensions in other areas would suggest that even in this declension this periphrasis was not limited to any particular area. Of interest, of course, is the fact that the earliest example of this "analytic" genitive is found in the *Italian* area around the middle of the fourth century, while attestations of same in *Gaul* and the *Iberian Peninsula* do not occur before the middle of the fifth and middle of the seventh centuries, respectively. This spread seems to indicate a chronological progression of this prepositional periphrasis with possibly *Rome* (the center of linguistic innovations) as a focal point.

The circumlocution with *ad* to express dative relationship is not attested with first declension nouns at all, but sporadic examples in other declensions would seem to authorize us to assume that the "analytic" dative was also used as an acceptable substitute for the synthetic one already during the period covered by our inscriptional material. Unfortunately, there are no dated examples available (according to Diehl (*AI*, 2), non-dated examples do not antedate the fifth century), so that it is not possible to attempt drawing any conclusions as to a possible chronology.

Let us finally recall that accusative/ablative often also appear spelled with *-am* as an orthographic alternative. With the probable disappearance of final *-m* from speech by the fifth century, at the latest,[9] forms in *-am* do not, to our mind, represent a spoken variant.

In the *plural*, the *-as* ending seems to dominate in the *Italian* area due to its use in the nominative also. (As suggested already, this fact appears to constitute an important regional differentiation between this area, on the one hand, and *Gaul* and the *Iberian Peninsula* which hold on to the nominative in *-e*.) Beside the synthetic genitive in *-arum*, there is a single attestation of a periphrastic construction with *de* followed by an oblique form in *-as* also. Despite the very limited

---

[9] Higgins, 32.

evidence of this "analytic" genitive, however, we feel that in view of the periphrastic alternative to the synthetic form in the singular, there is no reason why the same alternative could not have been in current use in the plural as well.

While the classical dative/ablative *-is* ending is probably no more than a literary reminiscence, the "vulgäre Neubildungen" in *-abus* — as Hehl has called them — do not seem to have as yet been displaced by a general oblique form in *-as*, although this form appears to be the preferred one with prepositions.

Second Declension

	Singular		*Plural*
Nom.	*-us; -o*	Nom.	*-i; -a*
Gen.	*-i; -o* (except *Spain*) / *de* + *-o*	Gen.	*-orum; -oro* (Italy) / *ad* + *-os* (Gaul); *de* + *-os* (?)
Dat.	*-o; ad* + *-o* (?)	Dat.	*-is; ad* + *-os* (?)
Acc.	⟩ *-o*	Acc.	⟩ *-os, -us* (Gaul, Italy); *-a*
Abl.		Abl.	→ *-is*

The *singular* of second declension nouns and adjectives is characterized by the *-o* ending. Sporadic as it is in the nominative, it is nevertheless attested in virtually all areas under study, with the *Italian* area taking the lead in terms of frequency. It cannot be said, however, that this morphological form in *-o* has already usurped the traditional *-us* ending, which seems to be still firmly entrenched at this point in time.

While the possessive relationship expressed by an oblique form in *-o* appears to be an acceptable alternative in *Gaul* and *Italy*, it would appear that the classical genitive in *-i* is still in wide use and, in any event, seems to be more than a learned form used unconsciously. This genitive form in *-o* (which some scholars have interpreted as representing the classical "possessive dative," v. supra, 2.12, specifically note #25, p. 67) is especially frequent in *Lugdunensis* beginning with the sixth century, presaging one of the most characteristic features of Merovingian Latin.

The periphrastic genitive construction is also attested in this declension; in fact, it is found in all three major areas. Just as in the first declension, the earliest example is found at *Rome* and dates back to the fourth century. (*V. supra,* p. 201, our comments concerning a possible chronology of the extension of this construction.)

The periphrastic dative construction with *ad* is not attested. (But see our comments under "first declension," p. 201.)

Enough has already been said on the relationship of accusative and ablative and the emergence of a single oblique form in *-o* (also represented in orthography by forms in *-u* and *-um*). Let us recall, however, that in *Baetica* and *Lusitania* the accusative is always represented by the classical Latin form in *-um,* although here, too, we feel that these are residual forms and only orthographic variants. (Stonecutters better trained in traditional grammar than elsewhere?) As to the many forms in *-u* (in both ablative and accusative functions), these may well represent what we termed a "transitional spelling" in the process of restructuring the inflectional categories of the singular, as a result of the collapse of accusative/ablative opposition.

In the *plural,* the *-os* oblique form does not seem to have taken over all oblique functions to the extent that the oblique form in *-o* has in the singular. The classical genitive in *-orum* (almost consistently written *-oro* in the *Italian* area and probably pronounced [oro] in other areas as well) and the dative/ablative forms in *-is* seem to be quite viable still, except that with prepositions the balance is definitely in favor of the *-os* form for masculine and *-a* form for neuter nominals.

It is of interest to note, furthermore, that the nominative in *-i* is quite stable in all areas under investigation and that, contrary to what happens in the singular, there are no indications of an extension of the oblique form to the case of the subject.

Regarding periphrastic genitive and dative constructions (the only attested construction being the oft-quoted *ad duus fratres*), the comments just made in connection with the first declension plural are also valid here; there is no reason to assume that circumlocutions with *de* and *ad* should not have been in use as alternatives to synthetic forms.

Third Declension

	Singular		Plural
Nom.	-es	Nom.	-es; -is (Gaul, Italy)
Gen.	-is; -es; -e / de + e	Gen.	-orum; -oro (Italy); ad + -es/-is (Gaul) / de + -es/-is (?)
Dat.	-i; -e (Gaul, Italy) / ad + e	Dat.	-ibus; -is (Italy); ad + -es/-is (?)
Acc. Abl.	-e	Acc. Abl.	-es; -is (Gaul, Italy)

In the *singular*, the extension of the /e/ vowel phoneme of the oblique is quite evident. There is a general trend in the direction of *-es* in both the nominative and genitive cases at the expense of *-is* (*Baetica* and *Lusitania* being the only regions using *-is* consistently in the genitive). The extension of the oblique form in *-e* to both genitive and dative is also attested in *Gaul* and the *Italian* area.

Both the periphrastic genitive and dative constructions are attested in our material.

Concerning the orthographic alternative in *-em* appearing in both classical accusative and ablative functions, *v. supra* (p. 201) our comments on the *-am* spelling with first declension nouns and adjectives in the same function.

The most noteworthy feature in the *plural* seems to be the extension of the *-is* ending in both *Gaul* and the *Italian* area, in both subject and oblique functions.

The classical genitive in *-um* is more often than not replaced by the second declension form in *-orum*, also appearing as *-oro* in *Italian* epitaphs, *v. supra*, p. 203. (It must be pointed out, however, that occurrences of the plural genitive are only available from *Gaul* and *Italy*.)

While the periphrastic construction is only attested once in an inscription from *Gaul*, for reasons stated already, we believe that these constructions introduced by *de* -or *ad* were just as acceptable substitutes for the corresponding synthetic plural genitive and dative forms as they were in the singular.

If *Roman* epitaphs are any indication at all, it would seem that the trend toward eliminating the classical ablative form in favor of the oblique is more pronounced in this declension than in the others, suggesting that the *-ibus* form (residual in ablative absolute constructions and stereotyped formulae) may indeed have been among the first synthetic forms doomed to disappearance from the language.

Habes iudicium nostrum. To the extent that it is at all possible to ascertain the loss of the classical nominal flection in inscriptional material, we hope to have been able to point to certain unmistakable trends that were to result in the eventual collapse of the essentially synthetic multi-case system of Classical Latin and the ultimate emergence of an essentially analytic one-case system in the modern idioms that developed from the language reflected in our inscriptional material.

APPENDIX

TABLES OF MORPHOLOGICAL ENDINGS

APPENDIX

TABLE No. 1. FIRST DECLENSION SINGULAR

AREA	CENTURY	NOMINATIVE		GENITIVE			DATIVE		ACCUSATIVE			ABLATIVE		
		-a	dev.	-ae	-e	de + -a	-ae	-e	-am	$-a_1$	$-a_2$	-a	$-am_2$	$-am_3$
Baetica	4th-6th	56	0	0	5	0	0	0	2	1	0	1	1	2
	7th	11	0	3	12	0	0	1	3	0	0	4	0	0
Lusitania	4th-6th	48	0	1	6	0	2	0	3	0	0	9	0	0
	7th	4	0	1	1	0	0	3	2	1	0	4	0	0
Tarraconensis	4th-6th	5	0	3	5	0	8	3	0	2	1	3	2	1
	7th	3	0	0	9	0	0	0	1	0	0	0	1	0
Narbonensis	4th-5th	6	0	18	4	0	0	0	1	0	0	4	0	0
	6th-7th	29	0	40	30	0	0	0	4	1	0	19	0	0
Lugdunensis	4th-5th	9	0	10	12	0	1	0	2	1	0	1	0	0
	6th-7th	4	0	33	21	0	0	0	3	6	0	8	0	0
No. Italy	4th-5th	28	0	16	8	0	10	4	78	23	1	12	2	0
	6th	18	0	2	0	0	0	0	0	1	1	18	0	0
Ce. Italy	3rd-4th	8	0	5	3	0	8	8	3	0	0	4	0	0
	5th	8	0	2	0	0	1	0	1	0	0	0	0	0
	6th-7th	14	0	3	1	0	0	0	4	6	0	12	0	0
So. Italy	3rd-4th	14	0	3	9	0	8	3	2	0	0	3	0	0
	5th	8	0	4	2	0	6	0	3	1	2	3	0	0
	6th-7th	22	0	4	8	0	0	0	0	2	0	19	0	0
Rome	3rd-4th	112	0	37	18	2	36	42	4	3	0	25	0	0
	5th	57	0	9	3	0	9	3	1	0	6	34	0	0
	6th-7th	29	0	9	7	0	3	0	3	0	0	18	1	0

$-a_1$: after verbs
$-am/-a_2$: after prepositions
$-am_3$: absolute constructions

TABLE No. 2. FIRST DECLENSION PLURAL

AREA	CENTURY	NOMINATIVE -as	NOMINATIVE -e	NOMINATIVE -as	GENITIVE -arum	GENITIVE dev.	DATIVE -is	DATIVE dev.	ACCUSATIVE -as	ACCUSATIVE -a	ABLATIVE -is	ABLATIVE -abus	ABLATIVE -as₁
Baetica	4th-6th	0	0	0	0	0	0	0	24	0	0	0	0
	7th	1	7	0	0	0	0	0	14	0	0	0	0
Lusitania	4th-6th	0	0	0	0	0	0	0	36	0	0	0	0
	7th	0	0	0	1	0	0	0	7	0	0	0	0
Tarraconensis	4th-6th	0	1	0	0	0	0	0	3	0	0	0	0
	7th	0	3	0	0	0	0	0	2	0	0	0	0
Narbonensis	4th-5th	0	0	0	0	0	0	0	6	0	0	0	0
	6th-7th	0	0	0	0	0	0	0	36	0	0	0	0
Lugdunensis	4th-5th	0	0	0	0	0	0	0	11	0	0	0	0
	6th-7th	1	1	0	0	0	0	0	17	0	0	0	0
No. Italy	4th-5th	0	0	1	1	0	0	0	26	0	0	0	0
	6th	0	0	0	2	0	0	0	15	0	0	0	0
Ce. Italy	3rd-4th	0	0	0	0	0	0	0	6	0	0	0	0
	5th	0	0	0	2	0	0	0	7	0	0	0	0
	6th-7th	0	0	0	3	0	0	0	13	1	0	0	0
So. Italy	3rd-4th	0	0	0	1	0	0	0	8	0	0	0	0
	5th	0	0	0	0	0	0	0	15	0	0	0	0
	6th-7th	0	0	0	7	0	0	0	21	0	0	0	0
Rome	3rd-4th	1	0	0	1	0	0	0	43	0	2	0	0
	5th	1	0	2	3	0	0	0	44	0	2	0	0
	6th-7th	0	0	0	1	0	0	0	22	0	0	0	1

-as₁: after preposition

TABLE No. 3. SECOND DECLENSION SINGULAR

AREA	CENTURY	NOMINATIVE			GENITIVE			DATIVE		ACCUSATIVE				ABLATIVE			
		-us	-os	-u	-o	-i	-o	-o de +	-o	-i	-um	-u	-o₁	-o₂	-o	-u	-um₁ -um₂	-um₃
Baetica	4th-6th	28	0	1	0	38	0	0	0	0	1	0	0	0	17	0	0	0	0
	7th	16	0	0	0	42	0	0	0	0	3	0	0	0	26	0	3	0	0
Lusitania	4th-6th	49	1	2	1	71	0	0	2	0	4	0	0	0	16	0	0	0	0
	7th	9	0	0	0	6	0	0	1	0	2	0	0	0	8	0	0	0	0
Tarraconensis	4th-6th	14	0	0	0	18	0	1	8	0	2	0	2*	0	15	3	0	0	0
	7th	14	0	2	1	12	0	0	1	0	2	0	4*	0	19	0	0	0	0
Narbonensis	4th-5th	14	0	0	0	28	0	0	1	0	1	0	0	0	33	0	2	0	0
	6th-7th	25	2	0	0	53	1	0	1	0	11	0	0	0	71	3	0	0	0
Lugdunensis	4th-5th	15	0	0	0	12	0	0	3	0	1	1	1	0	33	1	0	0	0
	6th-7th	26	2	0	2	38	13	0	2	0	4	0	1	0	59	2	0	0	0
No. Italy	4th-5th	82	1	0	0	78	7	0	46	3	19	5	0	4	162	2	2	0	1
	6th	36	1	0	0	33	1	0	1	0	6	0	0	1	48	0	0	0	0
Ce. Italy	3rd-4th	22	0	0	0	9	0	0	26	0	9	0	0	0	43	0	0	1	0
	5th	11	0	0	0	15	5	0	12	0	5	1	0	0	27	2	1	1	0
	6th-7th	28	0	0	0	41	2	0	1	0	4	0	0	0	52	0	0	0	0
So. Italy	3rd-4th	23	0	0	0	17	0	0	29	0	7	3	0	0	46	1	0	0	0
	5th	19	0	0	0	25	2	0	5	0	3	1	0	0	38	2	1	1	1
	6th-7th	38	0	0	0	57	0	0	62	0	11	0	0	1	62	3	4	0	1
Rome	3rd-4th	111	1	0	0	52	16	1	91	0	39	9	1	1	432	11	8	0	0
	5th	92	1	2	0	98	7	1	21	0	31	0	1	0	163	10	8	2	1
	6th-7th	54	0	0	0	71	1	0	2	0	14	2?	0	0	86	4	2	1	1

* On the same epitaph.

-o₁: after verbs
-um/-o₂: after prepositions
-um₃: absolute constructions

TABLE No. 4. SECOND DECLENSION PLURAL

AREA	CENTURY	NOMIN.		GENITIVE			DATIVE		ACCUSATIVE			ABLATIVE			
		-i	dev.	-orum	-oru	-oro	-is	dev.	-os	-us	-is₂	-is₁	-is₂	-os₂	-a₂
Baetica	4th-6th	0	0	1	0	0	0	0	23	0	0	0	0	2	0
	7th	1	0	6	0	0	0	0	13	1	0	0	1	2	2
Lusitania	4th-6th	1	0	1	1	0	0	0	35	1	0	0	0	0	0
	7th	0	0	2	0	0	0	0	4	0	0	0	0	0	0
Tarraconensis	4th-6th	0	0	9	0	0	0	0	8	0	0	0	0	1	0
	7th	1	0	3	0	0	0	0	3	0	0	0	0	0	0
Narbonensis	4th-5th	0	0	1	0	0	0	0	4	3	0	3	0	0	0
	6th-7th	1	0	2	0	0	3	0	13	28	0	1	0	0	0
Lugdunensis	4th-5th	0	0	2	0	0	0	0	6	7	0	0	0	0	0
	6th-7th	0	0	2	0	0	3	0	13	26	0	1	1	1	0
No. Italy	4th-5th	9	0	32	2	0	5	0	30	8	0	2	3	0	1
	6th	1	0	2	0	0	0	0	14	6	0	1	1	0	0
Ce. Italy	3rd-4th	7	0	4	0	0	1	0	9	0	0	0	0	1	0
	5th	0	0	2	0	0	0	0	5	3	0	0	4	0	0
	6th-7th	2	0	9	0	0	3	0	1	12	0	0	0	1	0
So. Italy	3rd-4th	5	0	4	0	0	2	0	3	2	0	0	2	1	0
	5th	0	0	0	0	0	0	0	8	5	0	0	2	0	0
	6th-7th	7	0	9	0	0	0	0	17	16	0	0	0	0	0
Rome	3rd-4th	4	0	14	0	2	6	0	59	33	1	4	9	1	1
	5th	2	0	10	0	2	2	0	23	28	0	1	3	0	0
	6th-7th	0	0	5	0	0	3	0	8	19	0	5	0	0	0

-is₁: absolute constructions
-is₂: after prepositions
-os₂: after prepositions
-a₂: after prepositions

APPENDIX 213

TABLE No. 5. THIRD DECLENSION SINGULAR

AREA	CENTURY	NOMIN.		GENITIVE					DATIVE		ACCUSATIVE			ABLATIVE IN e				ABLATIVE IN i		
		-is	-es	-is	-es	-e	de+-e	-e	-is	-e	-em	$-e_1$	$-e_2$	-e	-i	$-em_2$	$-em_3$	-i	-e	-em
Bactica	4th-6th	4	1	1	0	0	0	0	2	0	1	1	0	44	0	0	0	2	0	0
	7th	6	0	9	0	0	0	0	0	0	0	0	2	26	0	0	0	1	3	0
Lusitania	4th-6th	1	0	1	0	0	0	0	1	0	6	0	0	53	0	1	0	0	0	0
	7th	0	0	2	0	0	0	0	2	0	0	0	0	8	0	0	0	1	0	0
Tarraconensis	4th-6th	6	2	5	1	0	0	0	7	0	2	0	1	29	0	1	0	0	0	0
	7th	0	0	2	0	0	4*	0	0	0	0	1	0	4	0	0	0	0	0	0
Narbonensis	4th-5th	4	0	3	0	0	1	0	0	0	2	0	0	22	0	0	0	1	0	0
	6th-7th	4	2	12	5	2	0	0	0	0	4	0	0	69	2	0	0	1	0	0
Lugdunensis	4th-5th	2	0	5	0	0	0	0	3	0	1	2	0	23	0	0	0	0	0	0
	6th-7th	6	1	8	2	0	0	0	1	1	3	0	0	46	1	1	1	1	0	0
No. Italy	4th-5th	13	1	12	0	1	0	0	9	1	2	2	0	59	0	0	0	2	0	0
	6th	1	0	10	3	0	0	0	0	0	0	0	0	51	0	0	0	0	0	0
Ce. Italy	3rd-4th	2	0	4	0	0	0	0	19	0	3	0	0	13	1	0	0	2	0	0
	5th	4	0	5	1	0	0	0	2	0	3	0	0	15	0	0	0	0	0	0
	6th-7th	1	0	16	0	0	0	0	1	1	4	1	3	44	0	1	0	1	0	0
So. Italy	3rd-4th	3	1	3	0	0	0	0	16	0	3	1	1	21	2	0	0	1	0	0
	5th	2	1	11	3	0	0	0	7	0	1	0	0	14	0	0	0	0	0	0
	6th-7th	3	1	31	2	0	0	0	1	0	0	1	2	47	0	0	0	1	0	0
Rome	3rd-4th	16	4	35	1	1	0	0	131	2	10	1	4	199	9	8	1	4	3	0
	5th	15	2	26	0	0	0	0	23	0	2	0	1	123	7	0	0	2	0	0
	6th-7th	9	0	12	1	1	0	1	2	0	4	0	1	74	0	2	0	2	1	0

$-e_1$: after verbs
$-em/-e_2$: after prepositions
$-em_3$: absolute constructions

* On the same inscription.

TABLE No. 6. THIRD DECLENSION PLURAL

AREA	CENTURY	NOMIN. -es	NOMIN. -is	GENIT. -um	GENIT. -orum	DATIVE -ibus	DATIVE -is	ACCUSATIVE -es	ACCUSATIVE -is	ACCUSATIVE -is	ACCUSATIVE -es	ABLATIVE -ibus$_1$	ABLATIVE -ibus$_2$	ABLATIVE -es/-is$_1$	ABLATIVE -es/-is$_2$	ABLATIVE -a$_2$
Baetica	4th-6th	0	0	0	0	0	0	8	0	0	2	0	1	0	0	0
	7th	0	0	3	0	0	0	7	0	1	12	0	1	0	0	0
Lusitania	4th-6th	0	0	0	0	0	0	11	0	0	7	0	0	0	0	0
	7th	0	0	0	0	0	0	0	0	0	1	0	0	0	0	0
Tarraconensis	4th-6th	0	0	0	0	0	0	2	2*	1	1	2	0	0	0	0
	7th	0	0	3	0	0	0	0	0	0	0	0	0	0	0	0
Narbonensis	4th-5th	0	0	0	0	0	0	2	1	5	0	3	0	0	0	0
	6th-7th	0	0	0	0	2	0	7	5	9	6	2	0	0	0	0
Lugdunensis	4th-5th	0	0	2	0	0	0	4	2	2	1	1	1	0	0	0
	6th-7th	0	0	2	0	1	0	1	4	10	1	2	1	0	0	0
No. Italy	4th-5th	1	0	13	0	11	0	6	4	8	4	2	0	0	0	0
	6th	1	0	0	0	1	0	4	2	5	1	0	0	0	0	0
Ce. Italy	3rd-4th	9	0	2	0	3	0	16	1	1	10	2	0	0	0	0
	5th	0	1	2	0	0	0	4	0	2	2	0	0	0	0	1
	6th-7th	0	0	1	0	2	0	3	2	4	0	0	0	0	0	0
So. Italy	3rd-4th	5	0	3	0	1	0	2	2	2	0	0	0	0	0	0
	5th	0	1	0	0	0	0	3	1	1	4	0	0	0	0	0
	6th-7th	3	0	4	0	1	0	7	3	15	3	0	0	0	1	0
Rome	3rd-4th	12	5	4	4	5	1	37	19	20	18	0	6	0	0	0
	5th	1	1	4	0	0	0	20	3	11	8	2	1	0	0	0
	6th-7th	1	0	3	0	2	0	2	2	9	0	3	0	0	1	0

* On the same epitaph.

-es/-is/-ibus$_1$: absolute constructions
-es/-is/-ibus$_2$: after prepositions
-a$_2$: after prepositions

TABLE No. 7. NOMINATIVE SINGULAR

AREA	CENTURY	1ST DECLENSION		2ND DECLENSION				3RD DECLENSION	
		-a	dev.	-us	-os	-u	-o	-is	-es
Baetica	4th-6th	56	0	28	0	1	0	4	1
	7th	11	0	16	0	0	0	6	0
Lusitania	4th-6th	48	0	49	1	2	1	1	0
	7th	4	0	9	0	0	0	0	0
Tarraconensis	4th-6th	5	0	14	0	0	0	6	2
	7th	3	0	14	0	2	1	0	0
Narbonensis	4th-5th	6	0	14	0	0	0	4	0
	6th-7th	29	0	25	2	0	0	4	2
Lugdunensis	4th-5th	9	0	15	0	0	0	2	0
	6th-7th	4	0	26	2	0	2	6	1
No. Italy	4th-5th	28	0	82	1	0	0	13	1
	6th	18	0	36	1	0	0	1	0
Ce. Italy	3rd-4th	8	0	22	0	0	0	2	0
	5th	8	0	11	0	0	0	4	0
	6th-7th	14	0	28	0	0	0	1	0
So. Italy	3rd-4th	14	0	23	0	0	0	3	1
	5th	8	0	19	0	0	0	2	1
	6th-7th	22	0	38	0	0	0	3	1
Rome	3rd-4th	112	0	111	1	0	0	16	4
	5th	57	0	92	1	2	0	15	2
	6th-7th	29	0	54	0	0	0	9	0

TABLE No. 8. GENITIVE SINGULAR

AREA	CENTURY	1ST DECLENSION				2ND DECLENSION				3RD DECLENSION			
		-ae	-e	-is	de+a	-i	-o	-um	de+o(-u)	-is	-es	-e	de+e
Baetica	4th-6th	0	5	0	0	38	0	0	0	1	0	0	0
	7th	3	12	0	0	42	0	0	0	9	0	0	0
Lusitania	4th-6th	1	6	0	0	71	0	0	0	1	0	0	0
	7th	1	1	0	0	6	0	0	0	2	0	0	0
Tarraconensis	4th-6th	3	5	1	0	18	0	0	0	5	1	0	0
	7th	0	9	0	0	12	0	0	1	2	0	0	4*
Narbonensis	4th-5th	18	4	0	0	28	0	0	1	3	0	0	1
	6th-7th	40	30	0	0	53	1	0	0	12	5	2	0
Lugdunensis	4th-5th	10	12	0	0	12	0	0	0	5	0	0	0
	6th-7th	33	21	0	0	38	13	3	0	8	2	0	0
No. Italy	4th-5th	16	8	0	0	78	7	0	0	12	0	1	0
	6th	2	0	0	0	33	1	0	0	10	3	0	0
Ce. Italy	3rd-4th	5	3	0	0	9	0	0	0	4	0	0	0
	5th	2	0	0	0	15	5	0	0	5	1	1	0
	6th-7th	3	1	0	0	41	2	0	0	16	0	0	0
So. Italy	3rd-4th	3	9	1	0	17	0	0	0	3	0	0	0
	5th	4	2	0	0	25	2	0	0	11	3	0	0
	6th-7th	4	8	0	0	57	0	0	0	31	2	0	0
Rome	3rd-4th	37	18	1	2	52	16	0	1	35	1	1	0
	5th	9	3	0	0	98	7	0	1	26	0	0	0
	6th-7th	9	7	0	0	71	1	0	0	12	1	1	0

* On the same inscription.

TABLE No. 9. DATIVE SINGULAR

AREA	CENTURY	1ST DECL. -ae	1ST DECL. -e	2ND DECL. -o	2ND DECL. -i	3RD DECL. -i	3RD DECL. -e
Baetica	4th-6th	0	0	0	0	2	0
	7th	0	1	0	0	0	0
Lusitania	4th-6th	2	0	2	0	1	0
	7th	0	3	1	0	2	0
Tarraconensis	4th-6th	8	3	8	0	7	0
	7th	0	0	1	0	0	0
Narbonensis	4th-5th	0	0	1	0	0	0
	6th-7th	0	0	1	0	0	0
Lugdunensis	4th-5th	1	0	3	0	3	0
	6th-7th	0	0	2	0	1	0
No. Italy	4th-5th	10	4	46	3	9	1
	6th	0	0	1	0	0	0
Ce. Italy	3rd-4th	8	8	26	0	19	0
	5th	1	0	12	0	2	0
	6th-7th	0	0	1	0	1	1
So. Italy	3rd-4th	8	3	29	0	16	0
	5th	6	0	5	0	7	0
	6th-7th	0	0	62	0	1	0
Rome	3rd-4th	36	42	91	0	131	2
	5th	9	3	21	0	23	0
	6th-7th	3	0	2	0	2	0

TABLE No. 10. ACCUSATIVE SINGULAR

AREA	CENTURY	1ST DECLENSION			2ND DECLENSION				3RD DECLENSION		
		$-am$	$-a_1$	$-a_2$	$-um$	$-u$	$-o_1$	$-o_2$	$-em$	$-e_1$	$-e_2$
Baetica	4th-6th	2	1	0	1	0	0	0	1	1	0
	7th	3	0	0	3	0	0	0	0	0	2
Lusitania	4th-6th	3	0	0	4	0	0	0	6	0	0
	7th	2	1	0	2	0	0	0	0	0	0
Tarraconensis	4th-6th	0	2	1	2	0	0	0	2	0	1
	7th	1	0	0	2	0	2*	0	0	1	0
Narbonensis	4th-5th	1	0	0	1	0	4*	0	2	0	0
	6th-7th	4	1	0	11	0	0	0	4	0	0
Lugdunensis	4th-5th	2	1	0	1	1	1	0	1	2	0
	6th-7th	3	6	0	4	0	1	0	3	0	0
No. Italy	4th-5th	78	23	1	19	5	0	4	2	2	1
	6th	0	1	1	6	0	0	1	0	0	0
Ce. Italy	3rd-4th	3	0	0	9	0	0	0	3	0	0
	5th	1	0	0	5	1	0	0	3	0	0
	6th-7th	4	6	0	4	0	0	0	4	1	3
So. Italy	3rd-4th	2	0	0	7	3	0	0	3	1	1
	5th	3	1	0	3	1	0	0	1	0	0
	6th-7th	0	2	2	11	0	0	1	0	1	2
Rome	3rd-4th	4	3	0	39	9	1	1	10	1	4
	5th	1	0	6	31	0	1	0	2	0	1
	6th-7th	3	0	0	14	2	0	0	4	0	1

* On the same epitaph.

$-a/-o/-e_1$: after verbs
$-a/-o/-e_2$: after prepositions

TABLE No. 11. ABLATIVE SINGULAR

AREA	CENTURY	1ST DECLENSION				2ND DECLENSION					3RD DECLENSION (cons. & *i*-stems)					
		-*a*	-*am*₂	-*am*₃		-*o*	-*u*	-*um*₂	-*um*₃		-*e*	-*i*	-*em*₂	-*em*₃	-*i*	-*e*
Baetica	4th-6th	1	1	2		17	0	0	0		44	0	0	0	2	0
	7th	4	0	0		26	0	3	0		26	0	0	0	1	3
Lusitania	4th-6th	9	0	0		16	0	0	0		53	0	1	0	0	0
	7th	4	0	0		8	0	0	0		8	0	0	0	1	0
Tarraconensis	4th-6th	3	2	1		15	3	0	0		29	0	1	0	0	0
	7th	0	1	0		19	0	0	0		4	0	0	0	0	0
Narbonensis	4th-5th	4	0	0		33	0	2	0		22	0	0	0	1	0
	6th-7th	19	0	0		71	3	0	0		69	2	0	0	1	0
Lugdunensis	4th-5th	1	0	0		33	1	0	0		23	0	0	0	0	0
	6th-7th	8	0	0		59	2	0	0		46	1	1	1	0	0
No. Italy	4th-5th	12	2	0		162	2	2	1		59	0	0	0	2	1
	6th	18	0	0		48	0	0	0		51	0	1	0	0	0
Ce. Italy	3rd-4th	4	0	0		43	0	0	0		13	1	0	0	2	0
	5th	0	0	0		27	2	1	1		15	0	1	0	0	0
	6th-7th	12	0	0		52	0	0	0		44	0	0	0	1	0
So. Italy	3rd-4th	3	0	0		46	1	0	0		21	2	0	0	1	0
	5th	3	0	0		38	2	1	0		14	0	0	0	0	0
	6th-7th	19	0	0		62	3	4	1		47	0	0	0	1	0
Rome	3rd-4th	25	0	0		432	11	8	0		199	9	8	1	4	3
	5th	34	0	0		163	10	8	2		123	7	0	0	2	0
	6th-7th	18	1	0		86	4	2	1		74	0	2	0	2	1

-*am*/-*um*/-*em*₂: after prepositions
-*am*/-*um*/-*em*₃: absolute constructions

TABLE No. 12. NOMINATIVE PLURAL

AREA	CENTURY	1ST DECL.			2ND DECL.		3RD DECL.	
		-ae	-e	-as	-i	other	-es	-is
Baetica	4th-6th	0	0	0	0	0	0	0
	7th	1	7	0	1	0	0	0
Lusitania	4th-6th	0	0	0	1	0	0	0
	7th	0	0	0	0	0	0	0
Tarraconensis	4th-6th	0	1	0	0	0	0	0
	7th	0	3	0	1	0	0	0
Narbonensis	4th-5th	0	0	0	0	0	0	0
	6th-7th	0	0	0	1	0	0	0
Lugdunensis	4th-5th	0	0	0	0	0	0	0
	6th-7th	1	1	0	0	0	0	0
No. Italy	4th-5th	0	0	1	9	0	1	0
	6th	0	0	0	1	0	1	0
Ce. Italy	3rd-4th	0	0	0	7	0	9	0
	5th	0	0	0	0	0	0	1
	6th-7th	0	0	0	2	0	0	0
So. Italy	3rd-4th	0	0	0	5	0	5	0
	5th	0	0	0	0	0	0	1
	6th-7th	0	0	0	7	0	3	0
Rome	3rd-4th	1	0	0	4	0	12	5
	5th	1	0	2	2	0	1	1
	6th-7th	0	0	0	0	0	1	0

TABLE No. 13. GENITIVE PLURAL

AREA	CENTURY	1ST DECL. -arum	1ST DECL. dev.	2ND DECL. -orum	2ND DECL. -oru	2ND DECL. -oro	3RD DECL. -um	3RD DECL. -orum
Baetica	4th-6th	0	0	1	0	0	0	0
	7th	0	0	6	0	0	3	0
Lusitania	4th-6th	0	0	1	0	0	0	0
	7th	1	0	2	0	0	0	0
Tarraconensis	4th-6th	0	0	9	0	0	0	0
	7th	0	0	3	0	0	3	0
Narbonensis	4th-5th	0	0	1	0	0	0	0
	6th-7th	0	0	2	0	0	0	0
Lugdunensis	4th-5th	0	0	2	0	0	2	0
	6th-7th	0	0	2	0	0	2	0
No. Italy	4th-5th	1	0	32	2	0	13	0
	6th	2	0	2	0	0	0	0
Ce. Italy	3rd-4th	0	0	4	0	0	2	0
	5th	2	0	2	0	0	2	0
	6th-7th	3	0	9	0	0	1	0
So. Italy	3rd-4th	1	0	4	0	0	3	0
	5th	0	0	0	0	0	0	0
	6th-7th	7	0	9	0	0	4	0
Rome	3rd-4th	1	0	14	0	2	4	4
	5th	3	0	10	0	2	4	0
	6th-7th	1	0	5	0	0	3	0

TABLE No. 14. DATIVE PLURAL

AREA	CENTURY	1ST DECL. -is	1ST DECL. -abus	2ND DECL. -is	2ND DECL. other	3RD DECL. -ibus	3RD DECL. -is
Baetica	4th-6th	0	0	0	0	0	0
	7th	0	0	0	0	0	0
Lusitania	4th-6th	0	0	0	0	0	0
	7th	0	0	0	0	0	0
Tarraconensis	4th-6th	0	0	0	0	0	0
	7th	0	0	0	0	0	0
Narbonensis	4th-5th	0	0	0	0	0	0
	6th-7th	0	0	3	0	2	0
Lugdunensis	4th-5th	0	0	0	0	0	0
	6th-7th	0	0	3	0	1	0
No. Italy	4th-5th	0	0	5	0	11	0
	6th	0	0	0	0	1	0
Ce. Italy	3rd-4th	0	0	1	0	3	0
	5th	0	0	0	0	0	0
	6th-7th	0	0	3	0	2	0
So. Italy	3rd-4th	0	0	2	0	1	0
	5th	0	0	0	0	0	0
	6th-7th	0	0	0	0	1	0
Rome	3rd 4th	0	0	6	0	5	1
	5th	0	0	2	0	0	0
	6th-7th	0	0	3	0	2	0

APPENDIX

Table No. 15. ACCUSATIVE PLURAL

AREA	CENTURY	1ST DECL.		2ND DECL.			3RD DECL. (CONS. & *i*-STEMS)			
		-*as*	-*a*	-*os*	-*us*	-*is*₂	-*es*	-*is*	-*is*	-*es*
Baetica	4th-6th	24	0	23	0	0	8	0	0	2
	7th	14	0	13	1	0	7	0	1	12
Lusitania	4th-6th	36	0	36	1	0	11	0	0	7
	7th	7	0	4	0	0	0	0	0	1
Tarraconensis	4th-6th	3	0	8	0	0	2	2*	1	1
	7th	2	0	3	0	0	0	0	0	0
Narbonensis	4th-5th	6	0	4	3	0	2	1	5	0
	6th-7th	36	0	13	28	0	7	5	9	6
Lugdunensis	4th-5th	11	0	6	7	0	4	2	2	1
	6th-7th	17	0	13	26	0	1	4	10	1
No. Italy	4th-5th	26	0	30	8	0	6	4	8	4
	6th	15	0	14	6	0	4	2	5	1
Ce. Italy	3rd-4th	6	0	9	0	0	16	1	1	10
	5th	7	0	5	3	0	4	0	2	2
	6th-7th	13	1	1	12	0	3	2	4	0
So. Italy	3rd-4th	8	0	3	2	0	2	2	2	0
	5th	15	0	8	5	0	3	1	2	4
	6th-7th	21	0	17	16	0	7	3	15	3
Rome	3rd-4th	43	0	59	33	1	37	19	20	18
	5th	44	0	23	28	0	20	3	11	8
	6th-7th	22	0	8	19	0	2	2	9	0

* On the same epitaph.   -*is*₂: after preposition

TABLE No. 16. ABLATIVE PLURAL

AREA	CENTURY	1ST DECL.		2ND DECL.				3RD DECLENSION				
		$-is_2$	$-as_2$	$-is_1$	$-is_2$	$-os_2$	$-a_2$	$-ibus_1$	$-ibus_2$	$-es$ / $-is_1$	$-es$ / $-is_2$	$-a_2$
Baetica	4th-6th	0	0	0	0	2	0	0	0	0	0	0
	7th	0	0	0	1	0	0	0	1	0	0	0
Lusitania	4th-6th	0	0	0	0	0	0	0	1	0	0	0
	7th	0	0	0	0	0	0	0	0	0	0	0
Tarraconensis	4th-6th	0	0	0	0	1	0	2	0	0	0	0
	7th	0	0	0	0	0	0	0	0	0	0	0
Narbonensis	4th-5th	0	0	3	0	0	0	3	0	0	0	0
	6th-7th	0	0	1	0	0	0	2	0	0	0	0
Lugdunensis	4th-5th	0	0	0	0	0	0	1	1	0	0	0
	6th-7th	0	0	1	1	1	0	2	1	0	0	0
No. Italy	4th-5th	0	0	2	3	0	1	2	0	0	0	0
	6th	0	0	1	1	0	0	0	0	0	0	0
Ce. Italy	3rd-4th	0	0	0	0	1	0	2	0	0	0	0
	5th	0	0	0	4	0	0	0	0	0	0	1
	6th-7th	0	0	0	0	0	0	0	0	0	0	0
So. Italy	3rd-4th	0	0	0	2	1	0	0	0	0	0	0
	5th	0	0	0	2	0	0	0	0	0	0	0
	6th-7th	0	0	0	0	0	0	0	0	0	0	0
Rome	3rd-4th	2	0	4	9	1	1	0	6	0	0	0
	5th	2	0	1	3	0	0	2	1	0	0	0
	6th-7th	0	1	5	0	0	0	3	0	0	1	0

$-es$/$-is$/$-ibus_1$: absolute constructions
$-es$/$-is$/$-ibus_2$: after prepositions
$-a_2$: after prepositions

INDEX NOMINUM RERUMQUE

NOTE: For reasons of space, this index lists important grammatical phenomena and references occurring only in the body of the text (excluding footnotes). It does not list words cited as examples of linguistic forms found in our inscriptional material, since these are referred to under the appropriate subject entry. Thus, for example, Lat. *opera* used in a feminine nominative singular function is indexed under "gender, shift of," and also "declension, shift of," rather than under a separate vocabulary entry.

a-stems, 104, 177, 182
ablative (classical), 35, 51, 81, 93, 99, 101, 113, 116, 118, 141, 150, 151, 169, 174, 180, 191-192, 205
   absolute, 45, 53, 71, 96-97, 116, 119, 133, 148, 167, 171, 178, 196, 205
   vs. accusative, 44-45, 46, 55, 93, 99, 114, 118, 123, 140, 149, 169-170, 171, 192, 197
   followed by "*ad*," 84, 86
   "fossilized," 152
   in -*abus*, 52, 57, 201
   in -*am*, 43-46, 55, 190
   in -*as*, 53, 57, 196
   in -*e* < -*ī*, 150-152, 173-174, 192
   in -*em*, 44, 147-150, 173-174, 182, 192
   in -*es* (-*is*) < -*ibus*, 168-170, 176, 197
   in -*i* < -*e*, 145-147, 173, 192
   in -*o* < -*ū*, 178, 180
   in -*os*, 114-119, 126, 197
   in -*u*, 73, 88-94, 122-123, 190-191, 203
   in -*um*, 94-99, 123, 190-191
   of means, 117, 148
   of origin, 43, 106
   of price, 97
   of specification, 63
   of time, 44, 77, 79, 81, 92, 104, 110, 114-115, 116, 122, 126
   substitute for, 53, 57, 116-117, 118, 126, 168-171, 190, 197
accusative (classical), 51, 73, 77-78, 81-82, 85, 87, 89, 92, 93, 97, 99, 101, 107, 112, 113, 114-115, 117, 118, 122-123, 125-126, 140-142, 149, 164, 168-169, 170-171, 174, 188-190, 191, 192, 197
   vs. ablative, 40-41, 45-46, 77, 93, 99, 123, 140, 149, 169-170, 176, 192
   absolute, 97, 119, 163, 171
   in -*a* (feminine), 38-43, 55, 149, 188, 190
   in -*a* (neuter), 102, 114-115, 116, 118, 124, 126, 158, 179-181, 197, 203
   in -*e*, 139-144, 173-174, 189-190
   in -*es* < -*īs*, 164-167, 175, 196
   in -*is* < -*ēs*, 162-167, 176, 182, 196, 200, 204
   in -*o*, 83-87, 122, 178, 188-189, 190
   in -*om*, 79
   in -*os* < -*ūs*, 177-178

in -*u*, 73, 77-83, 93, 122, 188, 190, 203
in -*us* < -*ōs*, 107-113, 125-126, 195
vs. oblique theory, 149-150, 169, 198
of time, 44, 77, 79, 92, 104, 110, 115, 122
substitute for, 86
Aebischer, Paul, 49
alternation
  morphological, 112, 125, 154, 163-164, 181, 195-196
  orthographic, 105, 112, 125, 156, 164-166, 175, 195, 200
analogical influence (pull), see analogy
analogical formation, 159-160, 183
analogy, 30, 88, 98, 110-111, 119, 126, 127, 134, 136, 152, 156, 158-159, 169, 172, 175-176, 179, 187, 197
Andecavenses, 35, 68
Appendix Probi, 130, 159, 177
assibilation, 145
assimilation, 104
Atellanae, 48
-*avit* > -*aut*, 30
Battisti, Carlo, 138, 152
Bennet, Charles E., 63
Bonnet, Max, 35
Bourciez, Edouard, 155, 167, 178
Carnoy, A., 28, 34, 52, 111, 117, 150, 165, 177, 194, 199
Cartulario de San Vicente, 34, 168
case, see also nominative, genitive, dative, accusative, and ablative
  confusion, 85, 92
  reduction, 177
casus obliquus, 74, 126, 139
casus universalis, 117, 126
Catalan, 76
Cato, 178
chronological continuity, 176, 196
Cisalpina, 51
classical norm, see under nominative, genitive, dative, accusative, and ablative
"compromise" spelling, 124, 194
consonant stems, 138, 144, 154, 162-163, 167, 173, 191, 196
content, see level
  vs. form, 190

Cooper, Paul, 34
cum followed by accusative, 100, 102, 114-116, 117, 148-150, 180
dative (classical), 65, 178
  analytic, 36, 37, 38, 160, 201
  in -*abus*, 52, 56, 194, 202
  in -*e* < -*ī*, 137-139, 173-174
  in -*i* < -*ō*, 75-76, 121, 188
  in -*is* < -*ibus*, 161-162, 175, 195
  in -*o* < -*ui*, 178-180
  in -*os*, 107, 125, 195
  periphrastic with "*ad*," 36-38, 139, 160-161, 173, 188, 201, 203-204
  possessive, 67, 76, 106, 161, 202
  sympathetic (*dativus simpateticus*), 67
  synthetic, 37, 38, 139, 173, 201, 204
declension
  first, 27-57, 139, 149, 177, 182-183, 184, 197
  second, 58-126, 134, 139, 142, 156, 158-159, 161, 168, 175, 176-177, 178-180, 181, 184, 187, 190, 194
  third, 127-176, 182, 185
  fourth, 177-181
  fifth, 181-183
  shift of, 42, 70, 107, 158, 177-178, 179-183
declinatio semi-graeca, 28
deviant form, 193
Díaz y Díaz, Manuel, 67
Diehl, Ernst, 23, 42, 71, 77-78, 111, 116, 119, 135, 201
dissimilation, 59
D'Ovidio, F., 156
ē-stems, 177, 182
Elcock, W. D., 30, 31
endings
  morphological, 184-185
  non-morphological, 184
Ewert, Alfred, 31
expressions of date, 57, 91, 94, 97, 121, 181
  of time, 70-71, 79-80, 89, 92-96, 110, 114-115, 116, 122-123, 167
form
  Romance, 104

INDEX NOMINUM RERUMQUE 227

vs. content, *see* content
residual, *see* orthography
formulaic expressions, *see* stereotyped formulae
Forum Judicum, 34, 107, 167
French, 75, 106, 113, 155, 166
  old, 106, 149
Gallic, 51, 74
Gallo-Roman, 51
Gallo-Romance, 196
gender
  feminine, masculine, and neuter *passim*
  shift of, 39, 42, 44, 65, 102-103, 124, 144, 158, 181, 193
genitive (classical), 34, 35, 66, 68, 73, 75, 103, 120, 121, 131, 136-137, 173, 185-187
  analytical, 32-35, 75, 106, 121, 186, 193, 201-202
  analogical, 32, 103, 104, 121, 131, 134-136, 175, 186-187
  appositional, 88
  in *-e* < *-is*, 132-133
  in *-es* < *-is*, 131-132, 172, 174, 187, 204
  in *-es (-aes)* < *-ae*, 27-29, 30, 54, 186
  in *-ii*, 66, 121
  in *-i* < *-is*, 31, 54, 73, 133-136, 172, 187
  in *-i* < *-ūs*, 178
  in *-is (die Lunis)*, 30-32, 54, 186
  in *-o*, 66-72, 121, 186, 199-200, 202
  in *-oro (-oru)*, 103-106, 124, 194, 203-204
  in *-orum* < *-um (-ium)*, 159-160, 175, 194, 204
  vs. oblique, 67-69, 72-73, 186-187
  of material, 69
  of possession, 34, 55, 67-68, 106, 125, 137, 172, 187
  of quality, 135, 136, 183
  of time, 104
  partitive, 34-35
  periphrastic with "*ad*," 35, 67, 106, 125, 160, 194
  periphrastic with "*de*," 32-36, 51, 54, 56, 73-75, 106, 121, 136-137, 172, 186-187, 193, 201, 203-204

sigmatic, 30-32, 54, 73, 186-187
  substitute for, 34-35, 55, 204
  synthetic, 34, 186, 201, 204
Gerola, Berengario, 49
graeco-latin hybrids, 27-30
Grandgent, C. H., 32, 36, 162, 167, 178
graphie archaïsante, 27
Greek influence, 27-30, 58, 111, 125, 184
Gregory of Tours, 35, 110
haplology, 93
Hehl, Albert, 27-28, 194, 202
Higgins, Robert, 201
hybrid constructions, 71-72, 133
hypercorrect forms, *see* hypercorrection
hypercorrection, 45, 66, 75, 93, 96, 100-101, 125, 148-149, 168, 171, 173, 178, 180, 182, 190, 192, 195
inflectional morpheme, 122, 175, 188-189
inflectional morphology, 101, 104
inflection in *-ane*, *-etis*, *-eti*, etc., 78, 138
i-stems, 138, 144, 147, 150, 154, 156-157, 159, 164-165, 167, 173-175, 192-193, 196, 200
io-stems, 66
innovation (linguistic), 26, 51, 201
innovative form, 189, 194
Italian, 31, 49, 50, 75, 113, 131, 172, 174, 176, 185, 192-193
  early, 158
  old, 106
  plurals, *first declension*: 49-51, 192-193; *third declension*: 155-158, 167, 174, 193
Italic dialects, 49, 192
-ivit > *-iut*, 92
Jennings, Augustus C., 34, 62, 117, 120
Konjetzny, Guilelmus, 119
Latin
  archaic, 156
  classical, 21, 23, 26, 43, 53, 71, 107, 112, 154, 160, 162, 164, 178, 189, 198, 200, 203, 205
  late, 22, 37, 51, 75, 85, 111, 117, 122, 160, 188
  Merovingian, 202

post-classical, 42
vulgar, 21, 26, 31-32, 34, 36, 37, 49, 51, 54, 77, 113, 155, 162, 167, 193
LeBlant, Edmond, 63
Lehmann, Winfred, 101
level (of)
    content, 55, 99, 101, 124, 140, 190
    expression (*parole*), 65, 105, 121-122, 140, 173, 185, 188-189, 191, 194
    form, 55, 99, 101, 112, 125, 155, 190
    orthography, 83
Lindsay, W. M., 66
Löfstedt, Bengt, 84, 93, 99, 111, 147
-*m*
    addition of, 178, 182
    loss (fall) of, 42, 76, 99, 123, 188, 190, 201
    omission of, 39, 42-43, 65, 77, 79, 82, 87, 89, 93, 99, 101, 103, 121-122, 139, 173, 189, 194
    retention of, 78, 82-83, 122, 189, 190
magister vici, 136
margine urgente, 42, 61, 93, 120, 139
Martin, Henry, 34
Maurer, Theodoro, 200
Menéndez Pidal, Ramón, 32
merger (coalescence)
    phonetic, 59, 63, 76, 110-112, 120, 127, 173, 184
    morpho-syntactic, 101, 169
Merovingian documents, 106, 117, 144, 151, 161, 176
monophthongization, 27, 187
morphological
    collapse, 46, 124, 191
    confusion, 69, 93, 123, 152, 174, 192
    extension, 65, 157, 166, 174, 185
    substitution (replacement), 62, 65, 83, 87, 94, 104, 120-121, 129, 138-139, 152, 161, 170, 185-186, 194, 197-198
morphology vs. phonology, 76, 110-113, 139, 147, 151, 157, 163-164, 175, 192, 195
morpho-syntactic substitution, 94, 123
Muller, Henri-F., 161
Muller, H.-F. - P. Taylor, 68

nominative (classical), 49, 50-51, 56-57, 59
    "fossilized," 112, 125
    grecized, 28, 184
    in -*a* (pl.), 181
    in -*as*, 46-51, 53, 56, 192-193, 196, 198-199, 201
    in -*e*, 46-51, 56, 192, 201
    in -*es* < -*is*, 127-131, 172, 174, 185, 204
    in -*i* < -*ūs*, 179
    in -*is* < -*es*, 128-130, 172
    in -*is* < -*ēs*, 152-158, 174, 182, 192, 200, 204
    in -*o*, 60, 62-66, 120, 180, 184, 202
    in -*os* < -*us*, 58-59, 120, 184
    in -*u*, 60-62, 120, 184-185
    vs. oblique, 59, 62, 65, 120, 180, 185
    sigmatic, 49, 56, 192-193
Norberg, Dag, 75-76, 121, 188
o-stems, 177-178, 181
oblique
    vs. accusative, *see* accusative
    extension of, 65, 67, 72, 132
    vs. genitive, *see* genitive
    vs. nominative, *see* nominative
    plural, 57, 176, 196-197, 198, 201-203, 205
    singular, 55-56, 59, 62, 72-73, 76, 87, 99, 101, 119, 120-122, 124, 126, 132, 140-143, 150, 169, 172-173, 185-186, 188-189, 191-192, 196, 198, 202-204
object
    direct, 82-83, 84, 86, 98, 100, 122, 139-140, 142, 173, 189
    indirect, 85
opposition (conflict)
    ablative vs. accusative, 45, 87, 94, 97, 99, 101, 117, 119, 122, 140, 149, 174, 189, 191, 203
    formal vs. grammatical, 86, 122, 189
orthography
    change (deviation) of, 76-77, 107, 119, 120, 122, 127-128, 130-131, 133, 139, 145, 147, 162, 164-165, 172-173, 175, 184, 188, 190, 191, 195
    confusion of, 44, 178, 179
    residual, 79, 85, 100, 168, 171,

INDEX NOMINUM RERUMQUE

173, 188-190, 194, 198, 203, 205
substitution of, 64, 110, 119, 123, 138, 164, 178, 188
traditional, 83, 124, 189, 194
orthographic alternative, 201, 204
Pannonia, 48
parisyllabics, 127-128, 172, 185
parole, see level of expression
Pei, Mario, 35, 36, 68, 117, 147, 150, 151, 161, 169
periphrastic future, 149
permutatio vocalium, 92-93
phonetic identity, 99
phonetic similarity, 92
phonology vs. morphology, see morphology
Pirson, Jules, 28, 30, 34, 52, 59, 66, 104, 110, 117, 147, 151, 154, 160, 178, 194
Pisaurum, 47
Plautus, 32, 36, 178, 181
Pompeian *graffiti*, 48, 171
Politzer, Robert, 36, 49, 161
praefectura urbi, 136
praefectus urbi, 136
Prinz, Otto, 59, 81, 92, 93, 104, 111
pro followed by accusative, 108, 115, 148-149, 169
pronouns (new formations), 41
proto-
French, 199
Italian, 199
Romance, 200
Spanish, 199
Provençal, 160
old, 149
Puşcariu, Sextil, 30, 156
reconstruction, 200
regional differences, 23, 26, 199, 201
residual form, see orthography
reverse spelling, see hypercorrection
Rhetian, 51
Rohlfs, Gerhardt, 31, 32, 181
Romance
pre-, 37, 199
speech (languages), 24, 149, 160
western, 21, 123-124
Rönsch, H., 181
Rumanian, 75, 156
-*s*
addition of, 119-120, 126, 185, 197

loss (fall) of, 31, 54, 118, 156, 158, 175
omission of, 60, 61-62, 120, 129, 134-135, 136, 170, 182, 185
survival of, 32
Sardinia, 75
Sas, Louis F., 35, 110, 117, 144, 161, 169, 199
Schuchardt, Hugo, 112, 123, 191
Sittl, Karl, 160
Sommer, Ferdinand, 30, 66, 181
Spanish, 131, 172, 185
speech, see spoken language
spoken language, 26, 83-84, 116, 117, 160, 185-186, 189-190
spoken vs. written form, 189
stereotyped formulae (phrases), 26, 71, 72, 78, 83, 84, 116, 147, 168, 171, 205
Stolz, F. - J. H. Schmalz, 167, 171
syntactic
confusion, 71-72, 76, 85, 94, 99, 121, 123
identity, 110
replacement, 53, 116, 117
Tarraco, 24
Terence, 178
terminus
in quem, 40, 86, 144
in quo, 40, 86, 94-95, 144
thematic vowel, 131, 172
time expressions, 70-71, 79-80, 89, 92, 96, 110, 114-115, 116, 122-123, 167
Tocqueville, 48
transitional spelling (stage), 101, 106, 124, 203
two-case system, 200
u-stems, 177, 181
Uddholm, A., 160
Universalkasus, 45, 53, 87, 121, 144, 169, 198
Väänänen, Veikko, 27, 30, 33, 36, 67, 171, 190
variation
formal, 105, 154
free, 112, 155, 157
morphological, 154, 157, 174
Vives, D. José, 23-24
vulgarism, 106, 202
vulgäre Neubildung, see vulgarism
v. Wartburg, Walther, 32, 38

NORTH CAROLINA STUDIES IN THE ROMANCE LANGUAGES AND LITERATURES

I.S.B.N. Prefix 0-88438

Recent Titles

THE ITALIAN VERB. A MORPHOLOGICAL STUDY, by Frede Jensen. 1971. (No. 107). -907-3.

A CRITICAL EDITION OF THE OLD PROVENÇAL EPIC "DAUREL ET BETON," WITH NOTES AND PROLEGOMENA, by Arthur S. Kimmel. 1971. (No. 108). -908-1.

FRANCISCO RODRIGUES LOBO: DIALOGUE AND COURTLY LORE IN RENAISSANCE PORTUGAL, by Richard A. Preto-Rodas. 1971. (No. 109). 909-X.

RAIMOND VIDAL: POETRY AND PROSE, edited by W. H. W. Field. 1971. (No. 110). -910-3.

RELIGIOUS ELEMENTS IN THE SECULAR LYRICS OF THE TROUBADOURS, by Raymond Gay-Crosier. 1971. (No. 111). -911-1.

THE SIGNIFICANCE OF DIDEROT'S "ESSAI SUR LE MERITE ET LA VERTU," by Gordon B. Walters. 1971. (No. 112). -912-X.

PROPER NAMES IN THE LYRICS OF THE TROUBADOURS, by Frank M. Chambers. 1971. (No. 113). -913-8.

STUDIES IN HONOR OF MARIO A. PEI, edited by John Fisher and Paul A. Gaeng. 1971. (No. 114). -914-6.

DON MANUEL CAÑETE, CRONISTA LITERARIO DEL ROMANTICISMO Y DEL POSROMANTICISMO EN ESPAÑA, por Donald Allen Randolph. 1972. (No. 115). -915-4.

THE TEACHINGS OF SAINT LOUIS. A CRITICAL TEXT, by David O'Connell. 1972. (No. 116). -916-2.

HIGHER, HIDDEN ORDER: DESIGN AND MEANING IN THE ODES OF MALHERBE, by David Lee Rubin. 1972. (No. 117). -917-0.

JEAN DE LE MOTE "LE PARFAIT DU PAON," édition critique par Richard J. Carey. 1972. (No. 118). -918-9.

CAMUS' HELLENIC SOURCES, by Paul Archambault. 1972. (No. 119). -919-7.

FROM VULGAR LATIN TO OLD PROVENÇAL, by Frede Jensen. 1972. (No. 120). -920-0.

GOLDEN AGE DRAMA IN SPAIN: GENERAL CONSIDERATION AND UNUSUAL FEATURES, by Sturgis E. Leavitt. 1972. (No. 121). -921-9.

THE LEGEND OF THE "SIETE INFANTES DE LARA" (Refundición toledana de la crónica de 1344 versión), study and edition by Thomas A. Lathrop. 1972. (No. 122). -922-7.

STRUCTURE AND IDEOLOGY IN BOIARDO'S "ORLANDO INNAMORATO," by Andrea di Tommaso. 1972. (No. 123). -923-5.

STUDIES IN HONOR OF ALFRED G. ENGSTROM, edited by Robert T. Cargo and Emmanuel J. Mickel, Jr. 1972. (No. 124). -924-3.

A CRITICAL EDITION WITH INTRODUCTION AND NOTES OF GIL VICENTE'S "FLORESTA DE ENGANOS," by Constantine Christopher Stathatos. 1972. (No. 125). -925-1.

LI ROMANS DE WITASSE LE MOINE. Roman du treizième siècle. Édité d'après le manuscrit, fonds français 1553, de la Bibliothèque Nationale, Paris, par Denis Joseph Conlon. 1972. (No. 126). -926-X.

EL CRONISTA PEDRO DE ESCAVIAS. Una vida del Siglo XV, por Juan Bautista Avalle-Arce. 1972. (No. 127). -927-8.

AN EDITION OF THE FIRST ITALIAN TRANSLATION OF THE "CELESTINA," by Kathleen V. Kish. 1973. (No. 128). -928-6.

When ordering please cite the ISBN Prefix plus the last four digits for each title.

Send orders to: University of North Carolina Press
Chapel Hill
North Carolina 27514
U. S. A.

NORTH CAROLINA STUDIES IN THE ROMANCE LANGUAGES AND LITERATURES

I.S.B.N. Prefix 0-88438

Recent Titles

MOLIÈRE MOCKED. THREE CONTEMPORARY HOSTILE COMEDIES: Zélinde, Le portrait du peintre, Élomire Hypocondre, by Frederick Wright Vogler. 1973. (No. 129). -929-4.

C.-A. SAINTE-BEUVE. Chateaubriand et son groupe littéraire sous l'empire. Index alphabétique et analytique établi par Lorin A. Uffenbeck. 1973. (No. 130). -930-8.

THE ORIGINS OF THE BAROQUE CONCEPT OF "PEREGRINATIO," by Juergen Hahn. 1973. (No. 131). -931-6.

THE "AUTO SACRAMENTAL" AND THE PARABLE IN SPANISH GOLDEN AGE LITERATURE, by Donald Thaddeus Dietz. 1973. (No. 132). -932-4.

FRANCISCO DE OSUNA AND THE SPIRIT OF THE LETTER, by Laura Calvert. 1973. (No. 133). -933-2.

ITINERARIO DI AMORE: DIALETTICA DI AMORE E MORTE NELLA VITA NUOVA, by Margherita de Bonfils Templer. 1973. (No. 134). -934-0.

L'IMAGINATION POETIQUE CHEZ DU BARTAS: ELEMENTS DE SENSIBILITE BAROQUE DANS LA "CREATION DU MONDE," by Bruno Braunrot. 1973. (No. 135). -934-0.

ARTUS DESIRE: PRIEST AND PAMPHLETEER OF THE SIXTEENTH CENTURY, by Frank S. Giese. 1973. (No. 136). -936-7.

JARDIN DE NOBLES DONZELLAS, FRAY MARTIN DE CORDOBA, by Harriet Goldberg. 1974. (No. 137). -937-5.

MYTHE ET PSYCHOLOGIE CHEZ MARIE DE FRANCE DANS "GUIGEMAR", par Antoinette Knapton. 1975. (No. 142). -942-1.

THE LYRIC POEMS OF JEHAN FROISSART: A CRITICAL EDITION, by Rob Roy McGregor, Jr. 1975. (No. 143). -943-X.

THE HISPANO-PORTUGUESE CANCIONERO OF THE HISPANIC SOCIETY OF AMERICA, by Arthur Askins. 1974. (No. 144). -944-8.

HISTORIA Y BIBLIOGRAFÍA DE LA CRÍTICA SOBRE EL "POEMA DE MÍO CID" (1750-1971), por Miguel Magnotta. 1976. (No. 145). -945-6.

LES ENCHANTEMENZ DE BRETAIGNE. AN EXTRACT FROM A THIRTEENTH CENTURY PROSE ROMANCE "LA SUITE DU MERLIN", edited by Patrick C. Smith. 1977. (No. 146). 0-8078-9146-0.

THE DRAMATIC WORKS OF ÁLVARO CUBILLO DE ARAGÓN, by Shirley B. Whitaker. 1975. (No. 149). -949-9.

A CONCORDANCE TO THE "ROMAN DE LA ROSE" OF GUILLAUME DE LORRIS, by Joseph R. Danos. 1976. (No. 156). 0-88438-403-9.

POETRY AND ANTIPOETRY: A STUDY OF SELECTED ASPECTS OF MAX JACOB'S POETIC STYLE, by Annette Thau. 1976. (No. 158). -005-X.

FRANCIS PETRARCH, SIX CENTURIES LATER, by Aldo Scaglione. 1975. (No. 159).

STYLE AND STRUCTURE IN GRACIÁN'S "EL CRITICÓN", by Marcia L. Welles, 1976. (No. 160). -007-6.

MOLIERE: TRADITIONS IN CRITICISM, by Laurence Romero. 1974 (Essays, No. 1). -001-7.

CHRÉTIEN'S JEWISH GRAIL. A NEW INVESTIGATION OF THE IMAGERY AND SIGNIFICANCE OF CHRÉTIEN DE TROYES'S GRAIL EPISODE BASED UPON MEDIEVAL HEBRAIC SOURCES, by Eugene J. Weinraub. 1976. (Essays, No. 2). -002-5.

STUDIES IN TIRSO, I, by Ruth Lee Kennedy. 1974. (Essays, No. 3). -003-3.

VOLTAIRE AND THE FRENCH ACADEMY, by Karlis Racevskis. 1975. (Essays, No. 4). -004-1.

When ordering please cite the *ISBN Prefix* plus the last four digits for each title.

Send orders to: University of North Carolina Press
                  Chapel Hill
                  North Carolina 27514
                  U. S. A.

NORTH CAROLINA STUDIES IN THE ROMANCE LANGUAGES AND LITERATURES

I.S.B.N. Prefix 0-88438

Recent Titles

THE NOVELS OF MME RICCOBONI, by Joan Hinde Stewart. 1976. (Essays, No. 8). *-008-4.*

FIRE AND ICE: THE POETRY OF XAVIER VILLAURRUTIA, by Merlin H. Forster. 1976. (Essays, No. 11). *-011-4.*

THE THEATER OF ARTHUR ADAMOV, by John J. McCann. 1975. (Essays, No. 13). *-013-0.*

AN ANATOMY OF POESIS: THE PROSE POEMS OF STÉPHANE MALLARMÉ, by Ursula Franklin. 1976. (Essays, No. 16). *-016-5.*

LAS MEMORIAS DE GONZALO FERNÁNDEZ DE OVIEDO, Vols. I and II, by Juan Bautista Avalle-Arce. 1974. (Texts, Textual Studies, and Translations, Nos. 1 and 2). *-401-2; 402-0.*

GIACOMO LEOPARDI: THE WAR OF THE MICE AND THE CRABS, translated, introduced and annotated by Ernesto G. Caserta. 1976. (Texts, Textual Studies, and Translations, No. 4). *-404-7.*

LUIS VÉLEZ DE GUEVARA: A CRITICAL BIBLIOGRAPHY, by Mary G. Hauer. 1975. (Texts, Textual Studies, and Translations, No. 5). *-405-5.*

UN TRÍPTICO DEL PERÚ VIRREINAL: "EL VIRREY AMAT, EL MARQUÉS DE SOTO FLORIDO Y LA PERRICHOLI". EL "DRAMA DE DOS PALANGANAS" Y SU CIRCUNSTANCIA, estudio preliminar, reedición y notas por Guillermo Lohmann Villena. 1976. (Texts, Textual Studies, and Translation, No. 15). *-415-2.*

LOS NARRADORES HISPANOAMERICANOS DE HOY, edited by Juan Bautista Avalle-Arce. 1973. (Symposia, No. 1). *-951-0.*

ESTUDIOS DE LITERATURA HISPANOAMERICANA EN HONOR A JOSÉ J. ARROM, edited by Andrew P. Debicki and Enrique Pupo-Walker. 1975. (Symposia, No. 2). *-952-9.*

MEDIEVAL MANUSCRIPTS AND TEXTUAL CRITICISM, edited by Christopher Kleinhenz. 1976. (Symposia, No. 4). *-954-5.*

SAMUEL BECKETT. THE ART OF RHETORIC, edited by Edouard Morot-Sir, Howard Harper, and Dougald McMillan III. 1976. (Symposia, No. 5). *-955-3.*

DELIE. CONCORDANCE, by Jerry Nash. 1976. 2 Volumes. (No. 174).

FIGURES OF REPETITION IN THE OLD PROVENÇAL LYRIC: A STUDY IN THE STYLE OF THE TROUBADOURS, by Nathaniel B. Smith. 1976. (No. 176). *0-8078-9176-2.*

A CRITICAL EDITION OF LE REGIME TRESUTILE ET TRESPROUFITABLE POUR CONSERVER ET GARDER LA SANTE DU CORPS HUMAIN, by Patricia Willett Cummins. 1977. (No. 177).

THE DRAMA OF SELF IN GUILLAUME APOLLINAIRE'S "ALCOOLS", by Richard Howard Stamelman. 1976. (No. 178). *0-8078-9178-9.*

A CRITICAL EDITION OF "LA PASSION NOSTRE SEIGNEUR" FROM MANUSCRIPT 1131 FROM THE BIBLIOTHEQUE SAINTE-GENEVIEVE, PARIS, by Edward J. Gallagher. 1976. (No. 179). *0-8078-9179-7.*

A QUANTITATIVE AND COMPARATIVE STUDY OF THE VOCALISM OF THE LATIN INSCRIPTIONS OF NORTH AFRICA, BRITAIN, DALMATIA, AND THE BALKANS, by Stephen William Omeltchenko. 1977. (No. 180). *0-8078-9180-0.*

OCTAVIEN DE SAINT-GELAIS "LE SEJOUR D'HONNEUR", edited by Joseph A. James. 1977. (No. 181). *0-8078-9181-9.*

THE LIFE AND WORKS OF LUIS CARLOS LÓPEZ, by Martha S. Bazic. 1977. (No. 183). *0-8078-9183-5.*

When ordering please cite the *ISBN Prefix* plus the last four digits for each title.

Send orders to: University of North Carolina Press
Chapel Hill
North Carolina 27514
U. S. A.

The Department of Romance Studies Digital Arts and Collaboration Lab at the University of North Carolina at Chapel Hill is proud to support the digitization of the North Carolina Studies in the Romance Languages and Literatures series.

www.ingramcontent.com/pod-product-compliance
Lightning Source LLC
Chambersburg PA
CBHW022013220426
43663CB00007B/1064